WITHDRAWN

W9-BLV-826

HENRY DAVID THOREAU

Henry David
Thoreau

A P R O F I L E

EDITED BY

WALTER HARDING

AMERICAN PROFILES

General Editor: Aïda DiPace Donald

American Century Series
HILL AND WANG : NEW YORK

COPYRIGHT © 1971 BY WALTER HARDING
ALL RIGHTS RESERVED
ISBN (CLOTHBOUND EDITION): 0–8090–9351–5
ISBN (PAPERBACK EDITION): 0–8090–0215–9
LIBRARY OF CONGRESS CATALOG CARD NUMBER: 74–163577
FIRST EDITION NOVEMBER 1971
MANUFACTURED IN THE UNITED STATES OF AMERICA
1 2 3 4 5 6 7 8 9 10

FOR
THOMAS BLANDING
WHO IS OPENING UP
WHOLE NEW VISTAS
IN THE STUDY
OF THOREAU

Oh, this study of souls, the inexhaustible charm of it, the puzzle, the perplexity, the complexity, the long wandering, the impossibility of ever arriving, yet with it all the growing magic, which enthralls you more and more. That is the real life to me, the only life, to probe and probe these strange, mysterious souls more deeply, whether souls of devils, like Arnold and Burr, or souls of angels, like Very; and the more one probes, the more one finds the souls of devils and angels both to be extremely like, and, above all, to be extremely like one's own. (Reprinted from Van Wyck Brooks, ed., *Journal of Gamaliel Bradford.* Boston: Houghton Mifflin, 1933.)

Contents

Contents

Introduction

Although Henry David Thoreau died more than a century ago, if we are to judge at all by the flood of new editions of his works, the multiplicity of books and articles about him, and the frequency with which he is talked about and quoted today, he is growing more pertinent (or, to use his own pun, more impertinent) every day. There is something about this man and his writings that fascinates us in the twentieth century. He refuses to die. He gets livelier every moment. He needles us with questions that we would like to ignore—but we find it impossible to forget them or him. He used to boast that he had been born "in the very nick of time," but, paradoxically, he has proved to be more meaningful to our century than to his own.

The breadth of Thoreau's appeal today is enormous. Lovers of nature first claimed him as their own and he is still without peer as a rhapsodist on the joys and rewards of contemplating the beauties of nature. It was he who perfected the nature essay as such and all modern nature writers are measured against his standard. Many find that his philosophy of the simple life is his greatest appeal. Here he came into his own during the Great Depression of the 1930's, when the man in the street (indeed, quite literally in the street) found himself forced to live the simple life willy-nilly and discovered in Thoreau a writer who did not insult him if he had no more than a nickel in his pocket. Yet with the ending of the Depression, the interest in Thoreau grew rather than declined, for, with the ever-increasing complexity of life, his insistence upon the *necessity* of living the simple life—if one is to make his life meaningful—has become more and more pertinent. Our young people today, who so understandably are revolting against the materialism of the older generation, are hailing Thoreau as their patron saint, as well they should. No phrase is more frequently on their lips than their reference to "a different drummer" (though perhaps not all those who quote that phrase realize it is from *Walden*). So far, in speaking of Thoreau's appeal today, I have been referring primarily to his *Walden*. Unquestionably, that is the work which first gained him his fame. But in recent years his essay on "Civil Disobedience" is challenging *Walden*'s place. This essay, which Gandhi put to such good use in India half a century ago and which the anti-Nazi resistance movements were using so effectively in Europe during World War II, has now come back to its home country to be one of the most discussed and most influential essays of our day.

I spoke of Thoreau's life *and* writings. The two are inextricably intertwined. He once complained that "My life hath been the poem I would have writ,/But I could not both live and utter it." Yet few writers have been so successful in making their lives and writings one. As Alfred Kazin has so felicitously said, "The greatest part of Thoreau's life was his writing. . . . The work of art he was seeking to create was really himself; his life was the explicit object that he tried to make in words."

The autobiographical nature of such works as *Walden,* "Civil Disobedience," the *Journal,* and *The Maine Woods* is obvious. Yet even when Thoreau was writing on Sir Walter Raleigh or Thomas Carlyle, he was unwittingly (or perhaps even wittingly) arguing ardently for his own way of life and writing rather than analyzing Raleigh or Carlyle. With Thoreau, perhaps more than with any other major writer, it is absolutely essential to understand the man first if we are to fully understand his work.

We have been fortunate in that over the years scholars have been diligently at work, and because of their great efforts an astonishing amount of factual information about Thoreau's day-to-day life has been accumulated. For few other writers is there such a comprehensive record of what was being done, and when. This present volume, however, is not an attempt to add to those details. Rather, it is an inquiry into the nature of Thoreau's personality and is not so much concerned with the *what* of his life as with the *why*. It tries to answer such questions as: Why was he the man he was? Why did he hold the opinions he did? Why did he write what he did? Such an inquiry, it is my hope, will increase our understanding of this challenging and enigmatic man.

This book is divided into two parts. The first, "Thoreau as Seen by His Contemporaries," is a collection of reminiscences of Thoreau by those who knew him well—some who were his age, some younger, some older; some who were of his station in life (if anyone as unique and individualistic as Thoreau can be said to have a station in life), some above, some below; some who understood him, some who were honestly baffled by him; some who liked him, some who did not. The reader may at times be puzzled because these reporters may not seem to be talking about the same man, so different are their reactions. Indeed, as George W. Cooke remarks in an essay included in this section, "There are evidently two Thoreaus—one that of his admirers and the other that of his detractors." But as Cooke concludes, "Thoreau must be understood from the point of view of the detractor as well as from that of the admirer, in order fully to appreciate him." And so we have intentionally tried to present him from many points of view. The more aspects of his nature we examine, the greater will be our knowledge of the man.

The second part, "Thoreau as Seen by the Critics," is a collection of studies of his personality, not by those who knew him personally, but by those who have studied his life and writings closely and have attempted to explain them. The studies represent the scholarship of nearly a century—from Daniel Gregory Mason writing in the 1890's to James Armstrong writing in the 1970's. Here again we find great dichotomies. The approaches are distinct;

the answers often very different. The critics at times seem to be talking about radically different men. If we could submit Thoreau in real life to the prolonged analysis of a trained psychiatrist or psychologist, *perhaps* we could come up with *the* definitive analysis of his life and personality. But Thoreau has been dead for more than a century, dead before modern science even began to think of the kinds of questions they would have to ask. We must therefore recognize the fact that these critics are necessarily limited. Their answers are theoretical and speculative. But that fact does not negate the validity of their attempts to explain Thoreau the man. He stands there challenging us. We want to know why. We want more than the simple facts of his life. To use a current phrase, we want to know what made Henry run. Among these theories and speculations here assembled may be some of the answers we seek.

I offer no particular brief for either the techniques these critics have employed or for their findings—except to say that each, I believe, has gone about his work with high seriousness and has come up with answers that we must consider thoughtfully, even if we do not necessarily accept them. If there seems to be an overemphasis on the Freudian approach, it is simply because Freud still unquestionably dominates the scene in psychology and personality analysis. It is inevitable that some Thoreau enthusiasts are going to be dismayed, even distressed by some of the suggestions made by the critics. They are going to feel that their hero has been tarnished. But I think that if they are willing to read these essays with an open mind, they will emerge with a better understanding of both Thoreau and his writings—and that, after all, is the purpose of this book.

I am happy to acknowledge the assistance, cooperation, and generosity of many people in my work on this volume. I am particularly indebted to Mr. and Mrs. Raymond Emerson of Concord, Massachusetts, for permission to edit and publish some of the manuscripts of Mr. Emerson's father, Dr. Edward Waldo Emerson; and to Professor James Armstrong of Laguna Beach, California, and Professor Raymond Gozzi of the University of Massachusetts at Amherst for revising their earlier unpublished studies for this volume and for their permission to publish them. I am also indebted to the staff of the Milne Library of the State University College of Arts and Science at Geneseo, New York—and, in particular, to Mr. William Lane—for patiently tracking down some of the essays in this book; and to the editor of this American Profiles series, Mrs. Aïda DiPace Donald, for her thoughtful advice and encouragement. I wish also to express my appreciation for permission to reprint copyright materials to Harper & Row, the Thoreau Society, Professor Paul Carroll, Stanford University Press, and Wesleyan University Press.

WALTER HARDING

State University College of Arts and Science
Geneseo, New York

Henry David Thoreau, 1817–1862

Henry David Thoreau was born in Concord, Massachusetts, on July 12, 1817, the only one of the famous Concord writers who was actually a native of that town. The third of four children in the Thoreau family, Henry grew up in genteel poverty when his father experienced a series of business failures. He was educated in the Concord schools, and when the family fortunes took a gradual turn for the better, with the establishment of a pencil manufacturing business, Henry was able to enroll at Harvard College. A shy, quiet boy, who was more interested in curling up with a book in the library or taking a solitary walk into the countryside, Thoreau took little part in the more boisterous collegiate activities, but graduated in 1837 with sufficiently high rank to read a paper at the commencement. In words that were to prove typical of his later philosophy and style he announced:

The order of things should be somewhat reversed; the seventh should be man's day of toil, wherein to earn his living by the sweat of his brow; and the other six his Sabbath of the affections and the soul,— in which to range this widespread garden, and drink in the soft influences and sublime revelations of nature.

He accepted the position of schoolmaster in Concord, but resigned after only two weeks when a school committee member insisted he use corporal punishment. Typically, Thoreau ferruled several children at random to "fulfill his obligation" to the committee, and then handed in his resignation. After nearly a year's unsuccessful search for another teaching position, in the summer of 1838 he established his own private school, in which he was later joined by his brother John. Despite (or perhaps because of) the fact that it was a highly experimental school using many of the techniques characteristic of the "progressive education" of a century later, it was an immediate success. He abandoned it in 1841 only because he wished to turn to other fields.

The great intellectual ferment of the New England of Thoreau's day was, of course, Transcendentalism, and its most famous exponent, Ralph Waldo Emerson, had settled in Concord in 1835. Upon Thoreau's return to Concord, the two soon became close friends. Emerson, fourteen years Thoreau's elder, took a fatherly interest in the younger man, introducing him to the other Transcendentalists and urging and encouraging him to turn to writing as a career. From 1841 to 1843 Thoreau lived in the Emerson household, and for six months in 1843 he lived with Emerson's brother's family on Staten Island—ostensibly in the former case as a handyman about the house and in the latter, as a tutor to William Emerson's children. In reality, however, both arrangements were made by Emerson to give Thoreau time to write and the opportunity to meet important editors and publishers.

In the fall of 1839, Thoreau and his brother John took a vacation—a rowboat journey down the Concord River and up the Merrimack River and back—which was later to become the subject of Thoreau's first book, *A Week on the Concord and Merrimack Rivers*. In the summer of 1840, both brothers fell in love with seventeen-year-old Ellen Sewall of Scituate, Massachusetts, the older sister of one of the pupils in their school. John proposed marriage and was refused because she preferred Henry, but when Henry later proposed, she turned him down too because her father, a conservative Unitarian minister, objected to the Thoreaus' association with anyone as "radical" as Emerson.

Thoreau for a number of years had wished to devote himself entirely to writing, but found his way blocked by the necessity of earning a living. When in the fall of 1844 Emerson bought some acreage on the shores of beautiful Walden Pond on the outskirts of Concord, Thoreau quickly asked permission to use the land. In the spring of 1845—at the cost of $28.12½—he built a sturdy little cabin, and by adopting the simplest possible mode of life, he soon found he could live on as little as 27 cents a week. Freed thus from the necessity of spending long hours earning a living— he found, in fact, that in six weeks of manual labor he could earn enough to live a year—he devoted his new-found free time to studying nature and writing. In the two years he remained at Walden Pond he not only succeeded in at last writing his long-projected book about his vacation journey with John, but also the first draft of what was to become his masterpiece, *Walden,* the account of his life at the pond. In September of 1847, having completed his announced task at Walden, he left the pond, first spending a year looking after the Emerson family while Emerson himself was abroad, and then living the rest of his life with his parents, but still following the simple life he had followed at Walden.

Thoreau grew up in the period of great conflict between the South and the North over the issue of slavery. He early took side with the abolitionists and in 1843, feeling that he should take a more effective stand against slavery, refused to pay his poll tax on the grounds that it supported a government which in turn supported slavery. For some unknown reason he was ignored until the summer of 1846, when he was arrested and placed in the Concord jail for nonpayment of his taxes. Someone—probably his Aunt Maria—under cover of darkness paid his taxes for him, and he was released in the morning, angry that his protest had been thus foiled. In 1849 he published "Resistance to Civil Government," later better known as "Civil Disobedience," a reasoned explanation of the course he had taken in going to jail—an essay that has become the Bible of such fighters for freedom as Gandhi and Dr. Martin Luther King, Jr. Thoreau incidentally continued his fight against slavery, speaking out frequently against it on the lecture platform and taking an active part in the Underground Railroad by aiding escaped slaves to freedom in Canada. When

John Brown made his raid on Harpers Ferry in 1859, Thoreau was the first to come to his defense with his eloquent "Plea for Captain John Brown."

In 1849, despairing of ever getting a book into print, he paid a commercial publisher to bring out his *A Week.* It was a dismal failure, selling only a few hundred copies. When the publisher returned the unsold stock to him, he sardonically wrote in his *Journal,* "I have now a library of nearly nine hundred volumes, over seven hundred of which I wrote myself." The failure of *A Week,* however, did not discourage Thoreau. He set to work to make his next book, *Walden,* a better book and in the process completely rewrote it eight times. In 1854 he persuaded Ticknor & Fields of Boston to publish it and while it was by no means a best seller, it did receive some laudatory reviews and sold two thousand copies in five years.

Although he liked to boast that he had "traveled much in Concord"—as indeed he had, for he spent four or five hours of each day exploring the woods and fields, the rivers and ponds of his native town—he also took delight in making what he called "excursions" to more distant points: trips to the woods of northern Maine in 1846, 1853, and 1857; trips to Cape Cod in 1849, 1850, 1855, and 1857; a trip to Quebec in 1850; and numerous shorter journeys. He prepared for each of these excursions by careful reading in advance and by taking gazetteers and other guidebooks with him. Many of these journeys were in large part made on foot or by canoe; they became the subjects of his lighthearted travel books *The Maine Woods, Cape Cod, A Yankee in Canada,* and other shorter travel sketches. But perhaps the major work of his life was his *Journal,* for which he made almost daily entries from 1837 to 1861. In it he reported not only his daily excursions into the Concord countryside, but, more importantly, his thoughts. It is one of the great records of a man's life—nearly two million words of it.

All of his adult life Thoreau suffered from bouts of tuberculosis. When in December of 1860 he developed a bad cold, it soon worsened into bronchitis and opened up the tubercular lesions in his lungs. Doctors despaired for his life. In the spring of 1861 he made a futile journey to Minnesota, hoping the drier climate there would aid him, but he returned in a few months fully aware he had not much longer to live. His last months he devoted, as long as he was able, to preparing his unpublished papers for the press. He died on May 6, 1862, a few months short of the age of forty-five, with only two books published and both of those out-of-print. *Walden* and *A Week* were very shortly reprinted and within five years, five more volumes of his writings had appeared. By the turn of the century his fame had grown sufficiently that in 1906 his complete *Journals* were published in fourteen volumes. But it has not been until the past few decades that Thoreau has really come into his own, and has been recognized as one of America's greatest writers.

W. H.

Part One

Thoreau as Seen by
His Contemporaries

✪

Thoreau

Henry David Thoreau was the last male descendant of a French ancestor who came to this country from the Isle of Guernsey. His character exhibited occasional traits drawn from this blood, in singular combination with a very strong Saxon genius. He was born in Concord, Massachusetts, on the 12th of July, 1817. He was graduated at Harvard College in 1837, but without any literary distinction. An iconoclast in literature, he seldom thanked colleges for their service to him, holding them in small esteem, whilst yet his debt to them was important. After leaving the University, he joined his brother in teaching a private school, which he soon renounced. His father was a manufacturer of lead-pencils, and Henry applied himself for a time to this craft, believing he could make a better pencil than was then in use. After completing his experiments, he exhibited his work to chemists and artists in Boston, and having obtained their certificates to its excellence and to its equality with the best London manufacture, he returned home contented. His friends congratulated him that he had now opened his way to fortune. But he replied that he should never make another pencil. "Why should

Reprinted from the revised version of the Centenary Edition of Emerson's works (Boston: Houghton Mifflin, 1904), X, 451–485.

Because of its great influence, this essay has been taken out of the chronological order that the remaining essays in this section have been placed in [ed.].

3

I? I would not do again what I have done once." He resumed his
endless walks and miscellaneous studies, making every day some
new acquaintance with Nature, though as yet never speaking of
zoology or botany, since, though very studious of natural facts, he
was incurious of technical and textual science.

At this time, a strong, healthy youth, fresh from college, whilst
all his companions were choosing their profession, or eager to
begin some lucrative employment, it was inevitable that his
thoughts should be exercised on the same question, and it required rare decision to refuse all the accustomed paths and keep
his solitary freedom at the cost of disappointing the natural expectations of his family and friends: all the more difficult that
he had a perfect probity, was exact in securing his own independence, and in holding every man to the like duty. But Thoreau
never faltered. He was a born protestant. He declined to give up
his large ambition of knowledge and action for any narrow craft
or profession, aiming at a much more comprehensive calling, the
art of living well. If he slighted and defied the opinions of others,
it was only that he was more intent to reconcile his practice with
his own belief. Never idle or self-indulgent, he preferred, when
he wanted money, earning it by some piece of manual labor agreeable to him, as building a boat or a fence, planting, grafting,
surveying or other short work, to any long engagements. With
his hardy habits and few wants, his skill in wood-craft, and his
powerful arithmetic, he was very competent to live in any part of
the world. It would cost him less time to supply his wants than
another. He was therefore secure of his leisure.

A natural skill for mensuration, growing out of his mathematical knowledge and his habit of ascertaining the measures and
distances of objects which interested him, the size of trees, the
depth and extent of ponds and rivers, the height of mountains
and the air-line distance of his favorite summits—this, and his
intimate knowledge of the territory about Concord, made him
drift into the profession of land-surveyor. It had the advantage
for him that it led him continually into new and secluded grounds,
and helped his studies of Nature. His accuracy and skill in this

work were readily appreciated, and he found all the employment he wanted.

He could easily solve the problems of the surveyor, but he was daily beset with graver questions, which he manfully confronted. He interrogated every custom, and wished to settle all his practice on an ideal foundation. He was a protestant *à outrance,* and few lives contain so many renunciations. He was bred to no profession; he never married; he lived alone; he never went to church; he never voted; he refused to pay a tax to the State; he ate no flesh, he drank no wine, he never knew the use of tobacco; and, though a naturalist, he used neither trap nor gun. He chose, wisely no doubt for himself, to be the bachelor of thought and Nature. He had no talent for wealth, and knew how to be poor without the least hint of squalor or inelegance. Perhaps he fell into his way of living without forecasting it much, but approved it with later wisdom. "I am often reminded," he wrote in his journal, "that if I had bestowed on me the wealth of Croesus, my aims must be still the same, and my means essentially the same." He had no temptations to fight against—no appetites, no passions, no taste for elegant trifles. A fine house, dress, the manners and talk of highly cultivated people were all thrown away on him. He much preferred a good Indian, and considered these refinements as impediments to conversation, wishing to meet his companion on the simplest terms. He declined invitations to dinner-parties, because there each was in every one's way, and he could not meet the individuals to any purpose. "They make their pride," he said, "in making their dinner cost much; I make my pride in making my dinner cost little." When asked at table what dish he preferred, he answered, "The nearest." He did not like the taste of wine, and never had a vice in his life. He said—"I have a faint recollection of pleasure derived from smoking dried lily-stems, before I was a man. I had commonly a supply of these. I have never smoked anything more noxious."

He chose to be rich by making his wants few, and supplying them himself. In his travels, he used the railroad only to get over so much country as was unimportant to the present purpose, walking hundreds of miles, avoiding taverns, buying a lodging in farmers' and fishermen's houses, as cheaper, and more agreeable to him, and because there he could better find the men and the information he wanted.

There was somewhat military in his nature, not to be subdued, always manly and able, but rarely tender, as if he did not feel himself except in opposition. He wanted a fallacy to expose, a blunder to pillory, I may say required a little sense of victory, a roll of the drum, to call his powers into full exercise. It cost him nothing to say No; indeed he found it much easier than to say Yes. It seemed as if his first instinct on hearing a proposition was to controvert it, so impatient was he of the limitations of our daily thought. This habit, of course, is a little chilling to the social affections; and though the companion would in the end acquit him of any malice or untruth, yet it mars conversation. Hence, no equal companion stood in affectionate relations with one so pure and guileless. "I love Henry," said one of his friends, "but I cannot like him; and as for taking his arm, I should as soon think of taking the arm of an elm-tree."

Yet, hermit and stoic as he was, he was really fond of sympathy, and threw himself heartily and childlike into the company of young people whom he loved, and whom he delighted to entertain, as he only could, with the varied and endless anecdotes of his experiences by field and river: and he was always ready to lead a huckleberry-party or a search for chestnuts or grapes. Talking, one day, of a public discourse, Henry remarked that whatever succeeded with the audience was bad. I said, "Who would not like to write something which all can read, like *Robinson Crusoe*? and who does not see with regret that his page is not solid with a right materialistic treatment, which delights everybody?" Henry objected, of course, and vaunted the better lectures which reached only a few persons. But, at supper, a young girl, understanding that he was to lecture at the Lyceum, sharply asked him, "Whether his lecture would be a nice, interesting story, such as she wished to hear, or whether it was one of those old philosophical things that she did not care about." Henry turned to her, and bethought himself, and, I saw, was trying to believe that he had matter that might fit her and her brother, who were to sit up and go to the lecture, if it was a good one for them.

He was a speaker and actor of the truth, born such, and was ever running into dramatic situations from this cause. In any circumstance it interested all bystanders to know what part Henry would take, and what he would say; and he did not disappoint expectation, but used an original judgment on each emergency. In 1845 he built himself a small framed house on the shores of Walden Pond, and lived there two years alone, a life of labor and study. This action was quite native and fit for him. No one who knew him would tax him with affectation. He was more unlike his neighbors in his thought than in his action. As soon as he had exhausted the advantages of that solitude, he abandoned it. In 1847,* not approving some uses to which the public expenditure was applied, he refused to pay his town tax, and was put in jail. A friend paid the tax for him, and he was released. The like annoyance was threatened the next year. But as his friends paid the tax, notwithstanding his protest, I believe he ceased to resist. No opposition or ridicule had any weight with him. He coldly and fully stated his opinion without affecting to believe that it was the opinion of the company. It was of no consequence if every one present held the opposite opinion. On one occasion he went to the University Library to procure some books. The librarian refused to lend them. Mr. Thoreau repaired to the President, who stated to him the rules and usages, which permitted the loan of books to resident graduates, to clergymen who were alumni, and to some others resident within a circle of ten miles' radius from the College. Mr. Thoreau explained to the President that the railroad had destroyed the old scale of distances—that the library was useless, yes, and President and College useless, on the terms of his rules—that the one benefit he owed to the College was its library—that, at this moment, not only his want of books was imperative, but he wanted a large number of books, and assured him that he, Thoreau and not the librarian, was the proper custo-

* No, 1846 [ed.].

dian of these. In short, the President found the petitioner so
formidable, and the rules getting to look so ridiculous, that he
ended by giving him a privilege which in his hands proved unlimited thereafter.

No truer American existed than Thoreau. His preference of
his country and condition was genuine, and his aversion from
English and European manners and tastes almost reached contempt. He listened impatiently to news or *bonmots* gleaned from
London circles; and though he tried to be civil, these anecdotes
fatigued him. The men were all imitating each other, and on a
small mould. Why can they not live as far apart as possible, and
each be a man by himself? What he sought was the most
energetic nature; and he wished to go to Oregon, not to London.
"In every part of Great Britain," he wrote in his diary, "are discovered traces of the Romans, their funeral urns, their camps,
their roads, their dwellings. But New England, at least, is not
based on any Roman ruins. We have not to lay the foundations
of our houses on the ashes of a former civilization."

But idealist as he was, standing for abolition of slavery, abolition of tariffs, almost for abolition of government, it is needless
to say he found himself not only unrepresented in actual politics,
but almost equally opposed to every class of reformers. Yet he
paid the tribute of his uniform respect to the Anti-Slavery party.
One man, whose personal acquaintance he had formed, he honored with exceptional regard. Before the first friendly word had
been spoken for Captain John Brown, he sent notices to most
houses in Concord that he would speak in a public hall on the
condition and character of John Brown, on Sunday evening, and
invited all people to come. The Republican Committee, the Aboli-
tionist Committee, sent him word that it was premature and not
advisable. He replied—"I did not send to you for advice, but to
announce that I am to speak." The hall was filled at an early
hour by people of all parties, and his earnest eulogy of the hero
was heard by all respectfully, by many with a sympathy that
surprised themselves.

It was said of Plotinus that he was ashamed of his body, and 'tis very likely he had good reason for it—that his body was a bad servant, and he had not skill in dealing with the material world, as happens often to men of abstract intellect. But Mr. Thoreau was equipped with a most adapted and serviceable body. He was of short stature, firmly built, of light complexion, with strong, serious blue eyes, and a grave aspect—his face covered in the late years with a becoming beard. His senses were acute, his frame well-knit and hardy, his hands strong and skilful in the use of tools. And there was a wonderful fitness of body and mind. He could pace sixteen rods more accurately than another man could measure them with rod and chain. He could find his path in the woods at night, he said, better by his feet than his eyes. He could estimate the measure of a tree very well by his eye; he could estimate the weight of a calf or a pig, like a dealer. From a box containing a bushel or more of loose pencils, he could take up with his hands fast enough just a dozen pencils at every grasp. He was a good swimmer, runner, skater, boatman, and would probably outwalk most countrymen in a day's journey. And the relation of body to mind was still finer than we have indicated. He said he wanted every stride his legs made. The length of his walk uniformly made the length of his writing. If shut up in the house he did not write at all.

He had a strong common sense, like that which Rose Flammock, the weaver's daughter in Scott's romance, commends in her father, as resembling a yardstick, which, whilst it measures dowlas and diaper, can equally well measure tapestry and cloth of gold. He had always a new resource. When I was planting forest trees, and had procured half a peck of acorns, he said that only a small portion of them would be sound, and proceeded to examine them and select the sound ones. But finding this took time, he said, "I think if you put them all into water the good ones will sink;" which experiment we tried with success. He could plan a garden or a house or a barn; would have been competent to lead a "Pacific Exploring Expedition;" could give judicious counsel in the gravest private or public affairs.

He lived for the day, not cumbered and mortified by his memory. If he brought you yesterday a new proposition, he would bring you to-day another not less revolutionary. A very industrious man, and setting, like all highly organized men, a high value on his time, he seemed the only man of leisure in town, always ready for any excursion that promised well, or for conversation prolonged into late hours. His trenchant sense was never stopped by his rules of daily prudence, but was always up to the new occasion. He liked and used the simplest food, yet, when some one urged a vegetable diet, Thoreau thought all diets a very small matter, saying that "the man who shoots the buffalo lives better than the man who boards at the Graham House." He said—"You can sleep near the railroad, and never be disturbed: Nature knows very well what sounds are worth attending to, and has made up her mind not to hear the railroad-whistle. But things respect the devout mind, and a mental ecstasy was never interrupted." He noted what repeatedly befell him, that, after receiving from a distance a rare plant, he would presently find the same in his own haunts. And those pieces of luck which happen only to good players happened to him. One day, walking with a stranger, who inquired where Indian arrow-heads could be found, he replied, "Everywhere," and, stooping forward, picked one on the instant from the ground. At Mount Washington, in Tuckerman's Ravine, Thoreau had a bad fall, and sprained his foot. As he was in the act of getting up from his fall, he saw for the first time the leaves of the *Arnica mollis.*

His robust common sense, armed with stout hands, keen perceptions and strong will, cannot yet account for the superiority which shone in his simple and hidden life. I must add the cardinal fact, that there was an excellent wisdom in him, proper to a rare class of men, which showed him the material world as a means and symbol. This discovery, which sometimes yields to poets a certain casual and interrupted light, serving for the ornament of their writing, was in him an unsleeping insight; and whatever faults or obstructions of temperament might cloud it, he was not disobedient to the heavenly vision. In his youth, he said, one day, "The other world is all my art; my pencils will draw no other; my jack-knife will cut nothing else; I do not use it as a means." This was the muse and genius that ruled his opinions, conversation, studies, work and course of life. This made him a searching judge of men. At first glance he measured his companion, and, though insensible to some fine traits of culture, could very well report his weight and calibre. And this made the impression of genius which his conversation sometimes gave.

He understood the matter in hand at a glance, and saw the limitations and poverty of those he talked with, so that nothing seemed concealed from such terrible eyes. I have repeatedly known young men of sensibility converted in a moment to the belief that this was the man they were in search of, the man of men, who could tell them all they should do. His own dealing with them was never affectionate, but superior, didactic, scorning their petty ways—very slowly conceding, or not conceding at all, the promise of his society at their houses, or even at his own. "Would he not walk with them?" "He did not know. There was nothing so important to him as his walk; he had no walks to throw away on company." Visits were offered him from respectful parties, but he declined them. Admiring friends offered to carry him at their own cost to the Yellowstone River—to the West Indies—to South America. But though nothing could be more grave or considered than his refusals, they remind one, in quite new relations, of that fop Brummel's reply to the gentleman who offered him his carriage in a shower, "But where will *you* ride, then?"—and what accusing silences, and what searching and irresistible speeches, battering down all defences, his companions can remember!

Mr. Thoreau dedicated his genius with such entire love to the fields, hills and waters of his native town, that he made them known and interesting to all reading Americans, and to people over the sea. The river on whose banks he was born and died he knew from its springs to its confluence with the Merrimack. He had made summer and winter observations on it for many years, and at every hour of the day and night. The result of the recent survey of the Water Commissioners appointed by the State of Massachusetts he had reached by his private experiments, several years earlier. Every fact which occurs in the bed, on the banks or in the air over it; the fishes, and their spawning and nests, their manners, their food; the shad-flies which fill the air on a certain evening once a year, and which are snapped at by the fishes so ravenously that many of these die of repletion; the conical heaps of small stones on the river-shallows, the huge nests of small fishes, one of which will sometimes overfill a cart; the birds which frequent the stream, heron, duck, sheldrake, loon, osprey; the snake, muskrat, otter, woodchuck and fox, on the banks; the turtle, frog, hyla and cricket, which make the banks vocal—were all known to him, and, as it were, townsmen and fellow creatures; so that he felt an absurdity or violence in any narrative of one of these by itself apart, and still more of its dimensions on an inch-rule, or in the exhibition of its skeleton, or the specimen of a squirrel or a bird in brandy. He liked to speak of the manners of the river, as itself a lawful creature, yet with exactness, and always to an observed fact. As he knew the river, so the ponds in this region.

One of the weapons he used, more important to him than microscope or alcohol-receiver to other investigators, was a whim which grew on him by indulgence, yet appeared in gravest statement, namely, of extolling his own town and neighborhood as the most favored centre for natural observation. He remarked that the Flora of Massachusetts embraced almost all the important plants of America—most of the oaks, most of the willows, the best pines, the ash, the maple, the beech, the nuts. He returned Kane's *Arctic Voyage* to a friend of whom he had borrowed it, with the remark, that "Most of the phenomena noted might be observed in Concord." He seemed a little envious of the Pole, for the coincident sunrise and sunset, or five minutes' day after six months: a splendid fact, which Annursnuc had never afforded him. He found red snow in one of his walks, and told me that he expected to find yet the *Victoria regia* in Concord. He was the attorney of the indigenous plants, and owned to a preference of the weeds to the imported plants, as of the Indian to the civilized man, and noticed, with pleasure, that the willow bean-poles of his neighbor had grown more than his beans. "See these weeds," he said, "which have been hoed at by a million farmers all spring and summer, and yet have prevailed, and just now come out triumphant over all lanes, pastures, fields and gardens, such is their vigor. We have insulted them with low names, too—as Pigweed, Wormwood, Chick-weed, Shad-blossom." He says, "They have brave names, too—Ambrosia, Stellaria, Amelanchier, Amaranth, etc."

I think his fancy for referring everything to the meridian of Concord did not grow out of any ignorance or depreciation of other longitudes or latitudes, but was rather a playful expression of his conviction of the indifferency of all places, and that the best place for each is where he stands. He expressed it once in this wise: "I think nothing is to be hoped from you, if this bit of mould under your feet is not sweeter to you to eat than any other in this world, or in any world."

The other weapon with which he conquered all obstacles in science was patience. He knew how to sit immovable, a part of the rock he rested on, until the bird, the reptile, the fish, which had retired from him, should come back and resume its habits, nay, moved by curiosity, should come to him and watch him.

It was a pleasure and a privilege to walk with him. He knew the country like a fox or a bird, and passed through it as freely by paths of his own. He knew every track in the snow or on the ground, and what creature had taken this path before him. One must submit abjectly to such a guide, and the reward was great. Under his arm he carried an old music-book to press plants; in his pocket, his diary and pencil, a spy-glass for birds, microscope, jack-knife and twine. He wore a straw hat, stout shoes, strong gray trousers, to brave scrub-oaks and smilax, and to climb a tree for a hawk's or a squirrel's nest. He waded into the pool for the water-plants, and his strong legs were no insignificant part of his armor. On the day I speak of he looked for the Menyanthes, detected it across the wide pool, and, on examination of the florets, decided that it had been in flower five days. He drew out of his breast-pocket his diary, and read the names of all the plants that should bloom on this day, whereof he kept account as a banker when his notes fall due. The Cypripedium not due till to-morrow. He thought that, if waked up from a trance, in this swamp, he could tell by the plants what time of the year it was within two days. The redstart was flying about, and presently the fine grosbeaks, whose brilliant scarlet "makes the rash gazer wipe his eye," and whose fine clear note Thoreau compared to that of a tanager which has got rid of its hoarseness. Presently he heard a note which he called that of the night-warbler, a bird he had never identified, had been in search of twelve years, which always, when he saw it, was in the act of diving down into a tree or bush, and which it was vain to seek; the only bird which sings indifferently by night and by day. I told him he must beware of finding and booking it, lest life should have nothing more to show him. He said, "What you seek in vain for, half your life, one day you come full upon, all the family at dinner. You seek it like a dream, and as soon as you find it you become its prey."

His interest in the flower or the bird lay very deep in his mind, was connected with Nature—and the meaning of Nature was never attempted to be defined by him. He would not offer a memoir of his observations to the Natural History Society. "Why should I? To detach the description from its connections in my mind would make it no longer true or valuable to me: and they do not wish what belongs to it." His power of observation seemed to indicate additional senses. He saw as with microscope, heard as with ear-trumpet, and his memory was a photographic register of all he saw and heard. And yet none knew better than he that it is not the fact that imports, but the impression or effect of the fact on your mind. Every fact lay in glory in his mind, a type of the order and beauty of the whole.

His determination on Natural History was organic. He confessed that he sometimes felt like a hound or a panther, and, if born among Indians, would have been a fell hunter. But, restrained by his Massachusetts culture, he played out the game in this mild form of botany and ichthyology. His intimacy with animals suggested what Thomas Fuller records of Butler the apiologist, that "either he had told the bees things or the bees had told him." Snakes coiled round his legs; the fishes swam into his hand, and he took them out of the water; he pulled the woodchuck out of its hole by the tail, and took the foxes under his protection from the hunters. Our naturalist had perfect magnanimity; he had no secrets: he would carry you to the heron's haunt, or even to his most prized botanical swamp—possibly knowing that you could never find it again, yet willing to take his risks.

No college ever offered him a diploma, or a professor's chair; no academy made him its corresponding secretary, its discoverer or even its member. Perhaps these learned bodies feared the satire of his presence. Yet so much knowledge of Nature's secret and genius few others possessed; none in a more large and religious synthesis. For not a particle of respect had he to the opinions of any man or body of men, but homage solely to the truth itself; and as he discovered everywhere among doctors some leaning of courtesy, it discredited them. He grew to be revered and admired by his townsmen, who had at first known him only as an oddity. The farmers who employed him as a surveyor soon discovered his rare accuracy and skill, his knowledge of their lands, of trees, of birds, of Indian remains and the like, which enabled him to tell every farmer more than he knew before of his own farm; so that he began to feel a little as if Mr. Thoreau had better rights in his land than he. They felt, too, the superiority of character which addressed all men with a native authority.

Indian relics abound in Concord—arrow-heads, stone chisels, pestles and fragments of pottery; and on the river-bank, large heaps of clam-shells and ashes mark spots which the savages frequented. These, and every circumstance touching the Indian, were important in his eyes. His visits to Maine were chiefly for love of the Indian. He had the satisfaction of seeing the manufacture of the bark canoe, as well as of trying his hand in its management on the rapids. He was inquisitive about the making of the stone arrow-head, and in his last days charged a youth setting out for the Rocky Mountains to find an Indian who could tell him that: "It was well worth a visit to California to learn it." Occasionally, a small party of Penobscot Indians would visit Concord, and pitch their tents for a few weeks in summer on the river-bank. He failed not to make acquaintance with the best of them; though he well knew that asking questions of Indians is like catechizing beavers and rabbits. In his last visit to Maine he had great satisfaction from Joseph Polis, an intelligent Indian of Oldtown, who was his guide for some weeks.

He was equally interested in every natural fact. The depth of his perception found likeness of law throughout Nature, and I know not any genius who so swiftly inferred universal law from the single fact. He was no pedant of a department. His eye was open to beauty, and his ear to music. He found these, not in rare conditions, but wheresoever he went. He thought the best of music was in single strains; and he found poetic suggestion in the humming of the telegraph-wire.

His poetry might be bad or good; he no doubt wanted a lyric facility and technical skill, but he had the source of poetry in his spiritual perception. He was a good reader and critic, and his judgment on poetry was to the ground of it. He could not be deceived as to the presence or absence of the poetic element in any composition, and his thirst for this made him negligent and perhaps scornful of superficial graces. He would pass by many delicate rhythms, but he would have detected every live stanza or line in a volume and knew very well where to find an equal poetic charm in prose. He was so enamoured of the spiritual beauty that he held all actual written poems in very light esteem in the comparison. He admired Aeschylus and Pindar; but when some one was commending them, he said that Aeschylus and the Greeks, in describing Apollo and Orpheus, had given no song, or no good one. "They ought not to have moved trees, but to have chanted to the gods such a hymn as would have sung all their old ideas out of their heads, and new ones in." His own verses are often rude and defective. The gold does not yet run pure, is drossy and crude. The thyme and marjoram are not yet honey. But if he want lyric fineness and technical merits, if he have not the poetic temperament, he never lacks the causal thought, showing that his genius was better than his talent. He knew the worth of the Imagination for the uplifting and consolation of human life, and liked to throw every thought into a symbol. The fact you tell is of no value, but only the impression. For this reason his presence was poetic, always piqued the curiosity to know more deeply the secrets of his mind. He had many reserves, an unwillingness to exhibit to profane eyes what was still sacred in his own, and knew well how to throw a poetic veil over his experience. All readers of *Walden* will remember his mythical record of his disappointments:

I long ago lost a hound, a bay horse and a turtle-dove, and am still on their trail. Many are the travellers I have spoken concerning them, describing their tracks, and what calls they answered to. I have met one or two who have heard the hound, and the tramp of the horse, and even seen the dove disappear behind a cloud; and they seemed as anxious to recover them as if they had lost them themselves.

His riddles were worth the reading, and I confide that if at any time I do not understand the expression, it is yet just. Such was the wealth of his truth that it was not worth his while to use words in vain. His poem entitled "Sympathy" reveals the tenderness under that triple steel of stoicism, and the intellectual subtility it could animate. His classic poem on "Smoke" suggests Simonides, but is better than any poem of Simonides. His biography is in his verses. His habitual thought makes all his poetry a hymn to the Cause of causes, the Spirit which vivifies and controls his own:

> I hearing get, who had but ears,
> And sight, who had but eyes before;
> I moments live, who lived but years,
> And truth discern, who knew but learning's lore.

And still more in these religious lines:

Now chiefly is my natal hour,
And only now my prime of life;
I will not doubt the love untold,
Which not my worth nor want have bought,
Which wooed me young, and woos me old,
And to this evening hath me brought.

Whilst he used in his writings a certain petulance of remark in reference to churches or churchmen, he was a person of a rare, tender and absolute religion, a person incapable of any profanation, by act or by thought. Of course, the same isolation which belonged to his original thinking and living detached him from the social religious forms. This is neither to be censured nor regretted. Aristotle long ago explained it, when he said, "One who surpasses his fellow citizens in virtue is no longer a part of the city. Their law is not for him, since he is a law to himself."

Thoreau was sincerity itself, and might fortify the convictions of prophets in the ethical laws by his holy living. It was an affirmative experience which refused to be set aside. A truth-speaker he, capable of the most deep and strict conversation; a physician to the wounds of any soul; a friend, knowing not only the secret of friendship, but almost worshipped by those few persons who resorted to him as their confessor and prophet, and knew the deep value of his mind and great heart. He thought that without religion or devotion of some kind nothing great was ever accomplished: and he thought that the bigoted sectarian had better bear this in mind.

His virtues, of course, sometimes ran into extremes. It was easy to trace to the inexorable demand on all for exact truth that austerity which made this willing hermit more solitary even than he wished. Himself of a perfect probity, he required not less of others. He had a disgust at crime, and no worldly success would cover it. He detected paltering as readily in dignified and prosperous persons as in beggars, and with equal scorn. Such dangerous frankness was in his dealing that his admirers called him "that terrible Thoreau," as if he spoke when silent, and was still present when he had departed. I think the severity of his ideal interfered to deprive him of a healthy sufficiency of human society.

The habit of a realist to find things the reverse of their appearance inclined him to put every statement in a paradox. A certain habit of antagonism defaced his earlier writings—a trick of rhetoric not quite outgrown in his later, of substituting for the obvious word and thought its diametrical opposite. He praised wild mountains and winter forests for their domestic air, in snow and ice he would find sultriness, and commended the wilderness for resembling Rome and Paris. "It was so dry, that you might call it wet."

The tendency to magnify the moment, to read all the laws of Nature in the one object or one combination under your eye, is of course comic to those who do not share the philosopher's perception of identity. To him there was no such thing as size. The pond was a small ocean; the Atlantic, a large Walden Pond. He referred every minute fact to cosmical laws. Though he meant to be just, he seemed haunted by a certain chronic assumption that the science of the day pretended completeness, and he had just found out that the *savans* had neglected to discriminate a particular botanical variety, had failed to describe the seeds or count the sepals. "That is to say," we replied, "the blockheads were not born in Concord; but who said they were? It was their unspeakable misfortune to be born in London, or Paris, or Rome; but, poor fellows, they did what they could, considering that they never saw Bateman's Pond, or Nine-Acre Corner, or Becky Stow's Swamp; besides, what were you sent into the world for, but to add this observation?"

Had his genius been only contemplative, he had been fitted to his life, but with his energy and practical ability he seemed born for great enterprise and for command; and I so much regret the loss of his rare powers of action, that I cannot help counting it a fault in him that he had no ambition. Wanting this, instead of engineering for all America, he was the captain of a huckleberry-party. Pounding beans is good to the end of pounding empires one of these days; but if, at the end of years, it is still only beans!

But these foibles, real or apparent, were fast vanishing in the incessant growth of a spirit so robust and wise, and which effaced its defeats with new triumphs. His study of Nature was a perpetual ornament to him, and inspired his friends with curiosity to see the world through his eyes, and to hear his adventures. They possessed every kind of interest.

He had many elegancies of his own, whilst he scoffed at conventional elegance. Thus, he could not bear to hear the sound of his own steps, the grit of gravel; and therefore never willingly walked in the road, but in the grass, on mountains and in woods. His senses were acute, and he remarked that by night every dwelling-house gives out bad air, like a slaughter-house. He liked the pure fragrance of melilot. He honored certain plants with special regard, and, over all, the pond-lily—then, the gentian, and the *Mikania scandens,* and "life-everlasting," and a bass-tree which he visited every year when it bloomed, in the middle of July. He thought the scent a more oracular inquisition than the sight—more oracular and trustworthy. The scent, of course, reveals what is concealed from the other senses. By it he detected earthiness. He delighted in echoes, and said they were almost the only kind of kindred voices that he heard. He loved Nature so well, was so happy in her solitude, that he became very jealous of cities and the sad work which their refinements and artifices made with man and his dwelling. The axe was always destroying his forest. "Thank God," he said, "they cannot cut down the clouds!" "All kinds of figures are drawn on the blue ground with this fibrous white paint."

I subjoin a few sentences taken from his unpublished manuscripts, not only as records of his thought and feeling, but for their power of description and literary excellence:

Some circumstantial evidence is very strong, as when you find a trout in the milk.

The chub is a soft fish, and tastes like boiled brown paper salted.

The youth gets together his materials to build a bridge to the moon, or, perchance, a palace or temple on the earth, and, at length the middle-aged man concludes to build a wood-shed with them.

The locust z-ing.

Devil's-needles zigzagging along the Nut-Meadow brook.

Sugar is not so sweet to the palate as sound to the healthy ear.

I put on some hemlock-boughs, and the rich salt crackling of their leaves was like mustard to the ear, the crackling of uncountable regiments. Dead trees love the fire.

The bluebird carries the sky on his back.

The tanager flies through the green foliage as if it would ignite the leaves.

If I wish for a horse-hair for my compass-sight I must go to the stable; but the hair-bird, with her sharp eyes, goes to the road.

Immortal water, alive even to the superficies.

Fire is the most tolerable third party.

Nature made ferns for pure leaves, to show what she could do in that line.

No tree has so fair a bole and so handsome an instep as the beech.

How did these beautiful rainbow-tints get into the shell of the fresh-water clam, buried in the mud at the bottom of our dark river?

Hard are the times when the infant's shoes are second-foot.

We are strictly confined to our men to whom we give liberty.

Nothing is so much to be feared as fear. Atheism may comparatively be popular with God himself.

Of what significance the things you can forget? A little thought is sexton to all the world.

How can we expect a harvest of thought who have not had a seed-time of character?

Only he can be trusted with gifts who can present a face of bronze to expectations.

I ask to be melted. You can only ask of the metals that they be tender to the fire that melts them. To nought else can they be tender.

There is a flower known to botanists, one of the same genus with our summer plant called "Life-Everlasting," a *Gnaphalium* like that, which grows on the most inaccessible cliffs of the Tyrolese mountains, where the chamois dare hardly venture, and which the hunter, tempted by its beauty, and by his love (for it is immensely valued by the Swiss maidens), climbs the cliffs to gather, and is sometimes found dead at the foot, with the flower in his hand. It is called by botanists the *Gnaphalium leontopodium,* but by the Swiss *Edelweisse,* which signifies *Noble Purity.* Thoreau seemed to me living in the hope to gather this plant, which belonged to him of right. The scale on which his studies proceeded was so large as to require longevity, and we were the less prepared for his sudden disappearance. The country knows not yet, or in the least part, how great a son it has lost. It seems an injury that he should leave in the midst his broken task which none else can finish, a kind of indignity to so noble a soul that he should depart out of Nature before yet he has been really shown to his peers for what he is. But he, at least, is content. His soul was made for the noblest society; he had in a short life exhausted the capabilities of this world; wherever there is knowledge, wherever there is virtue, wherever there is beauty, he will find a home.

"A Slight, Quaint-Looking Person"

It was my good fortune to know Henry D. Thoreau as a friend and correspondent during the last eight years of his life. I had been attracted by his fresh and manly thoughts as recorded in *Walden,* and sought his acquaintance by writing him an appreciative letter, and inviting him to visit me. My first interview with him was so peculiar that I will venture to state it. The season was winter, a snow had lately fallen, and I was engaged in shovelling the accumulated mass from the entrance to my house, when I perceived a man walking towards me bearing an umbrella in one hand and a leather travelling-bag in the other. So unlike my ideal Thoreau, whom I had fancied, from the robust nature of his mind and habits of life, to be a man of unusual vigor and size, that I did not suspect, although I had expected him in the morning, that the slight, quaint-looking person before me was the Walden philosopher. There are few persons who had previously read his works that were not disappointed by his personal appearance. As he came near to me I gave him the usual salutation, and supposing him to be either a pedler or some way-traveller, he at once remarked, "You don't know me." The truth flashed on my mind, and concealing my own surprise I at once

Reprinted from *Daniel Ricketson and His Friends,* ed. Anna and Walton Ricketson (Boston: Houghton Mifflin, 1902), pp. 11–19, where it was entitled "Thoreau."

took him by the hand and led him to the room already prepared
for him, feeling a kind of disappointment—a disappointment,
however, which soon passed off, and never again obtruded itself
to the philosopher's disadvantage. In fact, I soon began to see
that Nature had dealt kindly by him, and that this apparently
slender personage was physically capable of enduring far more
than the ordinary class of men, although he had then begun to
show signs of failure of strength in his knees. . . .

The names of Thoreau and Emerson are not properly placed
together on account of any great similarity in the character of
the two men; yet from some cause, probably from their being
fellow-townsmen more than any other, they are in many minds
associated as of the same class. Although Thoreau was many
years younger than Emerson, his mind was equally as mature,
and I place his name first out of respect to the dead. While Emerson is the product of New England institutions, the ripest fruit
and the best specimen, perhaps, Thoreau is one of those remarkable instances of wisdom and philosophy that grow out, as it
were, of the order of nature, and may be born in any age or nation. They who drink at the fountain-head of knowledge and
truth need not the artificial training of the schools. Still Henry
Thoreau had the best advantages of New England in his education. He was a graduate of Harvard College, a good classical
scholar, well versed in the mathematics, had been a teacher of
youth, and a land surveyor in his own town, which brought him
into an intimate acquaintance with the topography of the surrounding country.

He was an excellent naturalist, particularly in his knowledge
of plants and birds. In fact, nothing escaped his notice or interest. He was, indeed, a most consummate observer and recorder
of the works of nature and the ways of men.

It was my privilege to know him during the last eight years of
his life, when in the full maturity of his powers. The relationship
between Thoreau and his most intimate friends was not that of
great warmth of affection, but rather of respect for manly virtues.

If affection were wanting, a strong and abiding attachment took its place, and his friendship was one not liable to the usual ruptions of more ardent and emotional minds.

He was in its strictest sense a good man, sternly virtuous and temperate in all his habits; in fact, one who did not know how little he valued the ordinary manifestations of religion would have said that he was a real Christian, indeed a Bishop of the Church could not have comported himself with more dignity or propriety of conduct than he. His tastes and pursuits were all of a manly character. The morning hours were usually devoted to study or writing, and the afternoon to walking, or boating on his favorite river, the Musketaquid or Concord, with an occasional pedestrian tour to the mountains or Cape Cod, many of his experiences in which are recorded in his published works. Many a long ramble have I taken with him, and although I am a pretty good walker, he usually quite fatigued me before he had accomplished his object, perhaps the pursuit of some rare plant. In a boat of his own construction I have sailed with him up and down the slow gliding Concord River, and found him a good boatman, both in sailing and sculling. Once, during a winter visit to him, we took a tramp through the snow to White Pond, some two or three miles beyond Walden, then surrounded by heavy wood, and frequented by huntsmen. He was fond of hardy enterprises, and few of his companions could compete with him. In fact I have heard that he quite tired out an Indian guide, on one of his excursions in Maine. I do not remember of ever seeing him laugh outright, but he was ever ready to smile at anything that pleased him; and I never knew him to betray any tender emotion except on one occasion, when he was narrating to me the death of his only brother, John Thoreau, from lockjaw, strong symptoms of which, from his sympathy with the sufferer, he himself experienced. At this time his voice was choked, and he shed tears, and went to the door for air. The subject was of course dropped, and never recurred to again.

In person he was rather below the medium stature, though not decidedly short—of rather slender than robust habit of body, and marked for his drooping shoulders. Still he was vigorous and active, and when in good health could perform a good deal of physical labor. His head was of medium size, but well formed according to the rules of phrenology—his brow was full, and his forehead rather broad than prominent; his eyes grayish blue, his nose long and aquiline, and his hair inclined to sandy. When interested in conversation, and standing, he had a decidedly dignified bearing.

At first Thoreau was far from being understood by the public; a few there were, and but a few, who accepted him; he lived, however, long enough to create a public for himself, and if not among the most scholarly, at least it comprised the more thoughtful portion of the reading class of our people. I never heard him lecture or speak in public, but I believe he was not generally successful except, perhaps, in his more private readings. His thoughts were often too subtle to be readily interpreted, requiring a deliberate reading to fully understand them. He won for himself a name and fame, which had before his death reached the other side of the water, where his works are by a chosen few still known and cherished. Among those from abroad who sought him out was the late Thomas Cholmondeley, Esq., an Oxford graduate, and a gentleman of rare culture and polished manners. In order to see more of Thoreau he became an inmate of his family for several weeks, and on his return to England sent over as a present to Thoreau a valuable collection of oriental works. I had the pleasure of having this worthy gentleman and my friend Thoreau on a visit of a few days, during which time I formed a high respect for his truly noble and Christian qualities of heart. He married a lady of rank, and died on his marriage tour in Italy. He was, I believe, a nephew of the good and highly respected Bishop Heber.

About three years before his death, Thoreau began to complain of weakness in his knees, which in a good degree he recovered from; but soon after, the disease of which he died, that of the lungs, manifested itself by general increased weakness and a cough. He still kept about his pursuits as usual, and during the summer of 1861, the last one he saw, he made me a visit at New Bedford, and though suffering by night and by day with his troublesome cough, was able to ride about the country and by the seashore, as well as to take short rambles for his favorite plants, or in search of those not found in his own vicinity of Concord. . . .

As well as Thoreau wrote, only those whose privilege it was to listen to one of his long discursive conversations by the evening fireside know how full of interest and instruction he made the subject of his disquisition, apparently enjoying himself as much as interesting his hearers. Judging from my own relationship with him, I would say that he won rather the respect and admiration of his friends than their love. He was so superior to almost all other men that he inspired a certain amount of awe. "Why," said his eccentric friend, C——,* in his own peculiar manner, which of course implied no irreverence, "Thoreau is a god!" Whether a god or saint it matters not, he was, in almost every walk of life that makes a man honored and respected by his friends, a rare example. As a son and brother he was much beloved, in temperance and frugality an example worthy of following; and though no politician he was by no means an uninterested looker-on of the state of affairs in ours as well as other countries. Few men in any age of the world have more fully rounded their lives than he.

If he had any fault, it was that he was too true to nature and himself to become a decided Christian; but in most that is excellent in Christianity he possessed a large share, and I am too much a believer in the doctrine of the light within not to recognize the divine unction in the soul even if the form of sound words be wanting. But it was in the closing scenes of his life, and when confined to his room and bed, that this truly good and brave man showed the depth and power of divine wisdom in his soul, giving him strength in his weakness, and making the sick-

---

* Channing [ed.].

room and the chamber of death resplendent in beauty and hopefulness.

His inquisitive mind still found an interest in the change he was experiencing, and regarding death to be as natural as life, he accepted it with gracefulness, and investigated its approach with more than philosophic composure.

As a writer Thoreau was sententious rather than graceful or elegant; his style was his own, and well adapted to his subject-matter. Originality perhaps more than other quality marked his thought; yet at times he uttered old truths in a new dress so well adapted to his object of conveying practical ideas, that they have the charm of novelty, and are calculated to edify the attentive reader. More than any writer perhaps of his time does he require a careful reading to fully arrive at the pith of his matter, which is often marked by a subtlety that he appears to have chosen to conceal a too glaring expression of his meaning. He could, however, at will execute his thought in the most graceful and poetic manner, and a judicious selection of these passages from his works would form a volume of remarkable beauty. He was a voluminous writer; and although since his death several volumes have been added to his former works, it is probable that a large amount of manuscript yet remains.

During his lifetime, he was known to the public by his *Week on the Concord and Merrimack Rivers* and *Walden, or Life in the Woods*; the former published in 1849 and the latter in 1854.

The titles of these books give but a faint idea of their contents, for both are full of thought and observation upon man and nature, and are rather works of philosophy than simple narratives, as their names might suggest.

Although the life of Thoreau was mostly within himself, or rather with the company he entertained there, as he would probably have expressed it, still few men have found a keener relish for innocent out of door amusements than he. His boat, his spy-glass, and staff, though he rarely used the latter about home, comprised his equipage. So thoroughly had he learned the characteristics of his own neighborhood for miles around, that he probably knew more about its history than the proprietors themselves, even as to boundaries and titles tracing back to the days of the native Indians.

Few men have accomplished more than our late friend, or lived to better purpose.

Peace to his memory.

✪

"A Nature Keenly Alive"

Those who have perused with interest the pages of *Walden,* yet laughed at the eccentricities therein, or admired the simple narrative, together with the profound philosophy contained in *A Week on the Concord and Merrimack Rivers,* will lament the recent death of their gifted author. It is with feelings akin to reverence that we now recall the life of one whose simplicity of heart and beauty of character seemed but the reflection of all the sweetness in the pursuits to which he was so enthusiastically devoted; yet it is not without mingled feelings of joy that we were permitted to become acquainted with him, and in some measure learn to appreciate his worth.

It was during the year 1857, while revelling in our school-life at Concord, that we first became attracted by a singular person who might be seen each day pacing through the long village street, with sturdy step and honest mien, now pausing to listen to some rich warble from the elms high overhead, or stooping to examine some creeping thing, of interest only to him who knew its ways. A casual observer might have passed him in the street without noticing in him anything peculiar or interesting, for his dress was plain, befitting the man, and consistent with

Reprinted from Samuel A. Jones, ed., *Pertaining to Thoreau* (Detroit, 1901), pp. 117–126; originally published in the *Harvard Magazine,* VIII (May 1862), 313–318, originally entitled "Henry D. Thoreau."

his stoical principles respecting matters of this description; yet whoever penetrated deeper, could not fail to mark in him the "honest man," nor in his countenance, half hidden by a generous beard, his nut-brown complexion and soft blue eye, help discerning beneath them only a warm heart, and a nature keenly alive to what was most impressive in the world around him. Spite of the faded corduroy, this salient trait in his character shone forth with unmistakable sincerity. He seemed like some sturdy mountaineer or hardy lumberman, in whom a rugged life has left only yet sturdier strength, with finer traits awakened by a daily contemplation of stupendous mountains or primeval forests. This love for man formed his passport to the favor of all whom he chanced to meet. It procured for him respect among his townsmen, and a welcome greeting from every schoolboy, for he "carried his heart in his hand," as it were, always willing to offer it to him who might justly claim a share of it.

Our curiosity, once excited, increased daily. In the ramble after school, we often met him, sometimes far from the town, deep in the thickest of the wood, searching untiringly among the brambles or underbrush, as though he had yet something to find, for which his search had hitherto been vain; or oftener we passed him on the river, paddling in his strange craft, built long ago for visiting the Merrimack, gliding silently along so as hardly to ruffle the surface of the water, the prow, sturdy forerunner of himself, parting the lily-pads with gentle touch, quietly cleaving a way among them, or thrusting them impatiently beneath. As he glided on, the ripple at the bow appeared to herald unto each denizen of the stream the coming of a friend. All seemed to know him, and hail his approach with increased song. The "red-wing" kept his perch beside his mate, the little "yellow-throat" moved listlessly about, chasing his reflection in the water, or sang his kind welcome, "Don't you wish it? don't you wish it? don't you wish it?" Even the staid turtle thought twice before dropping from his seat, finally deciding, with wonted judgment, after the boat had passed. Every living thing, every leaf and flower, were known to him, nor did the smallest objects of interest escape the glance of his observing eye. There was no corner of the way but it contained something for him, though others might look in vain to find it. No barren twig but it held in its grasp some new chrysalis, or the ova of some strange insect. Thus did Nature reveal to him the richest treasures of her store, as if sure of finding in this disciple a worthy advocate.

It was with joy that we hailed our first approach to this man, and gradually came to know more in regard to his private life. As our acquaintance grew, we found him to be one of the rarest companions, beneath whose rugged exterior there lay a lively appreciation of all that is vivifying in nature, and a natural yearning toward his fellow-men, together with a kindly sympathy, which was but the basis of his simple philosophy. In place of affected eccentricity, we discovered in him only originality, every thought and action revealing to us a mind singularly individual, acknowledging no model save that fashioned by the dictates of conscience, and by the inferences drawn from a thoughtful contemplation of the natural world. He appeared to us more than all men to enjoy life, not for its hypocrisies, its conventional shams and barbarisms, but for its intrinsic worth, taking great interest in everything connected with the welfare of the town, no less than delight in each changing aspect of Nature, with an instinctive love for every creature of her realm.

In this he may have found the philosopher's-stone, or at least the pebble adjoining it, which all the world aspire to reach, yet few attain. This feature, which, as I have said, formed the predominating element in his character, was contagious. No one could approach without feeling himself irresistibly drawn yet nearer to him, for he bore his credentials for our esteem in his bronzed and honest countenance. Thus we could not fear, though we had great reverence for him, and must needs deem it the greatest privilege to associate with him. In the wood, his spirits were always most elastic and buoyant. At such times he evinced the liveliest interest in our conversation, entering into our feelings with an earnestness and warmth of sentiment which only bound us still closer to him, and taught us to look upon him rather as a glorious boy, than one who had arrived at full maturity; one whose healthy life and vigorous thought had put to flight all morbidness, leaving his mind yet unclouded by the sorrows which too often tinge the years of riper manhood. He climbed and leaped as though he knew every "rope" of the wood, and quite shamed our efforts, the results of bars, racks, and wooden contrivances unknown to him.

But he was to be to us more than a charming companion; he became our instructor, full of wisdom and consideration, patiently listening to our crude ideas of Nature's laws and to our juvenile philosophy, not without a smile, yet in a moment ready to correct and set us right again. And so in the afternoon walk, or the long holiday jaunt, he first opened to our unconscious eyes a thousand beauties of earth and air, and taught us to admire and appreciate all that was impressive and beautiful in the natural world around us. When with him, objects before so tame acquired new life and interest. We saw no beauty in the note of veery or wood-thrush until he pointed out to us their sad yet fascinating melancholy. He taught us the rich variety of the thrasher's song, bidding us compare with it the shrieks of the modern *prima donna*. The weary peep of Hyla had for us no charm until he showed us how well it consorted with the surrounding objects—the dark pool with the andromeda weeping over it, as if in fear of the little "sea-monster." Nor did we fancy the flaming red-wing, with his anxious cry, the Perseus of the story, who makes his home near by, to keep the maiden company, until by his very love he caused us too to like him. Then we sought to know more of the young gallant, and saw how wonderfully well he built his home, and laughed at the grotesque markings upon the eggs. He turned our hearts toward every flower, revealing to us the haunts of rhodora and arethusa, or in the fragrant wood, half hidden by the withered leaves,

> He saw beneath dim aisles, in odorous beds,
> The sweet Linnea hang its twin-born heads.

His ear was keenly alive to musical sounds, discriminating with astonishing accuracy between the notes of various songsters. This discernment enabled him to distinguish at once the songs of many birds singing together, selecting each one with great nicety of perception. A single strain was enough for him to recall the note at once, and he always had some English translation, or carefully marked paraphrase of it, singularly expressive and unique.

His love of nature was unbounded. No subject of the animate creation was beneath his notice; no uncouth reptile, no blade of grass nor wayside weed, but it might confidently claim a share in his esteem. To him Nature seemed to speak a language clear, intelligible. He never wearied of her; but from whatever he found uncongenial and prosaic in daily life—from the cares which must come home to him, from bereavement and sorrow—he always returned again, with renewed devotion unto her sweet embrace.

His philosophy contained little that could be called visionary, but every tenet of it was made subservient to some practical end. He had a passion for Oriental literature, especially admiring, as he tells us, the *Bhagvat Geeta,* full of sublimity and divine thought. From these heathen writings his keen discernment enabled him to gather much practical good, gleaning from them maxims which to-day may help to shape the perfect mind and character.

It seemed part of his generous heart, that in all his researches, he rarely injured the smallest insect, never indulging in wanton slaughter, that he might stock cabinets, but respecting the life of every creature. Life, with its gushing melody and happy enjoyment, was to him far dearer than death with its "pickled victims," designed to show every little dimension, to the extent of a barleycorn.

> *Hast thou named all the birds without a gun,*
> Loved the wood-rose, and left it on its stalk,—
> O be my friend, and teach me to be thine!

Nothing seems to me more touching in the life of this man than his veneration for every little songster of the wood, which appeared to minister to him, and answer the inmost cravings of his nature. These were his pets, for whom he ever had a ready sympathy, regarding them with an affection almost paternal.

Thus the good man seemed to be Nature's child, rather than ours. By her was he fostered, under her willing guidance he grew up, and now within her bosom he sleeps the long sleep. From her he learned the lesson of forbearance, of sympathy for his fellow-men, of pity for the needy, nay, more, of godlike trust and holy reverence. His life was moulded from a serious contemplation of her laws, and a careful study of the world in which he lived. For him Nature donned her costliest dress, that he might view her in her fairest attire. Nor did he ever desert her, but passively yielded to her charms, and suffered no rude hand to tear him away. The freshness of spring, the long monotony of the dreamy summer, the changing glories of autumn, and the crisp and merry winter—all had for him a significance deeper than we could conceive, and lent their influence to quicken and intensify his life.

But Nature needed him, and with firm but gentle hand broke down his mighty strength, and with the fair May morning lifted him away within herself. As was his life, so was his lingering decline, and death the same beautiful dream, as it were, in which he clung yet closer to the haunts he loved, though unable longer to revisit them. . . .

✪

"Cold and Unimpressible"

Upon the tablet which friendship and delicate appreciation have raised to exhibit their record of Thoreau's genius, there is still space where a classmate's pen may leave some slight impressions, without claiming either advantage or authority to do so beyond a late but ever-deepening regard. This bids the thoughts return and drop themselves for holding-ground into some recollections of his collegiate career.

He would smile to overhear that word applied to the reserve and unaptness of his college life. He was not signalized by a plentiful distribution of the parts and honors which fall to the successful student. The writer remembers that a speech which was made at a highly inflammatory meeting in Dr. Beck's recitation room, during the Christopher Dunkin Rebellion, claimed, in allusion to Dunkin's arbitrary marking, that "our offence was *rank.*" It certainly was not Thoreau's offence; and many of the rest of us shared, in this respect, his blamelessness. We could sympathize with his tranquil indifference to college honors, but we did not suspect the fine genius that was developing under that impassive demeanor. Of his private tastes there is little of consequence to recall, excepting that he was devoted to the old

---

Reprinted from Samuel A. Jones, ed., *Pertaining to Thoreau* (Detroit, 1901), pp. 129–160; originally published in the *Christian Examiner,* LXXIX (July 1865), 96–117, originally entitled "Thoreau."

English literature, and had a good many volumes of the poetry from Gower and Chaucer down through the era of Elizabeth. In this mine he worked with a quiet enthusiasm, diverting to it hours that should have sparkled with emulation in the divisions where other genius stood that never lived, like his, to ripen. For this was the class of C. S. Wheeler, of Hildreth, Hayward, Eustis; scholars and poets all, to whom the sky stretched a too eager diploma.

We owe to those studies not named in the programme, the commencement of a quaint and simple style, and a flavor of old thinking, which appears through all the works of Thoreau. His earliest masters were thus the least artificial of the minds which have drawn from the well of undefiled English. And the phrase "mother-tongue" was cherished by him, and gained his early homage. He did not care for the modern languages; nor was he ever seriously attracted, by the literature which they express, to lay aside his English worthies. His mind was in native harmony with them, and it sometimes produces modern speculation in sentences and fragments of speech and turns of phrase that make you wonder if old Sir Thomas Brown, or Owen Feltham, or Norris, were lodging for awhile with him in their progress upon some transmigrating tour. We wonder if he alludes to the University when he says that he has *heard* of "a Society for the Diffusion of Useful Knowledge." Heard of it, but not personally acquainted with it. For, though he was careful not to miss a recitation, it is plain that he was not present at it, but was already like the man he mentions, who, "in some spring of his life, saunters abroad into the Great Fields of thought, goes to grass like a horse, and leaves all his harness behind in the stable. I would say to the Society for the Diffusion of Useful Knowledge, sometimes —Go to grass." So many of us said most fervently, but not because we had attached ourselves to his shyness in order to saunter with him into the Great Fields of thought, where "a man's ignorance sometimes is not only useful, but beautiful."

But he passed for nothing, it is suspected, with most of us; for he was cold and unimpressible. The touch of his hand was

moist and indifferent, as if he had taken up something when he
saw your hand coming, and caught your grasp upon it. How
the prominent, gray-blue eyes seemed to rove down the path,
just in advance of his feet, as his grave Indian stride carried
him down to University Hall! This down-looking habit was
Chaucer's also, who walked as if a great deal of surmising went
on between the earth and him.

> And on the ground, which is my mother's gate,
> I knocké with my staff early and late,
> And say to her, "Levé mother, let me in."

But Chaucer's heart sent brisk blood to and fro beneath that
modest look, and his poetry is more teeming with the nature of
men and women than with that of the air and earth. Thoreau was
nourished by its simplicity, but not fanned by its passion. He
was colder, but more resolute, and would have gone to prison
and starvation for the sake of his opinions, where Chaucer weakly
compromised to preserve freedom and comfort. The vivid human
life in the Elizabethan writers did not wake a corresponding
genius in Thoreau: he seemed to be feeding only upon their
raciness and Saxon vigor, upon the clearly phrased and unaffected
sentiment. The rest of the leaf never bore the marks of any
hunger.

He did not care for people; his classmates seemed very remote.
This reverie hung always about him, and not so loosely as the
odd garments which the pious household care furnished. Thought
had not yet awakened his countenance; it was serene, but rather
dull, rather plodding. The lips were not yet firm; there was almost a look of smug satisfaction lurking round their corners. It
is plain now that he was preparing to hold his future views with
great setness, and personal appreciation of their importance. The
nose was prominent, but its curve fell forward without firmness
over the upper lip; and we remember him as looking very much
like some Egyptian sculptures of faces, large-featured, but brooding, immobile, fixed in a mystic egotism. Yet his eyes were sometimes searching, as if he had dropped, or expected to find, some-

thing. It was the look of Nature's own child learning to detect her wayside secrets; and those eyes have stocked his books with subtle traits of animate and inanimate creation which had escaped less patient observers. For he saw more upon the ground than anybody suspected to be there. His eyes slipped into every tuft of meadow or beach grass, and went winding in and out of the thickest undergrowth, like some slim, silent, cunning animal. They were amphibious besides, and slid under fishes' eggs and into their nests at the pond's bottom, to rifle all their contents. Mr. Emerson has noticed, that Thoreau could always find an Indian arrow-head in places that had been ploughed over and ransacked for years. "There is one," he would say, kicking it up with his foot. In fact, his eyes seldom left the ground, even in his most earnest conversation with you, if you can call earnest a tone and manner that was very confident, as of an opinion that had formed from granitic sediment, but also very level and unflushed with feeling. The Sphinx might have become passionate and exalted as soon.

In later years his chin and mouth grew firmer as his resolute and audacious opinions developed, the curves of the lips lost their flabbiness, the eyes twinkled with the latent humor of his criticisms of society. Still the countenance was unruffled: it seemed to lie deep, like a mountain tarn, with cool, still nature all around. There was not a line upon it expressive of ambition or discontent: the affectional emotions had never fretted at it. He went about, like a priest of Buddha who expects to arrive soon at the summit of a life of contemplation, where the divine absorbs the human. All his intellectual activity was of the spontaneous, open-air kind, which keeps the forehead smooth. His thoughts grew with all the rest of nature, and passively took their chance of summer and winter, pause and germination: no more forced than pine-cones; fragrant, but not perfumed, owing nothing to special efforts of art. His extremest and most grotesque opinion had never been under glass. It all grew like the bolls on forest-trees, and the deviations from stem-like or sweeping forms. No man was ever such a placid thinker. It was because his thinking was observation isolated from all the temptations of society, from the artificial exigencies of literature, from the conventional sequence. Its truthfulness was not logically attained, but insensibly imbibed, during wood-chopping, fishing, and scenting through the woods and fields. So that the smoothness and plumpness of a child were spread over his deepest places.

His simple life, so free from the vexations that belong to the most ordinary provision for the day, and from the wear and tear of habits helped his countenance to preserve this complacency. He had instincts, but no habits; and they wore him no more than they do the beaver and the blue-jay. Among them we include his rare intuitive sensibility for moral truth and for the fitness of things. For, although he lived so closely to the ground, he could still say, "My desire for knowledge is intermittent; but my desire to bathe my head in atmospheres unknown to my feet is perennial and constant. The highest that we can attain to is not knowledge, but sympathy with intelligence." But this intuition came up, like grass in spring, with no effort that is traceable, or that registers itself anywhere except in the things grown. You would look in vain for the age of his thoughts upon his face.

Now, it is no wonder that he kept himself aloof from us in college; for he was already living on some Walden Pond, where he had run up a temporary shanty in the depths of his reserve. He built it better afterwards, but no nearer to men. Did anybody ever tempt him down to Snow's, with the offer of an unlimited molluscous entertainment? The naturalist was not yet enough awakened to lead him to ruin a midnight stomach for the sake of the constitution of an oyster. Who ever saw him sailing out of Willard's long entry upon that airy smack which students not intended for the pulpit launched from port-wine sangarees? We are confident that he never discovered the back-parlor aperture through which our finite thirst communicated with its spiritual source. So that his observing faculty must, after all, be charged with limitations. We say, *our* thirst, but would not be understood to include those who were destined for the ministry, as no clergyman in the embryonic state was ever known to visit Willard's.

But Thoreau was always indisposed to call at the ordinary places
for his spiritual refreshment; and he went farther than most persons when apparently he did not go so far. He soon discovered
that all sectarian and denominational styles of thinking had their
Willard within economical distance; but the respective taps did
not suit his country palate. He was in his cups when he was out
of doors, where his lips fastened to the far horizon, and he tossed
off the whole costly vintage that mantled in the great circumference.

But he had no animal spirits for our sport or mischief. We
cannot recollect what became of him during the scenes of the
Dunkin Rebellion. He must have slipped off into some "cool retreat or mossy cell." We are half inclined to suppose that the
tumult startled him into some metamorphose, that corresponded
to a yearning in him of some natural kind, whereby he secured
a temporary evasion till peace was restored. He may also, in
this interim of qualified humanity, have established an understanding with the mute cunning of nature, which appeared afterwards in his surprising recognition of the ways of squirrels, birds,
and fishes. It is certainly quite as possible that man should take
off his mind, and drop into the medium of animal intelligence,
as that Swedenborg, Dr. Channing, and other spirits of just men
made perfect, should strip off the senses and conditions of their
sphere, to come dabbling about in the atmosphere of earth among
men's thoughts. However this may be, Thoreau disappeared while
our young absurdity held its orgies, stripping shutters from the
lower windows of the buildings, dismantling recitation rooms,
greeting tutors and professors with a frenzied and groundless
indignation which we symbolized by kindling the spoils of sacked
premises upon the steps. It probably occurred to him that fools
might rush in where angels were not in the habit of going. We
recollect that he declined to accompany several fools of this
description, who rushed late, all in a fine condition of contempt,
with Corybantic gestures, into morning prayers—a college exercise which we are confident was never attended by the angels.

It is true he says, "Give me for my friends and neighbors wild

men, not tame ones;" and a little after, in the same essay, "I rejoice that horses and steers have to be broken before they can
be made the slaves of men, and that men themselves have some
wild oats still left to sow before they become submissive members of society." But, in fact, there is nothing so conventional as
the mischief of a boy who is grown large enough to light bon-
fires, and run up a bill for "special repairs," and not yet large
enough to include in such a bill his own disposition to "haze" his
comrades and to have his fits of anarchy. Rebellion is "but a
faint symbol of the awful ferity with which good men and lovers
meet."

There was no conceit of superior tendencies and exclusive
tastes which prevented him from coming into closer contact with
individuals. But it was not shyness alone which restrained him,
nor the reticence of an extremely modest temperament. For he
was complacent; his reserve was always satisfactory to himself.
Something in his still latent and brooding genius was sufficiently
attractive to make his wit "home-keeping;" and it very early occurred to him, that he should not better his fortunes by familiarity
with other minds. This complacency, which lay quite deep over
his youthful features, was the key to that defect of sympathy
which led to defects of expression, and to unbalanced statements
of his thought. It had all the effect of the seclusion that some men
inflict upon themselves, when from conceit or disappointment they
restrict the compass of their life to islands in the great expanse,
and become reduced at last, after nibbling every thing within
the reach of their tether, to simple rumination, and incessant returns of the same cud to the tongue. This, and not listlessness,
nor indolence, nor absolute incapacity for any professional pursuit, led him to the banks of Walden Pond, where his cottage,
sheltering a self-reliant and homely life, seemed like something
secreted by a quite natural and inevitable constitution. You might
as well quarrel with the self-sufficiency of a perfect day of Nature,
which makes no effort to conciliate, as with this primitive disposition of his. The critic need not feel bound to call it a vice of
temper because it nourished faults. He should, on the contrary,

accept it as he sees that it secured the rare and positive characteristics which make Thoreau's books so full of new life, of charms
unborrowed from the resources of society, of suggestions lent by
the invisible beauty to a temperate and cleanly soul. A greater
deference to his neighborhood would have impaired the peculiar
genius which we ought to delight to recognize as fresh from a
divine inspiration, filled with possibilities like an untutored America, as it hints at improvements in its very defects, and is for-
tunately guarded by its own disability. It was perfectly satisfied
with its own ungraciousness, because that was essential to its private business. Another genius might need to touch human life at
many points; to feel the wholesome shocks; to draw off the subtile
nourishment which the great mass generates and comprises; to
take in the reward for parting with some effluence: but this would
have been fatal to Thoreau. It would have cured his faults and
weakened his genius. He would have gained friends within the
world, and lost his friends behind it. . . .

✪

"Apostle of Solitude"

If any American deserves to stand as a representative of the experience of recluseness, Thoreau is the man. His fellow-feelings and alliances with men were few and feeble; his disgusts and aversions many, as well as strongly pronounced. All his life he was distinguished for his aloofness, austere self-communion, long and lonely walks. He was separated from ordinary persons in grain and habits, by the poetic sincerity of his passion for natural objects and phenomena. As a student and lover of the material world he is a genuine apostle of solitude, despite the taints of affectation, inconsistency, and morbidity which his writings betray. At twenty-eight, on the shore of a lonely pond, he built a hut in which he lived entirely by himself for over two years. And, after he returned to his father's house in the village, he was for the chief part of the time nearly as much alone as he had been in his hermitage by Walden water. The closeness of his cleaving to the landscape cannot be questioned: "I dream of looking abroad, summer and winter, with free gaze, from some mountain side, nature looking into nature, with such easy sympathy as the blue-eyed grass in the meadow looks in the face of the sky." When he describes natural scenes, his heart lends a sweet charm to the

---

Reprinted from *Solitudes of Nature and Man; or the Loneliness of Human Life* (Boston: Roberts Brothers, 1866), pp. 329–338. The essay was originally entitled "Thoreau."

44

pages he pens: "Paddling up the river to Fair-Haven Pond, as the sun went down, I saw a solitary boatman disporting on the smooth lake. The falling dews seemed to strain and purify the air, and I was soothed with an infinite stillness. I got the world, as it were, by the nape of the neck, and held it under, in the tide of its own events, till it was drowned; and then I let it go down stream like a dead dog. Vast, hollow chambers of silence stretched away on every side; and my being expanded in proportion, and filled them."

In his little forest-house, Thoreau had three chairs, "one for solitude, two for friendship, three for society." "My nearest neighbor is a mile distant. It is as solitary where I live as on the prairies. It is as much Asia or Africa as New England. I have, as it were, my own sun and moon and stars; and a little world all to myself." "At night, there was never a traveller passed my door, more than if I were the first or last man." "We are wont to imagine rare and delectable places in some remote and more celestial corner of the system,—behind the constellation of Cassiopea's Chair, far from noise and disturbance. I discovered that my house actually had its site in such a withdrawn, but forever new and unprofaned, part of the universe." "I love to be alone. I never found the companion that was so companionable as solitude." In this last sentence we catch a tone from the diseased or disproportioned side of the writer. He was unhealthy and unjust in all his thoughts on society; underrating the value, overrating the dangers, of intercourse with men. But his thoughts on retirement, the still study and love of nature, though frequently exaggerated, are uniformly sound. He has a most catholic toleration, a wholesome and triumphant enjoyment, of every natural object, from star to skunk-cabbage. He says, with tonic eloquence, "Nothing can rightly compel a simple and brave man to a vulgar sadness: while I enjoy the friendship of the seasons, I trust that nothing can make life a burden to me." But the moment he turns to contemplate his fellow-men, all his geniality leaves him —he grows bigoted, contemptuous, almost inhuman: "The names of men are of course as cheap and meaningless as Bose and Tray,

the names of dogs. I will not allow mere names to make distinctions for me, but still see men in herds." The cynicism and the
sophistry are equal. His scorn constantly exhales: "The Irishman
erects his sty, and gets drunk, and jabbers more and more under
my eaves; and I am responsible for all that filth and folly. I find
it very unprofitable to have much to do with men. Emerson says
that his life is so unprofitable and shabby for the most part, that
he is driven to all sorts of resources, and, among the rest, to men.
I have seen more men than usual, lately; and, well as I was
acquainted with one, I am surprised to find what vulgar fellows
they are. They do a little business each day, to pay their board;
then they congregate in sitting-rooms, and feebly fabulate and
paddle in the social slush; and, when I think that they have sufficiently relaxed, and am prepared to see them steal away to their
shrines, they go unashamed to their beds, and take on a new
layer of sloth." Once in a while he gives a saner voice out of a
fonder mood: "It is not that we love to be alone, but that we
love to soar; and, when we soar, the company grows thinner and
thinner, till there is none at all." But the conceited and misanthropic fit quickly comes back: "Would I not rather be a cedar
post, which lasts twenty-five years, than the farmer that set it; or
he that preaches to that farmer?" "The whole enterprise of this
nation is totally devoid of interest to me. There is nothing in it
which one should lay down his life for,—nor even his gloves.
What aims more lofty have they than the prairie-dogs?"

This poisonous sleet of scorn, blowing manward, is partly an
exaggerated rhetoric; partly, the revenge he takes on men for not
being what he wants them to be; partly, an expression of his un-
appreciated soul reacting in defensive contempt, to keep him from
sinking below his own estimate of his deserts. It is curious to note
the contradictions his inner uneasiness begets. Now he says, "In
what concerns you much, do not think you have companions;
know that you are alone in the world." Then he writes to one of
his correspondents, "I wish I could have the benefit of your
criticism; it would be a rare help to me." The following sentence
has a cheerful surface, but a sad bottom: "I have lately got back

to that glorious society, called solitude, where we meet our friends continually, and can imagine the outside world also to be peopled." At one moment, he says, "I have never felt lonesome, or the least oppressed by a sense of solitude, but once; and then I was conscious of a slight insanity in my mood." At another moment he says, "Ah! what foreign countries there are, stretching away on every side from every human being with whom you have no sympathy! Their humanity affects one as simply monstrous. When I sit in the parlors and kitchens of some with whom my business brings me—I was going to say—in contact, I feel a sort of awe, and am as forlorn as if I were cast away on a desolate shore. I think of Riley's narrative, and his sufferings." That his alienation from society was more bitter than sweet, less the result of constitutional superiority than of dissatisfied experience, is significantly indicated, when we find him saying, at twenty-five, "I seem to have dodged all my days with one or two persons, and lived upon expectation"; at thirty-five, "I thank you again and again for attending to me"; and at forty-five, "I was particularly gratified when one of my friends said, 'I wish you would write another book,—write it for me.' He is actually more familiar with what I have written than I am myself."

The truth is, his self-estimate and ambition were inordinate; his willingness to pay the price of their outward gratification, a negative quantity. Their exorbitant demands absorbed him; but he had not those powerful charms and signs which would draw from others a correspondent valuation of him and attention to him. Accordingly, he shut his real self in a cell of secrecy, and retreated from men whose discordant returns repelled, to natural objects whose accordant repose seemed acceptingly to confirm and return, the required estimate imposed on them. The key of his life is the fact that it was devoted to the art of an interior aggrandizement of himself. The three chief tricks in this art are, first, a direct self-enhancement, by a boundless pampering of egotism; secondly, an indirect self-enhancement, by a scornful depreciation of others; thirdly, an imaginative magnifying of every trifle related to self, by associating with it a colossal idea

of the self. It is difficult to open many pages in the written record
of Thoreau without being confronted with examples of these three
tricks. He is constantly, with all his boastful stoicism, feeling
himself, reflecting himself, fondling himself, reverberating himself, exalting himself, incapable of escaping or forgetting himself.
He is never contented with things until they are wound through,
and made to echo himself; and this is the very mark of spiritual
disturbance. "When I detect," he says, "a beauty in any of the
recesses of nature, I am reminded, by the serene and retired spirit
in which it requires to be contemplated, of the inexpressible
privacy of a life." In the holiest and silentest nook his fancy con-
jures the spectre of himself, and an ideal din from society for
contrast. He says of his own pursuits, "The unchallenged bravery
which these studies imply is far more impressive than the trum-
peted valor of the warrior." When he sees a mountain he sings:

> Wachuset, who, like me,
> Standest alone without society,
> Upholding heaven, holding down earth,—
> Thy pastime from thy birth,—
> Not steadied by the one, nor leaning on the other,
> May I approve myself thy worthy brother!

This self-exaggeration peers out even through the disguise of
humor and of satire: "I am not afraid of praise, for I have practised it on myself. The stars and I belong to a mutual-admiration
society." "I do not propose to write an ode to dejection, but to
brag as lustily as chanticleer in the morning, standing on his
roost." "The mass of men lead lives of quiet desperation." But
he—he is victorious, sufficing, royal. At all events he will be
unlike other people. "I am a mere arena for thoughts and feelings,
a slight film, or dash of vapor, so faint an entity, and make so
slight an impression, that nobody can find the traces of me." "I
am something to him that made me, undoubtedly, but not much
to any other that he has made." "Many are concerned to know
who built the monuments of the East and West. For my part, I
should like to know who, in those days, did not build them,—who

were above such trifling." "For my part, I could easily do without the post-office. I am sure that I never read any memorable news in a newspaper." This refrain of opposition between the general thoughts and feelings of mankind and his own, recurs until it becomes comical, and we look for it. He refused invitations to dine out, saying, "They make their pride in making their dinner cost much; I make my pride in making my dinner cost little." One is irresistibly reminded of Plato's retort, when Diogenes said, "See how I tread on the pride of Plato."—"Yes, with greater pride."

But he more than asserts his difference; he explicitly proclaims his superiority: "Sometimes when I compare myself with other men, it seems as if I were more favored by the gods than they." "When I realize the greatness of the part I am unconsciously acting, it seems as if there were none in history to match it." Speaking of the scarlet oaks, he adds with Italics: "These are *my* china-asters, *my* late garden-flowers; it costs *me* nothing for a gardener." The unlikeness of genius to mediocrity is a fact, but not a fact of that relative momentousness entitling it to monopolize attention. He makes a great ado about his absorbing occupation; his sacred engagements with himself; his consequent inability to do anything for others, or to meet those who wished to see him. In the light of this obtrusive trait the egotistic character of many passages like the following becomes emphatic: "Only think, for a moment, of a man about his affairs! How we should respect him! How glorious he would appear! A man about *his business* would be the cynosure of all eyes." He evidently had the jaundice of desiring men to think as well of him as he thought of himself; and, when they would not, he ran into the woods. But he could not escape thus, since he carried them still in his mind.

His quotations are not often beautiful or valuable, but appear to be made as bids for curiosity or admiration, or to produce some other sharp effect; as they are almost invariably strange, bizarre, or absurd: culled from obscure corners, *Damodara, Iamblichus,* the *Vishnu Purana,* or some such out-of-the-way source. He seems to take oddity for originality, extravagant singularity for depth and force. His pages are profusely peppered with pungent paradoxes and exaggerations—a straining for sensation, not in keeping with his pretence of sufficing repose and greatness: "Why should I feel lonely? is not our planet in the Milky Way?" "All that men have said or are, is a very faint rumor; and it is not worth their while to remember or refer to that." He exemplifies, to an extent truly astonishing, the great vice of the spiritual hermit; the belittling, because he dislikes them, of things ordinarily considered important; and the aggrandizing, because he likes them, of things usually regarded as insignificant. His eccentricities are uncorrected by collision with the eccentricities of others, and his petted idosyncrasies spurn at the average standards of sanity and usage. Grandeur, dissociated from him, dwindles into pettiness; pettiness, linked with his immense ego, dilates into grandeur. In his conceited separation he mistakes a crotchet for a consecration. If a worm crosses his path, and he stops to watch its crawl, it is greater than an interview with the Duke of Wellington.

It is the wise observation of Lavater, that whoever makes too much or too little of himself has a false measure for everything. Few persons have cherished a more preposterous idea of self than Thoreau, or been more persistently ridden by the enormity. This false standard of valuation vitiates every moral measurement he makes. He describes a battle of red and black ants before his wood-pile at Walden, as if it were more important than Marathon or Gettysburg. His faculties were vast, and his time inexpressibly precious: this struggle of the pismires occupied his faculties and time; therefore this struggle of the pismires must be an inexpressibly great matter. A trifle, plus his ego, was immense; an immensity, minus his ego, was a trifle. Is it a haughty conceit or a noble loftiness that makes him say, "When you knock at the Celestial City, ask to see God,—none of the servants"? He says, "Mine is a sugar to sweeten sugar with: if you will listen to me, I will sweeten your whole life." Again, "I would put forth sublime thoughts daily, as the plant puts forth leaves." And yet again, "I shall be a benefactor if I conquer some realms from the night, —if I add to the domains of poetry." After such manifestos, we expect much. We do not find so much as we naturally expect.

He was rather an independent and obstinate thinker than a powerful or rich one. His works, taken in their whole range, instead of being fertile in ideas, are marked by speculative sterility. "He was one of those men," a friendly but honest critic says, "who, from conceit or disappointment, inflict upon themselves a seclusion which reduces them at last, after nibbling everything within reach of their tether, to simple rumination and incessant returns of the same cud to the tongue." This unsympathetic temper is betrayed in a multitude of such sentences as this: "O ye that would have the cocoanut wrong side outwards! when next I weep I will let you know." Thoreau is not the true type of a great man, a genuine master of life, because he does not reflect greatness and joy over men and life, but upholds his idea of his own greatness and mastership by making the characters and lives of others little and mean. Those who, like Wordsworth and Channing, reverse this process, are the true masters and models. A feeling of superiority to others, with love and honor for them, is the ground of complacency and a condition of chronic happiness. A feeling of superiority to others, with alienation from them and hate for them, is the sure condition of perturbations and unhappiness.

Many a humble and loving author who has nestled amongst his fellow-men and not boasted, has contributed far more to brace and enrich the characters and sweeten the lives of his readers than the ill-balanced and unsatisfied hermit of Concord, part cynic, part stoic, who strove to compensate himself with nature and solitude for what he could not wring from men and society. The extravagant estimate he put on solitude may serve as a corrective of the extravagant estimate put on society by our hives of citizens. His monstrous preference of savagedom to civilization may usefully influence us to appreciate natural unsophisticatedness more highly, and conventionality more lowly. As a teacher, this is nearly the extent of his narrow mission. Lowell, in a careful article, written after reading all the published works of Thoreau, says of him: "He seems to us to have been a man with so high a conceit of himself, that he accepted without questioning, and insisted on our accepting, his defects and weaknesses of character, as virtues and powers peculiar to himself. Was he indolent,—he finds none of the activities which attract or employ the rest of mankind worthy of him. Was he wanting in the qualities that make success,—it is success that is contempitible, and not himself that lacks persistency and purpose. Was he poor, —money was an unmixed evil. Did his life seem a selfish one,— he condemns doing good, as one of the weakest of superstitions."

In relation to the intellectual and moral influence of solitude, the example of Thoreau, with all the alleviating wisdom, courage, and tenderness confessedly in it, is chiefly valuable as an illustration of the evils of a want of sympathy with the community. Yet there is often a deep justice, a grandly tonic breath of self-reliance, in his exhortations. How sound and admirable the following passage: "If you seek the warmth of affection from a similar motive to that from which cats and dogs and slothful persons hug the fire, because your temperature is low through sloth, you are on the downward road. Better the cold affection of the sun, reflected from fields of ice and snow, or his warmth in some still wintry dell. Warm your body by healthful exercise, not by cowering over a stove. Warm your spirit by performing independently noble deeds, not by ignobly seeking the sympathy of your fellows who are no better than yourself."

Though convinced of the justice of this sketch, the writer feels rebuked, as if it were not kind enough, when he remembers the pleasure he has had in many of the pages of Thoreau, and the affecting scene of his funeral on that beautiful summer day in the dreamy town of Concord. There was uncommon love in him, but it felt itself repulsed, and, too proud to beg or moan, it put on stoicism and wore it until the mask became the face. His opinionative stiffness and contempt were his hurt self-respect protecting itself against the conventionalities and scorns of those who despised what he revered and revered what he despised. His interior life, with the relations of thoughts and things, was intensely tender and true, however sorely ajar he may have been with persons and with the ideas of persons. If he was sour, it was on a store of sweetness; if sad, on a fund of gladness.

While we walked in procession up to the church, though the bell tolled the forty-four years he had numbered, we could not deem that *he* was dead whose ideas and sentiments were so vivid in our souls. As the fading image of pathetic clay lay before us, strewn with wild flowers and forest sprigs, thoughts of its former occupant seemed blent with all the local landscapes. We still recall with emotion the tributary words so fitly spoken by friendly and illustrious lips. The hands of friends reverently lowered the body of the lonely poet into the bosom of the earth, on the pleasant hillside of his native village, whose prospects will long wait to unfurl themselves to another observer so competent to discriminate their features and so attuned to their moods. And now that it is too late for any further boon amidst his darling haunts below,

> There will yet his mother yield
> A pillow in her greenest field,
> Nor the June flowers scorn to cover
> The clay of their departed lover.

GEORGE W. COOKE

⭐

The Two Thoreaus

There are evidently two Thoreaus—one that of his admirers, and the other that of his detractors. His admirers include such persons as Mr. Frank B. Sanborn and Mr. H. S. Salt, who have both written biographies of Thoreau, and who cannot easily accept any criticism of one they love almost to excess. Whatever of genius there was in him they are quick to recognize; but his faults they ignore or prefer to overlook. The other class, whose chief representative is Lowell, are inclined to see what was odd in Thoreau; they emphasize his excesses, and do not fully credit the genius which he undoubtedly possessed.

A willingness to recognize both phases of Thoreau's nature led me, the other day, to seek out two persons who knew him well— the one a most ardent admirer, and the other, not so much a detractor as one who is inclined to emphasize his faults. I will permit the detractor to speak first, in order that the admirer may give the last and most important word.

The detractor said that he went to school with Thoreau in the Concord Academy, that he was an odd stick, not very studious or devoted to his lessons, but a thoughtful youth and very fond of reading. He was not given to play or to fellowship with the boys; but he was shy and silent. When he was in college at Harvard he

Reprinted from the *Independent*, XLVIII (December 10, 1896), 1671–1672.

was not inclined to hard study, but spent much of his time in the library, had no special rank in his class, and took no part at commencement. As a teacher in Concord Academy he was a failure, and only remained for a short time.

Then Thoreau spent a year or two in Emerson's family, as the tutor of his children and as his literary assistant. This resulted in his becoming a thorough-going imitator of Emerson, whose manner, speech and ideas he copied with great fidelity and success. This was carried to such an extent as to make a decided change in Thoreau's life; and the change was for the better. When he sometimes gave lectures, as he did before the Concord Lyceum, and on other occasions, his manner of speaking was a coarse imitation of Emerson's, and so badly done as to make it painful to listen to him. He caught Emerson's hesitating manner, with all that was ungraceful and awkward in it. On these occasions Thoreau had but a small audience, no one but his personal friends turning out to hear him; and he had only a small personal following in the village.

Thoreau was an odd, shy, recluse man, an intense egotist, who thoroughly believed in himself and his own ideas. He was an Indian in his nature, with the advantages of the Harvard library and Plato's philosophy. He was a good deal of a Stoic; and he always judged of everything, even that Nature which he loved so well, with reference to himself. He could not see anything except with his own personality as its test, and with reference to what bearings it had upon his own life and thought. In his books he loved to play upon words, and cultivated a punning, alliterative style. The mere jingle of words seemed to attract him; and what was odd or bizarre gave him much pleasure.

The detractor went to visit Thoreau half-a-dozen times while he was living in his hut on Walden Pond. His life there was helped out by many tea-drinkings and dinners to which he was invited by his relatives and friends in the village, as well as by food which was frequently sent to him. He enjoyed his stay there, and had the feeling that he was performing a great feat to live without the trappings of civilization. He did not much care for the con-

ventionalities of life, and readily broke away from its customs and
ceremonies. In the last years of his life he became a thorough
convert to not blacking his shoes, put them on and never did
anything to them until they were worn out. He thought it a waste
of time to blacken and polish them, and a useless concession to
mere custom.

His attitude toward society was shown in his refusal to pay
taxes. Being an extreme individualist, he felt that he had no use
for Government; that it hampered him, and did not permit him
to do as he liked. He refused to yield obedience to it, or to add
anything to its means of support. When called upon by the tax
gatherer he excused himself on the ground of not caring to pay.
After repeated requests for the dollar and a half which the tax
roll had put down against his name, the tax collector, who was
also the constable, grew impatient of the delay, and took Thoreau
away to jail. In a few hours the tax was paid by one of his friends,
and he was liberated. He protested against any one paying for
him, but walked away as if nothing had happened.

Thoreau greatly enjoyed talking with the quaint people of the
town, those who were racy in speech and personal in character.
The more of oddity he found in them the greater liking he had
for their society, and the greater enjoyment he found in their
expressions and ideas. He talked with the old farmers of nature
and outdoor life, of what they had learned on their farms, and of
what they had gained of practical wisdom. He seldom came into
close contact with the educated people of the village, with the
exception of Emerson, Hawthorne, Channing, and the few others
who were his special admirers and friends.

The detractor said that he knew quite well that his way of
regarding Thoreau was that of the Philistine; but it was that of
the people generally in Concord who knew Thoreau intimately.
He said that he had all of Thoreau's books, had read them carefully, and enjoyed much of what was in them. He procured *Walden* and *The Week* when they first appeared, and he had recently read the books on the four seasons. Thoreau's descriptions

he regards as accurate and delightful; but his philosophy he always skips, as he does not care for it or agree with it. Those who knew Thoreau personally have found nothing so surprising as the cult which has grown up about him or so difficult of a rational explanation.

The admirer gave me a very different account of Thoreau, for he grew up with him, being only a few years younger. He had a boy's admiration for his friend, took lessons of him in wood-craft, came to love the woods and its creatures under his guidance, and had that enthusiasm about him which the boy conceives for his hero. Even now he does not like to hear a word said against Thoreau; and he has never yet forgiven Lowell for his cruel word of detraction and misrepresentation. By the admirer Thoreau is regarded with that fondness which would have been natural if he had been an older brother; and this is, in reality, the rela-tion in which they stand to each other, not by blood, but in the feeling which is cherished for the intimate friend of now so many years past. Thoreau's memory is not only cherished, but most warmly defended by this admirer of whatever was good and noble in him. He is talked of with the keenest zest, and all his bright qualities, his genius, his gifts which appealed to a boy's admira-tion, are described with strong appreciation.

Thoreau's room in his later years was in a back attic of the house in Concord where he died, and which was afterward owned by the Alcott family. It was sparsely furnished, with Spartan-like simplicity. There was in it a bureau, in which he kept a collection of bird's eggs and one of arrowheads. A rude cot on which he slept, a chair or two, and a wash-stand, bowl and pitcher, made up all the room contained.

He was a true companion of the boys of the village, entered into their sports, and was delighted in their outdoor life. He was pleased to show them bird's-nests; but he was shy of those who had not a genuine love of the life of the wood, and who hunted merely because they followed the other boys. Those who loved outdoor life found in him a true companion, one who was always willing and glad to serve them, and who entered into all their interests with a delight equal to their own. He was ready to initiate them into a knowledge of the country around, and into all the mysteries of woodcraft and the hidden secrets of Nature.

According to his admirer Thoreau was an impressive speaker, and had a large hearing whenever he spoke in Concord. There was a tang, something queer, in his manner of speech and in his ideas, which attracted people. On the day when John Brown was hanged he sent a boy about to notify people that he would speak in the vestry of the church. The boy returned, and said that Mr. Sanborn thought it a bad thing to do, that the time was dangerous, and it would be better to wait until there was a better feeling among the people. Thoreau sent the boy back with this message: "Tell Mr. Sanborn that he has misunderstood the announcement, that there is to be a meeting in the vestry, and that Mr. Thoreau will speak."

The vestry was full, but people came in shyly, as if afraid to be seen there; but they listened to the end, and then went out without discussion or comment. Thoreau was full of his subject on this occasion, was deeply agitated, and was so moved by his feelings as scarcely to be able to speak or to control his voice. It was a bold, strong argument he made, but in a time of fear and doubt. He had no hesitation himself, knew clearly his own attitude, and what he wished to say. Few other persons had a definite opinion or dared utter their thoughts openly. He was himself a non-resistant, decidedly preferred the interests of the individual to those of the State, would not pay taxes because he did not believe in the attitude of the nation on the great moral questions of the hour; but he saw at once to the core of Brown's character, was his earnest champion, and had for him the greatest admiration.

Thoreau's lectures were listened to with delight, and admired for their fresh and unique qualities. His descriptions of scenery and outdoor life were much appreciated and admired, and were fully understood by the farmers and other such people. He had a poetic fervor and charm which made his speaking attractive and pleasant for the listener.

The gossip about his being furnished with doughnuts, pies, and other delicacies, while he was living at Walden, is not worth listening to; for he was quite capable of living in the woods on his own fare. He did in no sense depend upon the supplies from the village; but these were accepted out of good will to the donors, not from any desire on his part to receive them. The fact is, he loved society in a way of his own, desired the companionship of people, cared for all simple, sincere and genuine persons, and went to see them at their houses from time to time. He could depend upon himself, but he was no misanthrope, no mere recluse, certainly not one to distrust or to hate his kind. He sought the company of the people of the village when he found it convenient to do so or the impulse called. He did not shun good food, but accepted it willingly; yet he was not in any degree dependent upon it. He did not seek it or beg for it; when it was offered he used it, but not to his own detriment.

He was a genuine man, sound, wholesome, thoroughly natural, and of noble impulses and purposes. His life was without any moral taint, and it was clean throughout. He was not narrow or warped, but sound in his principles and upright in his conduct. There was no deceit about him, no pretense, no stunted elements of character; but he was genuinely loyal and faithful in all the relations of life. In his relations to his friends he was fidelity itself; and to those who were in any way dependent upon him or who appealed to his sympathies he gave the most unfailing loyalty. To an elderly woman, a dependent and complaining person, he gave much of his time, made great efforts to cheer her and to give her courage, constituted himself her protector, and was persistent in his acts of kindness. He was patient, sympathetic and self-forgetful in her behalf, would run on errands for her, and did not fail in even the most lowly service.

Thoreau loved the society of boys, he knew boy character intimately, and he thoroughly sympathized with them; but he would not tolerate bad language or meanness in any boy who was in his company. Evil habits he scorned, and he used his best effort to destroy them in all the boys who associated with him.

He sought to develop whatever was good in the characters of his boy friends, and to give them moral backbone and manliness.

By nature Thoreau was independent in character and opinion, institutions were indifferent to him, while social forms and requirements repulsed him. He was an individualist of the most pronounced type, maintaining that institutions oppressed the individual, and were not to be trusted or their arbitrary laws obeyed. This faith of his he carried into daily life, not in an aggressive or offensive manner, but in his disregard of mere conventionalities. He was one of the most sturdy and uncompromising democrats who ever lived. He dressed plainly, like a farmer; not slovenly, but with no extra care or nicety. He fitted his dress to his outdoor life and its requirements. He was scrupulously clean, but did not love show or parade.

When Thoreau lived at Walden he read and wrote much, carried there the best books and read them diligently. It was a time of quiet thought with him, and of putting his thoughts upon paper. He had many visitors; and all those who had raciness of speech or any native force of character he was glad to welcome. He loved native fruit, at least among men, that with the flavor of the soil. One such man in Concord, the constable and tavern-keeper, had the warmest appreciation of Thoreau, and said of him that he was a good fellow and a delightful man to meet. Such was the testimony of all who knew him intimately on any side of his life, and who got close to that which was best within him.

Thoreau must be understood from the point of view of the detractor as well as from that of the admirer, in order fully to appreciate him. He was a genuine product of the soil of New England, a crab apple from the woods, transplanted to a cultivated garden, but retaining the old flavor along with the new. He was a hunter and backwoodsman, who knew Plato and could talk the language of the latest form of intellectual speculation. Through it all, however, there is something so racy, genuine and incisive about him that he commands our admiration, in spite of all his limitations. The very defects give us a greater love for him;

and we read him with the more delight that he is always himself, wild, rebellious and scornful. There is a raciness about his books, a manly, robust quality, and a freshness as of a spring morning, which commends them, and will keep them alive.

ANONYMOUS

⭐

"In Virtue of Noble Living"

Midsummer days, the sparkling hours of winter, somber, pensive autumn, the budding life of spring, all weathers and moods of nature, awaken remembrances of Concord and the Thoreau family. I knew the town in my younger life, but through all the shifting scenes of the passing years my memories of its quiet landscapes, sedate streets, cultivated people, and hospitable homes have always remained fresh and tender. I hear of changes, of growth, of the passing away of the old and advent of the new; changes there must have been, for a whole generation has moved off the earth to other homes and activities since those I knew were living their serene and benevolent lives, which were at once an example and a benediction to all within their influence.

What suggestions of harmony and peace the word Concord conveys, and how "the light that never was on sea or land" illumines the reveries of long ago, as I recall the happy hours spent in the dear Thoreau home! There was about all the household a perennial spring of vivacious life that made its members interesting and attractive even to the young and immature. Its members possessed large stores of anecdote and historical information relative to old Boston and neighboring towns that were always entertaining and instructive. Mr. Thoreau, the elder, and

Reprinted from *Outlook*, LXIII (December 2, 1899), 815–821. The article was originally entitled "Reminiscences of Thoreau."

myself were excellent friends; he was quiet and gentle, often humorous, expressing his thoughts in graphic, forcible language; in fact, a ready and copious vocabulary was characteristic of every member of his family, and life went on with them so evenly and calmly that talking seemed the principal business of the days. The arrival of the mails formed the excitement of the morning. Henry usually retired to his study after breakfast, and later would reappear ready for a jaunt through field or forest, or by the river, or, if in winter, for a long skate on its frozen surface, once going sixteen miles before turning homeward—this was, however, an exceptional achievement. But wherever he wandered, on his return he always had some new and instructive fact to relate, often all aglow with enthusiasm over some discovery he had made or treasure he had found.

Henry seemed to regard Concord and its vicinity as an epitome of the universe. . . . Nature revealed its secrets to his sympathetic soul; his searching eyes saw far, wide, and deep; he heard, nay, knew when to expect to hear, the first bluebird's note; indeed, no harbinger of the seasons escaped his alert observation. Before we had begun to think of spring flowers Henry came in from a ramble and surprised us with a handful of early violets. Sophia with her gifted pencil made a drawing of them for me, appending Henry's poem, suggested years before by precisely such a bunch tied round by a wisp of straw:

Sic Vita

I am a parcel of vain strivings tied
    By a chance bond together,
Dangling this way and that; their links
    Were made so loose and wide,
        Methinks,
      For milder weather.

A bunch of violets without their roots,
    And sorrel intermixed,
Encircled by a wisp of straw
    Once coiled about their shoots,

The law
By which I'm fixed.

A nosegay which Time clutched from out
Those fair Elysian fields,
With weeds and broken stems, in haste,
Doth make the rabble rout
That waste
The day he yields.

And here I bloom for a short hour unseen,
Drinking my juices up,
With no root in the land
To keep my branches green,
But stand
In a bare cup.

Some tender buds were left upon my stem
In mimicry of life.
But ah! the children will not know,
Till time has withered them,
The woe
With which they're rife.

But now I see I was not plucked for naught,
And after in life's vase
Of glass set while I might survive,
But by a kind hand brought
Alive
To a strange place.

That stock thus thinned will soon redeem its hours,
And by another year,
Such as God knows, with freer air,
More fruits and fairer flowers
Will bear,
While I droop here.

This graceful sketch, so exquisitely drawn, is a beautiful illustration of Sophia's artistic temperament and skill. She had an admirably balanced nature, and plenty of sentiment of a healthy kind; there was no waste or superfluity in any direction; and this equilibrium was her defense, and sustained her under the clouds of sorrow and sickness which overshadowed much of her life.

Henry and Sophia were in perfect accord (as indeed were all the family), and her thorough knowledge of botany formed a special bond of sympathy between them. Henry placed great reliance—as did all who knew her—on his sister's rare judgment and ability in practical matters, and he was himself a shrewd, practical man in affairs of every-day life; he once said, "I have as many trades as fingers." A comical illustration of his readiness to cope with sudden emergencies occurred late one warm afternoon in summer, just as a short, sharp thunder-storm had passed and the sun was breaking through the dispersing clouds. We had finished supper, but were lingering at the table, when the servant threw open the door, exclaiming, with wild excitement, "Faith! th' pig's out o' th' pin, an' th' way he's tearin' roun' Jege Hoore's fluer-bids es enuf ter scare er budy." Henry and his father at once rushed out in pursuit of the marauder, and the ladies flew to the windows to see the fray. Never was practical strategy more in evidence; plotting and counter-plotting on both sides, repeated circumvention of well-laid plans, and a final cornering and capture of the perverse beast, who, after his delicious taste of freedom, protested loudly and vigorously against being forced to return to his prison pen. It was truly a triumph of the intellectual over the animal nature, whose brief enjoyment of wild destructive liberty was suddenly ended by the power of a superior will. It was remarked at the time how much mental and physical strength had to be expended to subdue so inferior an animal. . . .

Henry often showed playful instincts, yet he *was* serious. Life was no play-day for himself or others; he seemed tremendously in earnest in trying to find the key to right living. He impressed one as being interested in all humanity and its work in the world, provided it was not sordid. Low expedients, no matter what they accomplished in the making of fame or fortune, were utterly repugnant to him. There was a conspicuous Spartan fortitude in the family character; the mother had taught it both by precept and example. They took high ground on every subject, had stern views of duty, and tolerated no vacillating or compromising measures in disposing of moral questions. This attribute of the family character was strikingly manifested when Henry submitted to be imprisoned for refusing to pay taxes during the Mexican war. He believed all war to be wrong, and that the then existing struggle was for the extension of slavery, which he abhorred. Soon after his incarceration, Mr. Emerson, whom he had always supposed was of like sentiments with himself, called at the jail, and on meeting his friend exclaimed, "Henry, why are you here?" and received for answer, "Mr. Emerson, why are *you* not here?"

The family were noteworthy not only for their mental gifts, but for their lofty character; they seemed incapable of pettiness, and made a principle of not being cast down or vanquished; their high spirit was temperamental on both sides of the house. Mrs. Thoreau kept her hopefulness and courage under the constant disability of feebleness of body; for she suffered under the family scourge, consumption, for many years; yet complaints she never uttered, and her stately though frail figure sitting year after year in her straight-backed chair was a picture of patience and brave endurance. Ever ready to be interested in passing events, expressing keen opinions or offering valuable suggestions, her hold on life was firm, and it was almost a surprise when she at last yielded to the inevitable and submitted to lie several days in bed before the end came. To a friend who visited her at this period Mrs. Thoreau recited Cato's soliloquy with perfect composure and contentment. Well might a gifted woman exclaim, "She looks like a queen," when death at last had claimed the resolute spirit, and she lay silently receiving her guests for the last time.

Notwithstanding the sturdy attitude of the family respecting all ethical questions, how delightful they were in social life!—most kind, generous, and winning. There conversation, animated and entertaining, always surrounded them with an atmosphere of cheerfulness—a genuine cheerfulness that looked upon life and all its crookedness with more than philosophic resignation.

They were spirited in the best sense; their mirthfulness had the spice of original wit, native pluck, and coherent strength, and was a natural development from their varied ancestry, by whom they were endowed with the French vivacity, Scotch shrewdness, and Puritan rectitude.

The house was a veritable haven of refuge to one who fled thither from the weary tread and turmoil of the city. Recollections crowd upon me: its undisturbed orderliness, the restful sitting-room, where the sun lay all day, passing around the corner of the house and shining in again at the west window in the late winter afternoons, making Sophia's window-plants all-glorious, which some magic in her touch or magnetism of genuine love for the floral family always conjured into wonderfully luxuriant bloom. In memory I walk among her flower-beds (hardly a garden) enjoying the fragrance of the old-time favorites; I see the graceful laburnum in blossom, and a few steps further bring me to the little pine grove in the corner of their front yard (long since sacrificed to the opening of a new street), where in an instant I am in perfect seclusion; I see the sun glinting through the moving boughs, making a dancing mosaic of light and shade on the floor of pine needles; I hear the chirping of birds and the gentle, sighing voice of the wind through the soft green branches—a lovely retreat, to which no footsteps but those of memory will evermore wander.

I recall the reading aloud of fresh new books; the evening games of chess and backgammon; the bright, often distinguished, people who came to the house; the tea-parties and evening visits; the lyceum lectures on cold winter nights; the walks by field and river, sometimes to the old battle-ground, where, one early June morning, we turned in to the shady inclosure and Sophia pointed out the unnamed graves of the British soldiers who fell in the fight, their resting-place marked by rough gray stones. A narrow field lay between us and the historic "Old Manse," brown with age. We sat on a large boulder beneath a grand spreading

tree, near the plain granite shaft commemorating the patriotic
valor of the "embattled farmers" who "fired the shot heard round
the world." We looked across the slow-flowing river, where at
the time of the battle stood "the old North Bridge," to an ancient
house with quaint projecting second story, memorable as one of
the depositories of the warlike stores of the American patriots;
the drives to Fairhaven cliffs, to Walden woods,[1] before those
grand solitudes had been invaded and transformed; and walks
to Sleepy Hollow years before it became a place of burial. If
Henry happened to be with us, although we were unobservant
of what was beneath our feet, his acute eyes, ever active, would
detect Indian arrow-heads, or some implement for domestic purposes made of flint or other hard stone. I have seen him with a
stick bring to light great numbers of clam-shells, remnants of
Indian feasts of long ago. It was noticeable that these shell de-
posits were always found in places evidently selected for their
pleasant situation and outlook.

Occasionally Henry would invite us to go with him in his boat.
One of these excursions was in late November, and the weather
was of almost unearthly beauty; bees in great multitudes hummed
loudly as they lazily floated in the golden slumberous haze only
seen in the true Indian summer. At a particular spot Henry
turned the boat toward the bank, saying: "We will make a call
upon a wild flower that is not ordinarily at home at this date, but
the unusually warm days and nights of the past fortnight may
have prevented its departure; so we will knock at its door," tap-
ping at the upper leaves of a low-growing plant; and, verily, there
was the shy, dainty little blossom underneath—welcomed by at
least one pair of alert, sympathetic eyes. . . .

It was often amusing to observe Henry's want of gallantry; in
getting in or out of a boat, or if a fence or wall were to be sur-

1. It may be considered strange that the author of this paper does not
speak of Henry Thoreau's life as an amateur hermit on the shore of
Walden Pond; this omission is due to the fact that her acquaintance with
the Thoreau family did not begin until about two years after that most
interesting experiment in "plain living and high thinking" had been
abandoned.

mounted, no hand did he stretch forth; he assumed that a woman should be able to help herself in all such matters; but if she were defenseless, his inborn chivalry could be relied on; as in the case of a terrified girl pursued through the woods by a couple of young ruffians, sons of influential parents, Henry's valiant rescue was most timely; and by his persistent efforts due punishment was inflicted upon the shameless offenders. Again, when a weary mother with a heavy child in her arms was struggling to reach the station, where the train had already arrived, her feet sinking in the hot sand at every step, with one glance Henry took in the situation. He bounded over the fence, transferred the child to his own arms, and, with strides that seemed to disdain the shifting sand, he moved over the ground with a conquering air that appeared to impress the inanimate engine and compel it to tarry till the belated mother and child were safely aboard the train.

No one could more heartily enjoy his family life than Henry. He invariably came down from his study for a while in the evening for conversation; the sound of the piano was sure to draw him.

Tears dim my eyes as those scenes arise before me; Sophia playing the old-time music, notably Scotch melodies, which so well suited her flexible voice, and those quaint ballads of a past generation, whose airs were often so plaintive and with so much of heartbreak in the words. All the family had rich, sweet voices. If the song was a favorite, the father would join in, and thrilling was their singing of that gem, "Tom Bowline." I hear now the refrain:

His soul has gone aloft.

Often Henry would suddenly cease singing and catch up his flute, and, musical as was his voice, yet it was a delight never to be forgotten to listen to the silvery tones that breathed from the instrument.

For general society or mixing with throngs Henry had no inclination. He once said: "I would rather sit on a pumpkin and have it all myself than be crowded on a velvet cushion." In 1860 there was a general muster of all the militia of Massachusetts at Concord, and, Henry being asked if he went to see the evolutions of the troops, answered: "I had occasion to ascend a hill in the neighborhood of the encampment, and was much surprised to find how small a space so large a body of men occupied in the landscape." Henry's first book (*A Week on the Concord and Merrimack Rivers*) was far from a pecuniary success, very few volumes having been sold. This was not only a disappointment but caused no small monetary embarrassment. To discharge this, he for a time turned his attention to surveying, in which he was regarded as very skillful.

The unsold portion of the above-named work—somewhat over nine hundred copies—was stored in his father's house. The disappointment and struggle occasioned by the failure of the reading public to appreciate his first book were met by Henry in his usual philosophic way. About this time, in speaking of his library, he remarked that it consisted of "about one thousand volumes, nine hundred of which were written by myself." Once, after a day so stormy that he had not taken his customary outdoor exercise, Henry came flying down from his study when the evening was half spent. His face was unusually animated; he sang with zest, but evidently needed an unrestricted outlet for his pent-up vitality, and soon began to dance, all by himself, spinning airily round, displaying most remarkable litheness and agility; growing more and more inspirited, he finally sprang over the center-table, alighting like a feather on the other side—then, not in the least out of breath, continued his waltz until his enthusiasm abated.

I know not why I was surprised at hearing his mother refer to his "dancing days," for I had never associated Henry with any fashionable follies, even in his boyhood; but it seems he had been taught the usual accomplishments of well-bred children.

In sad contrast to the memory of Henry in his strength arises another, some years later—of him in his decline; he had returned from the West, whither he had been in search of health, and by

evening a flush had come to his cheeks and an ominous brightness and beauty to his eyes, painful to behold. His conversation
was unusually brilliant, and we listened with a charmed attention
which perhaps stimulated him to continue talking until the weak
voice could no longer articulate.

This was the autumn before his death; in a few months his life
on earth was ended. I was told that he retained his splendid
courage and fortitude to the last.

> Say not that Caesar was victorious.
> With toil and strife he stormed the house of Fame.
> In other sense this youth was glorious,
> Himself a kingdom whereso'er he came.

Several years after, one late summer morning, I accompanied
Sophia on a pilgrimage to an old "burying-ground" near the heart
of the town. She told me of her intention of removing the remains
of her immediate family to Sleepy Hollow Cemetery. "You
know," she said, "when dear mother is gone I shall be left alone,
the last; so it must be done soon." The graves of her kindred
were all around us. We were close to the village street, but the
high stone wall was a barrier between the living and the dead;
if any passed on the highway, they were unseen and gave no
sound; we were shut in with the dead of two centuries. As we
sat on a gray slab, Sophia related incidents of family history and
personal characteristics of her ancestors slumbering at our feet,
and of many others, townspeople bearing the well-known names
prominent in early Concord annals; legends of the farmers who
cultivated the soft slopes which are such pleasing features in the
local landscape, the smithy on the mill-dam, the country store-
keeper, the squire in his office, the dignified parson in his study
—all were portrayed in her vivid sketches so full of quaint humor
and tender pathos.

As she talked, those long-quiet sleepers seemed to stand before
us, with all their eccentricities and idiosyncrasies, as when they
formed a part of the life of a century ago; and as she finished

her graphic word-picture they vanished into the invisible, leaving but a memory of her wonderful power of delineation behind them.

We turned to leave the place—truly "God's acre"; the air was alive with butterflies fluttering noiselessly, alighting now on purple thistle and then on a belated wild rose; that impressive description of the end of the life of the Hebrew king came to mind —"He slept with his fathers." We took a last look at the venerable stones and grassy mounds, and as we passed from the sacred inclosure birds and insects seemed to be singing nature's requiem for the dead.

Sauntering along the elm-shaded streets to the house whence so many of her beloved had disappeared into the great unknown, our thoughts naturally turned to the problems of life and immortality.

The religious belief of the family was, to state it briefly, the Fatherhood of God and the Brotherhood of Man. Their confidence in the eternal beneficence and justice of their Creator could not be shaken, but for dogmas and sectarian creeds they had little respect, living and dying firm in the faith that He who observes every falling sparrow could not fail the human soul when, tired of earth and hungry for immortality, it lays down its burden of flesh as it enters the eternal mansion prepared for it "from the foundation of the world."

These Concord friends have all passed from this world to a better. They made an ineffaceable impress upon their generation in virtue of noble living; they endeavored to elevate, and were stalwart friends of the poor and downtrodden. . . .

EDWARD WALDO EMERSON

✪

"A Different Drummer"

In childhood I had a friend, a free, brave, youthful-seeming man, who wandered in from unknown woods or fields without knocking,

> Between the night and day
> When the fairy king has power,

passed by the elders' doors, but straightway sought out the children, brightened up the wood-fire forthwith and it seemed as if it were done by a wholesome brave north wind, instead of by the armful of "cat-sticks" which he brought in from the yard. His type was Northern, strong features, light brown hair, an open-air complexion, with suggestion of a seafaring race; the mouth pleasant and flexible when he spoke; aquiline nose, deep-set but wide-open eyes of clear blue-grey, sincere but capable of a twinkle, and again of austerity, but not of softness; those eyes could not be made to rest on what was unworthy, saw much and keenly (but yet in certain worthy directions hardly at all), and did not fear the face of day. A figure short and narrow, but thick; a carriage assuring sturdy strength and endurance. When he walked to get over the ground, one, seeing his long uniform pace, was instinctively reminded of some tireless machine. His body was

Reprinted from the special "Thoreau Centenary" number of the London *Bookman*, LII (June 1917), 81–84, and there entitled "Personal Recollections," by permission of Mr. and Mrs. Raymond Emerson.

73

active, well-balanced, and his step could be light, as of one who could leap, or dance, or skate well at will.

His dress was strong and plain. He was not one of those little men who try to become great by exuvial methods of length of hair or beard, or broad collars, or conspicuous coat.

This youthful, cheery figure was a familiar one in our house, and when he, like the "Pied Piper of Hamelin," sounded his note in the hall, the children must needs come and hug his knees, and he struggled with them, nothing loth, to the fire-place, sat down and told stories, sometimes of the strange adventures of his childhood, or more often of squirrels, muskrats, hawks, he had seen that day, the Monitor-and-Merrimac duel of mud-turtles in the river, or the Homeric battle of the Red and Black Ants. Then he would make our pencils and knives disappear; and redeem them presently from our ears and noses; and last would bring down the copper warming pan from the oblivion of the garret and unweariedly shake it over the blaze till reverberations arose within, and then opening it, let a white-blossoming explosion of pop-corn fall over the little people on the rug.

Later, this magician often appeared in house or garden, and always to charm.

This youth who could pipe and sing himself, made for children pipes of all sorts, of grass, of leaf-stalk, of squash and pumpkin, handsome but fragrant flageolets of onion tops, but chiefly of the golden willow shoot. As the children grew older he led them to choice huckleberry hills, guided them to the land of the chestnut and barberry, and more than all, opened that land of enchantment into which, among dark hemlocks, blood-red maples and yellowing birches, we floated in his boat, and freighted it with leaves and gentians and fragrant grapes from the festooning vines.

A little later he opened another romantic door to boys full of "Robin Hood," made us know for ourselves that nothing was truer than

> 'Tis merry! 'tis merry in the good green wood
> When mavis and merle are singing!

Taught us how to camp and cook. Taught us also the decorum and manners of the wood, which gives no treasures or knowledge to the boisterous and careless; the humanity, not to kill a harmless snake because we thought it ugly, or in revenge for a start; and that the most zealous collector of eggs must always leave the mother-bird most of her eggs, and not go too often to watch the nest. He showed boys with short purses, but legs stout, if short, how to reach the nearest mountains—Wachusett and Monadnoc—and live there in a bough-house, on berries and meal and beans, happy as the gods on Olympus, and like them, in the clouds and among the thunders. He always came, after an expedition afar, to tell his adventures and wonders, and all his speech was simple, and clean and high. Yet he was associated with humble offices also, for, like the friendly Troll in the tale, he deftly came to the rescue when any lock or hinge or stove needed the hand of a master.

I saw this man, gravely and simply courteous, quietly and effectively helpful, always spoken of with affection and respect by my parents and other near friends; knew him strongly, but not noisily, interested on the side of Freedom in the great struggle that then stirred the country. When the red morning began to dawn in Kansas and at Harper's Ferry, I saw him deeply moved, and though otherwise avoiding public meetings and organised civic action, come to the front and, moved to the core, speak among the foremost against oppression.

Fatal disease laid hold of him at this time and I saw him face his slow death with cheerful courage.

Then I went away from home, and began to read his books; but I read them in the light of the man I knew. I met persons who asked questions about him; they had heard strange rumours and made severe criticisms; then I read essays and satires in which he was held lightly, or ridiculed—heard that he was pompous, rustic, conceited, that his thoughts were not original, that he strove to imitate another; that even his observations on natural history were of no value, and not new. Even in Concord I found that, while his manifest integrity commanded respect, he was regarded unsympathetically by many, and that not only the purposes, but many of the events of his life were unknown.

But it must be remembered that this was half a century ago. Even so, Thoreau's elevation and independence would not have made him popular in any age, and he was well in advance of his own. Let us fairly review the ground and see if with the light of latter years, and the better perspective, we may not find values there, passed by as naught, or as faults, in earlier years.

Thoreau once said that he was born in the best place in the world, among good people, "and in the very nick of time." John Thoreau, his father, a Jersey Breton by descent, was a kindly, quiet man, a pencil manufacturer. The mother, of Scottish ancestry, was spirited, capable and witty, with an edge to her wit on occasion, but generous, often showing great kindness, especially to young people, and with a rare talent for making home pleasant, for this woman knew how to keep work and care in their proper places, and give life and love precedence. These parents early introduced their children to the woods and their treasures.

Henry prepared for Harvard in the Concord schools. Out of hours he attended the Dame School taught by Nature—one of her best boys. In college, Henry did not suffer the rigid curriculum to trammel him too much, but haunted the library, acquiring there a knowledge of good authors, remarkable then as now.

I must pass over the period when, with his brother, he taught a private school far in advance of its day; then the happy river voyage together, and the, to Henry, almost crushing loss of this brother. They were just enough unlike to increase the interest and happiness of their relation. It was one of closest sympathy. It is believed that they were both charmed by one young girl; but she was denied them and passed out of their horizon. In reading what Thoreau says of Love and the poem relating to his loss, one sees that even his disappointment elevated his life.

In the next few years he worked with his father in the pencil shop, and wrote constantly, and the woods and river drew him

to them in each spare hour. He wrote for the *Dial* as the organ
of the new thought of the region and hour, and he generously
helped edit it. He relieved his friend Emerson from tasks which
to him were hopeless, by his skill in gardening and general household works, and twice took charge of his house and family during
his long absence.

After Henry's death, his sister gave me some account of their
black-lead business, and years later, after her death, I looked up
the matter with some care. Full details would take up too much
space, but I wish here to clear my honoured friend's memory
from the imputation of idleness to the neglect of his family's support and welfare. He brought his reading, his thought, and his
notable mechanical skill to the service of his father's humble
business of grinding plumbago and making pencils, and soon, by
their experiments and invention, in which the evidence is strong
that Henry bore an important, and probably the principal, part,
made the best American lead-pencil of their day, and put their
powdered plumbago, for fineness and quality, ahead of all manufactured in that country. The newly-discovered art of electro-
typing vastly increased the demand for their product which, because of the excellence of their secret process, had, for years,
practically the monopoly of the market.

Thus it appears that this ne'er-do-well so helped on the im-
provement of his father's business that he left it in advance of
competitors. Then, though he declined to put his life into that
trade, preferring trade with the Celestial City, he found time,
after his father's death, to oversee for his family the business
which gave them a very good maintenance and, when it was
necessary, to work at it with his own hands while health remained. Yet he did not think fit to button-hole his neighbours
on the street and say, "You mistake, I am not idle."

His own Spartan wants of plain food, strong clothing, and
telescope and a few books, with occasional travel in the cheapest
style, were supplied in a variety of ways. For he had what is
called in New England, "faculty"; was a good gardener, me-

chanic, and emergency-man. But his leading profession was that
of a land-surveyor. In this, as in his mechanics, he did the best
possible work.

Thoreau enjoyed his surveying, and the more if it led him
into wild lands "East of the Sun, West of the Moon." But he
construed his business largely, looking deeper than its surface.
While searching for their bounds with his townsmen and neighbours in village, swamp and woodlot, he found everywhere,
marked far more distinctly than by blazed oak-tree or stake and
stones, lines, imaginary truly, but forming bounds to their lives
more impassable than stone. Many he saw imprisoned for life,
and he found these walls already beginning to hedge in his horizon, shut out the beautiful free life of his hope.

> Heaven lies about us in our infancy,

sang the poet, and Thoreau, mainly to save a view of those
heavens and, that the household clatter and village hum drown
not the music of the spheres, went into the woods for a time.

His sojourn for two happy wholesome years by Walden's
shores, which he did not pretend were primeval wildness, was a
spiritual, intellectual, social, and economic experiment. He did
not go there as a Jonah crying out on Nineveh, but to mind his
own business, away from entanglement in village or household
affairs where he was not needed; studying Nature, writing his
first book, keeping his charming *Journal,* he could not forbear

> To chant the bliss of his abode
> To men imprisoned in their own.

Of what his wood-walks were to him he said: "I do not go
there to get my dinner, but to get that sustenance which dinners
only preserve me to enjoy, without which dinners were a vain
repetition." His genius was solitary, and though his need for
friendly and social relation with his kind was great, it was occasional, and to his lonely happiness the world will owe the best
gifts he has left. "It is not that we love to be alone," he said,

"but that we love to soar, and, when we do soar, the company grows thinner, till there is none at all."

Thoreau was a strong, loyal and helpful friend; never a caressing or flattering one. He was a good talker, unless led away by a certain hereditary enjoyment, from Scottish ancestry, of intellectual fencing. Paradoxical statement of his highly original thought sometimes interfered with pleasantest relations. His friend Emerson, honouring and valuing him, complained of this foible. Thoreau held this trait in check with women and children and humble people who were no match for him; with them he was simple, gentle, friendly and amusing; and all testify his desire to share the pleasant things he knew from his own experiences. But to a conceited gentleman from the city, or a dogmatic or patronising clergyman or editor he would, as Emerson said, appear as a "gendarme, good to knock down cockneys with."

He could afford to be a philosopher, for he was first a good common man. It takes good iron to receive a fine polish. His simple, direct speech and look and bearing were such that labourers, mechanics, farmers, would not put him down in their books as a fool, or visionary, or helpless, as the scholar, writer or reformer might probably do.

He has been accused of copying Emerson; the charge is frivolous. Thoreau's course in college and as a teacher, his original and sincere writing in college themes and early *Journals* prove that Thoreau was Thoreau, and not the copy of another. His close association, under the same roof, for months, with the maturer Emerson may, not unnaturally, have tinged his early writings, and some superficial trick of manner or of speech been unconsciously acquired, as often happens. But this is all that can be granted. Entire independence, strong individuality, was Thoreau's distinguishing trait, and his foible was not subserviency, but combativeness in conversation, as his friends knew almost too well. Conscious imitation was not to be thought of as a possibility of this strong spirit. Nor was he a product of the Transcendental epoch, though stimulated by it.

Thoreau was humane in the widest sense. He felt real respect for the personality and character of animals, and could never have been guilty of asking, with Paul, "Doth God care for oxen?" He respected his little forest neighbours, and felt that, until men showed higher behaviour, the less they said about the "lower animals" the better. For all life he had reverence, and just where the limits of conscious life began and ended he was too wise and too hopeful to say. He was more than naturalist. He said of Nature: "She must not be looked at directly, but askance, or by flashes; like the head of the Gorgon Medusa, she turns the men of science to stone." How Thoreau felt when alone with Nature, may be gathered from his own words about her: "At once our Destiny and Abode, our Maker and our Life."

In his early books, the youth tried to wake up people, a little roughly, to see the poor mill-round of their days, and show freedom and joy within reach; this many resented. Have the conduct and words of most poets, prophets, even the founders of the great religions, been considered sagacious "on 'Change"? But later, in the *Journals,* he drops the north wind method, and the enchanting haze of a poet's thought brings out the beauty in commonest things. Thoreau was half a century in advance of his time. "If I do not keep step with others"—he writes in his *Journal,* "it is because I hear a different drummer." * "Let a man step to the music which he hears—however measured, and however far away."

B. W. Lee of Newport, New York, said, "The year I was sixteen, I went to the Thoreau school in the Old Academy for two months. Henry Thoreau had a very small class of boys in Greek and Latin and maybe had young ladies in French. He used to come in just before recess both morning and afternoon. He came in at a rapid pace, commenced work at once in his peculiar odd way and the boy that had not got his lesson did not receive much mercy or taffy. He was very strict in that matter. As well

---

* This quotation is from *Walden* [ed.].

as I can remember, he was a thin, spare man, thin-faced, light complexion[ed], and weighed perhaps 140 pounds, rather on his dignity, and so far as I can remember not inclined to joking and fun, with his scholars outside of the school house." *

Edward Hoar [son of Concord's most prominent family and Thoreau's companion on numerous excursions] seemed glad that I was going to write about Thoreau and showed affectionate interest in him and high regard. Not being allowed by his parents to have or use a gun, he was delighted with the chances he had to go with Henry Thoreau when he went gunning. Henry had a single-barrel fowling piece with a flint lock, in the use of which he was very expert. But he did not long continue to use a gun. Hoar felt that with Thoreau's life something went out of Concord woods and fields and rivers that never would return.

William Ellery Channing [Thoreau's lifelong friend and companion] says that the work that Henry did in the family pencil factory was just in proportion to the needs of the family. When they were straitened in means because of any special needs, like building the house, then he would go to work and do more; but, for himself, he would never have done any of the mechanical work.

---

* There was, however, much material which Dr. Emerson did not use in *Henry Thoreau as Remembered by a Young Friend* and which was generously made available to me by his son and daughter-in-law, Mr. and Mrs. Raymond Emerson of Concord, Massachusetts, when I was working on the biography, *The Days of Henry Thoreau*. Once again, they have generously granted permission for me to publish here further extracts from those unpublished notes. I have printed them approximately in the order in which they occur in Dr. Emerson's notes, rather than making any attempt to force them into any chronological order. Since they were rough notes, I have taken the liberty of expanding abbreviations, regularizing punctuation, omitting repetitive material, and generally polishing the text for publication. In no case, however, I believe, has the sense of Dr. Emerson's notes been at all altered, though I have omitted silently large sections of his notes that did not particularly pertain to facets of Thoreau's personality [ed.].

Benjamin Tolman told me, "Once or twice Thoreau came to my printing office to look over the proof of something of his that I was printing—his Cattle Show address and some other things, and I went to his home, too, about proof. He was agreeable and pleasant, but I didn't see much of him or talk with him because he knew so much more and was so superior a man to me that I didn't feel like it." But when I asked, "But you don't mean that he put on airs of superiority; he was companionable and friendly, wasn't he?" He replied, "Always! Oh, yes, he was a very pleasant person."

Warren Miles, who worked in the Thoreau pencil factory, when asked if he knew Thoreau, replied, "Yes, I knew him very well." "What should you say of him?" "He was a good mechanic—rather inclined to improvements of arts as well as mechanical matters. He was better educated on Nature than any man I ever saw. I remember a long talk we had about mud turtles and about wildflowers. He would almost always get up some argument so as to get one interested. He liked creatures. He told me that he rather tamed a squirrel that lived close by him, and that he was about as much company as a person after he got him used to him."

George Keyes told me that he attended the Academy when it was taught by the Thoreau brothers. "How were they as school-masters?" "Very pleasant indeed. Yes, I have a very pleasant impression left in my mind of that school. I remember how interesting his stories were. One evening shortly after his return from Cape Cod, he told us about that expedition and about the old worn copper coin he found on the beach. Another time he was delighted because, being out very early in the morning, he had found the track of some very rare wild animal in the snow leading right up the meadow. He was light-haired, better looking than his portraits, had a healthy complexion with a bright color, though rather pale for an out-of-doors man. He had a strong

prominent nose and good eyes; a face that you would long remember."

Talked with James Garty about H.D.T. I asked, "Suppose I
did not know of him and asked you what kind of man he was,
what would you say of him?" *"Well, it wouldn't do to have
everybody like him,* of his way of thinking. Oh, he was a good
sort of man and was straight and I think would pay every cent
he owed to any man—I don't know whether he had any debts—
but what I mean when I say it would be bad if everybody thought
as he did that he didn't believe in government."

Frank C. Brown [Emerson's nephew] remembers Thoreau's
singing "Tom Bowline" and "that he put his heart into it." He
knew that he used to entertain his mother (Mrs. Lucy C. Brown)
by singing and by dancing (*pas seul*). Thoreau used to give
Frank natural history information, especially about the forest
trees, and found him always willing, even eager, to impart. He
doesn't clearly recollect his personal appearance, except his
prominent nose and that his skin seemed dark, probably from
out-of-door exposure, tan. (Mrs. Frank Brown said that his look
and complexion and eye reminded one of a longshoreman.)
Frank said that the principal impression left by Thoreau was his
universal knowledge—that he went to him with every question
as to birds, trees, etc., and he could tell him about them. He
recalls him as good-humored and talkative and as habitually in
good spirits.

Mrs. Edwin Bigelow knew the Thoreau family well for years,
when they lived opposite in the Parkman House. Her first recollection of Henry is seeing him a youth with fair hair and erect,
a serious face with mouth drawn together in a characteristic
curve, come out of the yard and walk towards the Academy
where he then taught. She knew at once by his gait and bearing
that he was a gentleman. As a neighbor, Henry was pleasant and
helpful, but by no means aggressive or vain or egotistical, drop-

ping in and out and lending a hand naturally as it came his way
to do so. He was friendly to his Irish neighbors and good to
stray cats and dogs and always humane to animals, and more
than this, *respected* them.

Mrs. Bigelow tells how at the "Little Woods" picnics, Henry
would tell all to sit absolutely quiet and close together—then he
would go forward cautiously, sprinkle crumbs before them, and
then, retreating, seat himself a little before the others and begin
a sort of rolling or humming sound and would draw squirrels
to come and eat at last out of his hands. He would open his hands
in the river and let the fish swim into them.

One Sunday as the congregations were coming home from
church, Henry Thoreau came up the street with a tree in his
hand which he had dug up to plant. His old aunt, the Orthodox
Miss Dunbar, hastened out to reprove him and abate this scandal
in the family, but he answered her pleasantly, "Aunt Louisa, I
have been worshipping in my way, and I don't trouble you in
your way."

I asked Mrs. Bigelow about Thoreau's connection with the
Underground Railroad. While Henry Thoreau was in the woods,
the slaves sometimes were brought to him there, but obviously
there was no possible concealment in his house, so he would look
after them by day, and at nightfall, get them to his mother's or
another house of hiding. He was always ready to help with
service and didn't count risk, and also, although he had little
money, always gave or advanced money to a slave who needed
it. Sometimes this was repaid from the fund. It was no part of
his plan in making the Walden hermitage to make there a refuge
for fugitives, that was only incidental.

Dr. Thomas Hosmer of Bedford (scholar of the Thoreaus at
the Academy in the years 1838–1839) went with the Thoreaus
in search of Indian relics. Once he found a sort of hollow,
scooped like a small amphitheatre, on the side of the bluff over
the Great Meadows and showed it to Thoreau who said, "This
is artificial, made by the Indians, and we ought to find evidences

of their fires here." They accordingly dug at the center and found charcoal and Indian relics, a mortar and pestle, etc. Hosmer also found a large block of the dark-grey flint with white specks such as most of the arrow and spearheads found in the neighborhood were made of, the mass weighing nearly fifty pounds. He showed it to the Thoreaus who told him that the nearest place where that stone was native to the soil, geographically, was Norwich, Connecticut.

[Reminiscing further of his days as a student in the Thoreau school] Hosmer said Thoreau spoke of the certainty we must feel of a wise and friendly power over us. He bade the boys and girls think, if any of them should go into a shop and see all the nicely finished wheels, pinions, springs and frame pieces of a watch lying spread out on a bench and again came to find them exactly put together and working in unison to move the hands on a dial and show the passage of time—whether they could believe that this had come by chance or rather should know that somebody with thought and plan and power had been there. This, I believe, used to be a familiar argument and example in philosophical and religious treatises, but its use in the Grammar School by the young schoolmaster showed that he knew himself there to teach broadly and awaken thought and not merely his lessons in the rudiments of letters.

There was a class in Natural Philosophy. If any pupil seemed to care for the study and took pains with [his] drawings on the blackboard illustrating the principles, Henry would take much interest and pains to help him along. The brothers would sometimes come out into the school yard at recess and join the children in their amusements; John more than Henry who was not so familiar with all the children as his elder brother but was interested in individual children.

Sometimes in winter the Bedford boys came swiftly and smoothly up the frozen river on skates. One day three Concord boys derided their old-fashioned skates and strapping which the Bedford boys defended by appealing to the test of best performance. Henry, hearing this, said, "Come boys, that's a good challenge. I move we accept it and go down to the river in the afternoon. If they find fault with the skates they must show that they can do better on theirs." It was agreed on and as they went to the river, Hosmer argued with Henry Thoreau that the race ought to begin from the moment they knelt on the ice to buckle on the skates, saying that in the quality of the skates should properly be included the care and speed with which they could be put on. But Henry said, "No, I shall overrule that: the question is now of speed in skating." Afterward he visited Thoreau [who was] living at Walden [and] who talked with him, inquiring of him of what use he found his school studies in life.

Edward Neally told me that when he was a boy he carried the chain for Thoreau on a survey near Fairhaven. Later he did so often, and his interest in natural history (birds, beasts and fishes; he never took to botany) was first awakened by him and afterwards he cared greatly for it and collected for the Natural History Society and sometimes for the Smithsonian Institute at Washington.

Thoreau seemed a careful manager, and he found him very different from what some people think; he always seemed jolly and social, liked a joke. The difference between him and other scientific men that he had seen, like Agassiz and Horace Mann, was they liked to have the creature killed and dissect and examine it carefully in every way to see how it was made, "but Thoreau liked to study 'em living. He didn't like to have 'em killed (oh, he didn't mind if I'd shoot a duck when we were out together), but he would rather know what they'd do. He had more patience than any man I ever knew. He would keep still and watch what they would do for more than an hour and a half. I would get tired waiting, but he wouldn't. He was a very strong man for his size, thick-set though he wasn't very large. He always walked with easy long steps; it would tire me well to keep up with him."

"How did people in general like him; what did the folks on the Milldam [Concord's main street] think of him?" "They rather liked him as a rule. Some of them couldn't understand him. He had a few who were his enemies. One of them was a farmer, a good man, too, but he thought ill of Thoreau and always spoke badly of him. But the trouble began years ago when the Thoreaus set his woods afire by accident and they was burned over. Another thing he never liked was that Thoreau said to him one day when he met him on his farm that he got all the hard work and trouble out of it and Thoreau got all the beauty out of it. You see, he didn't know how to take it. Thoreau didn't mean any harm. There was another man that was always down on Thoreau, but then for that matter, he lost wood by that same fire. Most people rather liked him, but many didn't understand him." Neally said (in answer to my inquiry as to whether he thought Thoreau a helpful, friendly man to his kind), "Yes, if I had been in trouble and needed assistance I don't know but I'd have turned to him as quick as to any man."

Sam Staples told me, "I used to go surveying with Thoreau a great deal. We've run a great many lines together. He was a good surveyor and very careful. Albert Wood'll tell you that he never in his surveying finds any better work done than that that Henry Thoreau did.

"When I bought that farm next to your father's, I had him run the lines for me. I guess 'twas about the last work he did. Well, the line against your father's pear orchard and meadow running down to the brook I'd always supposed was right, as his hedge ran, and so I dug that ditch between his meadow and mine, right in the line of the hedge. Well, when we come to run the line, the corner of the hedge on the Turnpike was right, but when we got to the other end of the hedge, 'twas several feet over on to what I'd bought. And at the brook, the ditch which I'd dug to it from the hedge-corner, supposing that was the line, came much as a rod into my meadow by the deed. That tickled Thoreau mightily. 'We'll call Emerson down and show it to him,' says he. 'Oh, never mind,' says I, 'he don't know about it; let it be as it is.' 'No,' says he, 'I'll get Emerson down.' So he went up to the house and told him we got something to show him down

at the meadow, and he put on his hat and came down along with
Henry. Well, when we got him down there, Thoreau, says he,
'I didn't think this of you, Mr. Emerson, stealing so much land
of Staples here.' Well, your father was troubled when he saw
where the ditch was over in my land. 'I'll pay you for the land,'
says he, 'what's it worth?' 'Oh, no,' says I, 'I dug the ditch there
supposing the hedge was the line. 'Twan't your fault. 'Twas the
man you bought of showed you where to put the hedge. Let it
be as the ditch is now.' It pleased Thoreau to get that joke on
him."

Elizabeth J. Weir went to school (1843) to Miss Sophia Thoreau in the Parkman House. She saw John and Henry as not
alike: John had less pronounced features and was plumper.
Henry had *fair* hair, large eyes—with outer parts of lids drooping, and large pupils—very blue. She listened eagerly for stories
of birds and squirrels. He had a pleasing appearance to young
people and children. So much life! She can see him with the
children around him standing on the door-steps with one foot on
the upper step telling stories and a circle of children about him.
People misunderstood him—on the street he didn't always stop
"to pass the time of day," but sometimes passed on his business
without noticing people—thinking. At his mother's house with
Sophia, all the little everyday things were made funny and agreeable. Henry would give such pleasant turns to conversation, make
things spicy and interesting. He saw the ludicrous side; enjoyed
the unusual. Like twins—he and Sophia; he opened his thought
to her.

[Miss Weir worked much at Mr. Emerson's.] Henry would
come in and offer to mend things. He saw what was waiting, as
an odd job, and mended it. If Mrs. Emerson were there, they
would have pleasant little conversations; get on deep subjects.
Henry was a help to Mrs. Emerson in all ways, being younger—
he appreciated her fine mind and beautiful thought, and she thus
helped educate him. He loved her elder sister Mrs. Brown, and
was as a son to her. She depended on him; she would say, "Run

over to Mr. Emerson's and see if Henry is there. Get him to come over and see if anything can be done about my stove's smoking." He would look at the damper or latch and mend and fit. While at work at these jobs, he would prolong the conversation. It seemed a favour to him to ask him to do something. He burned out the chimneys on rainy days, the excited children watching the process.

I met Daniel F. Potter this morning, November 17, 1904, and said to him, "Mr. Potter, I understand that Henry Thoreau once give you a thrashing." He was passing me to go into the post office, but turned instantly and said, "Yes, he did, and it smarts still." He spoke with energy, and I thought with a little feeling. "Then it wasn't justly given?" I asked. "No, sir, it wasn't," he replied. "I can tell you all about it if you want to know." And standing in the doorway to the post office, with a particularly sharp wind doing no good, I am sure, to his inflamed right eye, he told me the following, which I give in words as near to his as I can. He spoke as if he remembered the incident perfectly.

"I was a little fellow of ten, and was going to school in the brick school house that is now the Masonic Hall. There were men teachers there, but I'd just come from the district school, where I had a woman teacher. Now the women teachers taught, when we'd finished with a lesson, to put away our books and fold our arms." And the little old man illustrated, blinking through his spectacles. "Well, the rule at the Academy was that a boy should always have a book before him. First thing I knew, Henry Thoreau called me up and thrashed me. He thrashed twelve other boys that day, thirteen in all, and resigned the day after.

"I didn't understand the reason for this then, but I found out later. It seems he'd been taken to task by someone—I think 'twas Deacon Ball—for not using the rod enough. So Thoreau thought he'd give the other way a thorough trial, and he did, for one day. The next day he said he wouldn't keep school any longer, if that was the way he had to do it.

"When I went to my seat, I was so mad that I said to myself, 'When I'm grown up, I'll whip you for this, old feller.' But," and Mr. Potter chuckled, "I never saw the day I wanted to do it.—Why, Henry Thoreau was the kindest hearted of men. He only kept school in Concord for two weeks."

Horace Hosmer, another student in the school, states, "Henry told his mother to buy gold and plumbago at the commencement of the war; Louis F. Ball told me that he should have made twice as much as he did had he followed Henry's advice."

Part Two

Thoreau as Seen by the Critics

DANIEL GREGORY MASON

✪

The Idealistic Basis of Thoreau's Genius

One can hardly think of a literary figure more inviting to analysis than the solitary, uncouth student, often mistaken for a pedlar, who was spending his time, fifty years ago, ransacking the wood-lots and pastures of old Concord. As one reads of the thrifty habits, shrewd talk, and unusually ardent idealism of Thoreau, one feels that here is an absorbing subject to study. Yet of his various sides we have heard so far very unequally. Of the natural-ist, familiar with the ways of all his brute neighbors, we hear more and more; of the hermit, misanthropic and self-willed, we hear, to our honor as well as his, less and less. But of the phi-losopher, lighting up by his fine power of lucid vision the per-plexed fabric of human nature, and contrasting vividly its so varied elements, its power and impotence, its pettiness and gran-deur, we hear, strangely enough, scarcely anything at all. It may be that the appreciation of a quality so fundamental in the man as this profound spiritual insight will clarify our total conception of him. At any rate, the relations in which his perception and love of truth stood, on the one hand, with his social noncon-formity, and on the other, with his delight in Nature, are of themselves suggestive enough to invite examination.

The basis of Thoreau's idealism was an indomitable probity of mind. He had that keenness of sense which penetrates instan-

Reprinted from the *Harvard Monthly*, XXV (December 1897), 82–93.

taneously the mask of appearance, to discover the nucleus of actuality within. No taint of decay, however deeply hid or decorously incased, could escape him; his unerring intuition smelled out a sham inevitably. Many of us, even the most honest, are embarrassed by a slight bluntness of perception; with the best will in the world, we gloss over an inconsistency, or blink a harmless affectation. "What difference does it make?" we say; and indeed it makes very little, practically; but it obliterates for us just those subtle shades of contrast that give to the spectacle of life, for the fine artist in morals, all its charm and its appeal. These subtleties are for him what the most delicately elusive relations of color are for the artist of the picturesque; and for both men the ordinary practical way of looking, with its rough distinctions for purposes of utility, constitutes a sad lopping-off. If Thoreau saw a wonderfully varied pageant of truth and falsehood, reality and appearance, where his neighbors saw the dead surface of the usual, it may have made him, to be sure, a bit of a fanatic to live with, but it also made him a singularly absorbing, suggestive writer. Little as his townsmen may have relished having this sagacious surveyor plot out their characters while he measured their fields, we cannot be blamed for enjoying the resultant maps.

Of Thoreau's literary creed, then, the first tenet was attention to truth; and from that, since the truth is simply each man's particular way of seeing life, followed naturally the second, individuality of standpoint. He believed that the final aim of literature is always self-revelation; that nothing can be permanently valuable but the sincere thought of one man; and that, in a word, the only perennially interesting formula is "I think." Accordingly he made no attempt to conform his expressions to any standard, but only to reproduce as accurately as might be his own feelings and beliefs. His love for the wild was closely connected with his distrust of sophistication and tame conformity. He felt more deeply than most the sacredness of those dumb leadings of instinct or intuitive surmise that often forbid allegiance to accepted opinions. He wished his life to be egregious, in the primary sense of that word;

and he would not be dissuaded even when people applied the term to him in its commoner meaning. As philosophers clear the path for constructive thought by a systematic skepticism which burns up all accumulation of old sophistry, so Thoreau, to give himself breathing-space, made a grand bonfire of all dusty traditions and conventionalities. His elders must have been rather scandalized to see their ancestral hobby-horses crumbling in the lustral flames. But he wished to start unimpeded, and see what could be done by a brave push for truth.

Characteristically, he chose for guides in his quest not prudence or reason, but the finest, rarest intimations that came to him. With a naïveté worthy a woman, he believed the things he wanted to believe. The prosaic dicta of the intellect he thought misleading; the only voices safe to listen to were the intuitions, the supernatural suggestions of the imagination in ecstasy, the most extreme beliefs and wishes of the spirit. "Who that has heard a strain of music," he asks, "feared then lest he should speak extravagantly any more forever?" "I am convinced that I cannot exaggerate enough even to lay the foundation of a true expression." And in accordance with his belief he habitually followed, as solid practical guides, the remotest promptings of his genius in preference to the grosser prudential motives which govern most men. "The poet or the artist never yet had so fair and noble a design but some of his posterity at least could accomplish it."

Like other men who have tried the experiment of doing their own thinking, he found that independence of mind brought him happiness. Not from any ethical preconception, but spontaneously from a buoyant and romantic temperament, sprung his intense optimism. If he was a disciple of joy, it was not for the sake of the discipline, but of the joy. Morality was ever secondary for him, a means; happiness was the end, and beauty. His austerity was like the training of the athlete, dedicated to the establishment of health. And here it is interesting to note the fallacy of the ordinary view that Thoreau was a sort of miniature copy of Emerson, or "Emerson's independent moral man made flesh," as Mr. Henry James so cleverly called him. The fundamental traits which underlay the external similarities of the two men were exactly polar. Emerson was swayed by an ethical motive, Thoreau by an aesthetic; Emerson aimed at tranquillity and benignity, Thoreau at joy and delight; as Arnold would say, Emerson inclined naturally to Hebraism, Thoreau to Hellenism. The latter explicitly states that sheer and mere morality is not healthy. "Conscience is instinct bred in the house," he says in the *Week*; and in *Walden* he explains his meaning; "Our manners have been corrupted by communication with the saints. . . . There is nowhere recorded a simple, irrepressible satisfaction with the gift of life, any memorable praise of God. . . . If we would restore mankind by truly Indian, botanic, magnetic, or natural means, let us first be as simple and well as Nature ourselves, dispel the clouds which hang over our own brows, and take up a little life into our pores. Do not stay to be an overseer of the poor, but endeavor to become one of the worthies of the world." From this it is evident that his faithfulness, his vigorous adherence to moral principles, sprung from his conviction of the mutual dependence of conduct and happiness, of truth and beauty. He has been much misunderstood, because approached merely as a puritan, or at most a stoic: he was in reality a sort of spiritual epicurean, using stoicism as a means for attaining other than stoic ends. Like Wordsworth, he knew well that through duty, or a similar steadfastness for which that word may stand, "the most ancient Heavens are fresh and strong."

We may, then, consider it shown by our analysis of Thoreau's mental temper, that his radical probity made him an individualist, and that his deep idealism made him an optimist; and we may now go on to examine, in the light of this analysis, his attitude toward society, and toward Nature.

It is evident at the outset that one so bent on following only the suggestions of his own mind must soon run counter to the unwritten laws which tradition and custom institute everywhere. The attitude of opposition, however, was at first involuntary on his part, only later acquiring that element of propagandism which occasionally disfigures his writings, and at times even degenerates into pettishness. The reformer was not a fundamental character in him, but reform was in the air of his time, and he, unable to escape the contagion, ended by preaching to others the simplicity which he had at first practised merely for his own good. Of course the sharp and querulous passages in his books are the standing testimony always cited by those who consider him morbid or embittered. It is needless to attempt a defence of these passages; they are truly the blot upon his work. But that they are symptomatic of a thorough-going, pervasive cynicism is an untenable opinion. They exhibit simply the excess of qualities showing themselves normally in his antiseptic humor, so formidably hostile to the morally or mentally rotten. That great men should be faultless is no part of our desire.

We can hardly blame his contemporaries, nevertheless, for being unable to view him dispassionately. They cared for truth, to be sure, but they preferred the comfortable variety; and this lightning bolt, trying to purify the air, gave them a headache. Hence the antagonism which is generally attributed to Thoreau's acidity of disposition rather than to the annoyance of the worldlings whom he pestered out of their complacency. How could he conform to the abuses of society? Here as elsewhere, nonconformity was the beginning of wisdom. In "Life without Principle," one of the few essays in which he explicitly condemns the customs of men, he says, "We select granite for the underpinning of our houses and barns; we build fences of stone; but we do not ourselves rest on an underpinning of granitic truth, the lowest primitive rock. Our sills are rotten." And then he asks, with that terrible insistence of his, "What stuff is the man made of who is not coexistent in our thought with the purest and subtilest truth?"

This kind of plain dealing would make a man uneasy in any of the conventionalities, and we cannot wonder that he was as much a skeptic in religion as a nonconformist in society. Bad air, timid platitudes, and nasal hymnody could not be expected to appeal to one whose conceptions of religious truth were dominated by the idea of beauty; and Thoreau kept clear of them, simply and without ado. "As for positions, combinations, and details,—what are they? In clear weather, when we look into the heavens, what do we see but the sky and the sun?" Thus in various ways he endeavored to "work and wedge [his] feet downward through the mud and slush of opinion, and prejudice, and tradition, and delusion, and appearance, that alluvion which covers the globe." And among the genuine things his search revealed to him the supremely beneficent one was Nature.

His love of Nature is thus a corollary from the sincerity of his character. The freshness and vigor of tree and rock and sky meant for him an infinite relief from the arid, artificial life of the village. It was with a sense of vital exhilaration that he escaped from the close country parlor, with its hair sofas and ornamented mantelpiece, to the immense beauty and serenity of wild meadow and woodland. "It is as if I always met in those places," he says, "some grand, serene, immortal, infinitely encouraging, though invisible, companion, and walked with him. There, at last, my nerves are steadied, my senses and my mind do their office." Imagine a person of almost excessive sensibility living with people such as only Miss Wilkins* is able to describe, people among whom puritanism and poverty have bred so much gloom and ugliness, and you understand why Thoreau escaped to the woods for refreshment of mind, and for liberty to follow out quietly the thoughts which beckoned to him. Such liberty, together with the pleasures that his acutely sensuous nature found in the sights, sounds, and smells of his favorite haunts, would be in themselves enough to explain his love of open-air life; but there is a further reason for it.

The type of mind we call poetic looks habitually through material things to the spiritual existences beyond them, of which they are the symbols. The poet's imagination is a sort of added faculty by which he perceives an entire hierarchy of being unreal to the prosaic man, whose utilitarianism shuts out from him all

* Mary E. Wilkens Freeman, the New England writer known for her tales of rural life.

that does not directly affect his own well-being. Such a poet as Wordsworth, habitually taking a high, impersonal view, is able to discover the deep bonds that unite all things, and to show how the true reality is not that gross matter which sense reveals, but the most impalpable hints it breathes of remoter verities within, which the poetic faculty alone can discern. This faculty differs from the philosophic, on the other hand, in that it does not express itself abstractly, but uses the very matter it transcends as a medium by which to adumbrate its truths. Thus its attitude stands midway between that of the ordinary man and that of the philosopher; it contents itself with seeing neither the one aspect nor the other, but reads in the first the symbol of the second: it is characterized by a power which works through intuition, and expresses itself in metaphor and image.

Thoreau possessed this power in an extraordinary degree; it was the germinal seed of his intellect, just as sincerity was the energizing force of his spirit: and the domain in which he naturally chose to exert it was Nature. There he saw the emblems of a fairer, serener life than that we know; there were rainbow tints with which he might paint perhaps a just picture of man's destiny. Thus, like Wordsworth, he thought Nature no ultimate fact, but a wonderfully complete symbol of spiritual being. Both men were poets, and Nature meant to them largely—Metaphor. It was a language by which they could express movingly what without it would remain either inarticulate or abstract. No word but poetic can be applied, for instance, to the kind of imagination which makes Thoreau say of the scarlet fungus, so brilliant and yet, because it faces downwards, so unobtrusive, "Its ear is turned down listening to the honest praises of the earth"; and it is the same quality which describes the raying snow-crystals, heaped in a pile, as "the wreck of chariot wheels after a battle in the skies." A better example still, because of the equal dignity of thought and image, is the following: "The aspect of the world varies from year to year, as the landscape is differently clothed, but I find that the truth is still true, and I never regret any emphasis it may have inspired. Ktaadn is there still, but much more surely my conviction is there, resting with more than mountain breadth and weight on the world, the source still of fertilizing streams, and affording glorious views from its summit if I can get up to it again."

Thus mutually dependent were his conceptions of natural beauty and human happiness. "All Nature would be affected," he says, "and the sun's brightness fade, and the winds would sigh humanely, and the clouds rain tears, and the woods shed their leaves, and put on mourning in mid-summer, if any man should ever for a just cause grieve." But his rugged paganism gave him intelligence chiefly with the perennial vigor and fresh-ness of the world, and he had little tolerance for the querulous ailments of the sentimentalist. "How shall I complain," he cries, "who have not ceased to wonder?" Therefore, while men's latent nobility is one of his most frequent themes, men's infidelity sick-ened him more than is ordinary, even for the noblest minds. He had such high hopes for them, their faithlessness grieved him cruelly. And so he grew towards a remote and solitary way of life; nursed his ideals apart; and placed his trust ever more and more in the privatest intimations and suggestions of his own spirit. No doubt morbid in some of its effects, his isolation had the merit of developing in him a firm loftiness of character, and a resolute faith in the most intangible of intuitions, opposing single-handed the combined array of human prejudices, modes, and conventions; a faith which perhaps embodies, on the whole, the highest kind of heroism that the spiritual drama is capable of evoking. Thoreau could sing truly,

> The life that I aspire to live
> No man proposeth me;
> Only the promise of my heart
> Wears its emblazonry.

In beauty and distinction of literary style Thoreau is scarcely less extraordinary (and hardly more appreciated) than he is in vigorous elevation of thought. There are two notes in his writing constantly recurrent; one, a marvellously subtle suggestion of re-

mote, mystical, supramundane things, hidden relationships, veiled
identities, lurking significance; the other, a dry, corrosive humor,
to be found in no other books. Neither of these qualities can be
shown satisfactorily by quotations, but both are constantly felt
in *Walden,* or the *Week,* or the *Familiar Letters.* The first, the
suggestive or connotative quality, is the result partly of remote-
ness of thought (the mind dwelling amongst things communicable
only indirectly) and partly of a rare felicity of language, a skill
in marshalling the elements and the large masses of speech so
justly as to attain simultaneously the most succinct definiteness
and the most haunting aroma of latent meaning. There is hardly
any writer who manifests more mastery of his material, or who
gains by the nice adjustment of medium to thought a fine lucidity
and elegance. Careless of superficial ornaments in style, he yet
spared no pains to secure that constructive beauty of line, that
formal balance, which is of far greater import than luxuriance of
phrase. By elimination of the unnecessary—stern rejection of all
that Pater might call surplusage, he imparted to his diction a lithe
vigor comparable to that of the well-trained athlete. Except for
some inexplicable lapses in syntax, his style, notably pure in
idiom, has that peculiar distinction which attends deep conformity
to the genius of the language. None knew better than he how to
make each word tell, or how to bring out the hidden eloquence
of a single word by sudden revelation of its primitive or etymological value. Such qualities, combined with the imaginative beauty
of his thought, give many passages of his best writing a charm
not to be found elsewhere—a charm, however, which eludes
analysis, and which, because of its more than partial derivation
from large relationships and interconnexions of structure, half
evaporates in quotation: "To the sailor's eyes, it [the scarlet oak
leaf] is a much-indented shore. Is it not, in fact, a shore to the
aerial ocean, on which the windy surf beats? At sight of this
leaf we are all mariners—if not vikings, buccaneers, and fili-
busters. Both our love of repose and our spirit of adventure are
addressed. In our most casual glance, perchance, we think that
if we succeed in doubling those sharp capes we shall find deep,

smooth, and secure havens in the ample bays. How different from the White Oak leaf, with its rounded headlands, on which no lighthouse need be placed! That is an England, with its long civil history, that may be read. This is some still unsettled New-found Island or Celebes. Shall we go and be rajahs there?"

The second of his salient qualities, his humor, is as different from ordinary humor as his eloquence is different from ordinary eloquence. It arises, not from elegant trifling, or animal spirits, or from moral irresponsibility—as much charming humor in English does—but from the same lightning-like perception of actuality, transpiercing keenly all shams and surfaces, that is at the root of his power in the other kind. His elevation of thought comes from devotion to the truth; and from the same trait comes his humor. Nothing can be more delicious than to hear him quietly undermine an affectation, and bring it rattling down about the ears of its proprietor. All cowardice and superstition in thought are essentially ridiculous, and Thoreau is able in one vivid tableau to expose their folly. Thus, mentioning the old ladies who deplored the distance of his Walden hut from the doctor's, he remarks; "The amount of it is, if a man is alive, there is always *danger* that he may die, though the danger must be allowed to be less in proportion as he is dead-and-alive to begin with." When he was asked, shortly before his death, about his belief in a future life, he replied, "One world at a time." After he was let out of jail, where he had passed a night for refusing to pay his tax to a State which countenanced slavery, he went huckleberrying "to one of our highest hills, two miles off"; "and then," he adds drily, "the State was nowhere to be seen." Humor of this sort consists of wisdom made caustic by concentration. The large element of truth in his "knock-down blows at current opinion," as Stevenson declares, was what enabled them to "leave the orthodox in a kind of speechless agony." He did no juggling; he merely cleared away the mask and let the fact strike for itself. Pretentious hypocrisy would not care for such humor, but to haters of the canting and the facile, Thoreau's tart, sententious utterances do not lose their charm.

Humor, nevertheless, sanative as it is, "takes a lower view than enthusiasm"; and it is after all and in the end the enthusiasm of Thoreau's belief in the highest and remotest things that explains his power and seems to promise him literary longevity. Of faith, hope, and charity, he was richest in the first; by his invincible courage, his unflagging buoyancy of temper, and his childlike trust in the beneficence of the universe, he attained a rare serenity of spirit. Drawing his health directly from the eternal reservoirs of wild Nature, he was able to avoid the hectic excitements and depressions of artificial life, with all its pestilential modes of thought and mental valetudinarianism, and to discern that praise is the only appropriate prayer, and happiness the only sane religion. He gives, in *Walden,* the reason and the justification for that self-trust which led him to place so much stress on "listening to the faintest but constant suggestions of one's genius": "If the day and the night are such that you greet them with joy, and life emits a fragrance like flowers and sweet-scented herbs, is more elastic, more starry, more immortal,—that is your success."

Thoreau fairly earned his happiness; it was the reward of his faith. He had trusted the intimations that came to him, and he "learned this, at least, by his experiment; that if one advances confidently in the direction of his dreams, and endeavors to live the life which he has imagined, he will meet with a success unexpected in common hours. He will put some things behind, will pass an invisible boundary; new, universal, and more liberal laws will begin to establish themselves around and within him; or the old laws will be expanded and interpreted in his favor in a more liberal sense, and he will live with the license of a higher order of beings." Never was there a prophet whose life matched better with the tenor of his doctrines. Thoreau lived truly with the license of a higher order of beings; he trusted much, and was rewarded for his venturesomeness by an ability to dispense with many things, not only with tea, coffee, and broadcloth, but with care, complaint, boredom, and fretfulness. He was as fresh and happy as the morning he walked through; as brave and gallant as the dawn-heralding chanticleer, whose song he celebrated; as free and as pagan as the rabbit and the squirrel. There was an auroral vigor in him. He was a citizen of the New World, a worthy avatar of the American genius. "The singer can easily move us to tears or laughter," he says, "but where is he who can excite in us a pure morning joy?" And elsewhere, "There is no law so strong which a little gladness may not transgress."

Accordingly, with perennial courage, Thoreau was healthy and happy. Far from insensible to the gloomy element in life, he yet practically lived up to his belief that melancholy was a form of slovenliness: "Nothing can rightly compel a simple and brave man to a vulgar sadness." Surely no man had ever greater hope or greater faith; and the beauty and the strength of his work, permeated and immortalized by his indomitable ideality, is the fulfilment of that promise which must often have been in his heart as he suffered the misunderstandings of his townsmen and the more harassing obscurations and bewilderments of his own mind: "If ye have faith as a grain of mustard seed, nothing shall be impossible unto you."

✪

Thoreau: Nature's Musician

Thoreau was a great musician, not because he played the flute but because he did not have to go to Boston to hear "the Symphony." The rhythm of his prose, were there nothing else, would determine his value as a composer. He was divinely conscious of the enthusiasm of Nature, the emotion of her rhythms and the harmony of her solitude. In this consciousness he sang of the submission to Nature, the religion of contemplation, and the freedom of simplicity—a philosophy distinguishing between the complexity of Nature which teaches freedom, and the complexity of materialism which teaches slavery. In music, in poetry, in all art, the truth as one sees it must be given in terms which bear some proportion to the inspiration. In their greatest moments the inspiration of both Beethoven and Thoreau express profound truths and deep sentiment, but the intimate passion of it, the storm and stress of it, affected Beethoven in such a way that he could not but be ever showing it and Thoreau that he could not easily expose it. They were equally imbued with it, but with different results. A difference in temperament had something to do with this, together with a difference in the quality of expression between the two arts. "Who that has heard a strain of music feared lest he would speak extravagantly forever," says Thoreau.

Reprinted from *Essays Before a Sonata* (New York: Knickerbocker Press, 1920), pp. 56–77.

Perhaps music is the art of speaking extravagantly. Herbert
Spencer says that some men, as for instance Mozart, are so peculiarly sensitive to emotion . . . that music is to them but a
continuation not only of the expression but of the actual emotion,
though the theory of some more modern thinkers in the philosophy of art doesn't always bear this out. However, there is no
doubt that in its nature music is predominantly subjective and
tends to subjective expression, and poetry more objective tending
to objective expression. Hence the poet when his muse calls for a
deeper feeling must invert this order, and he may be reluctant
to do so as these depths often call for an intimate expression
which the physical looks of the words may repel. They tend to
reveal the nakedness of his soul rather than its warmth. It is not
a matter of the relative value of the aspiration, or a difference between subconsciousness and consciousness but a difference in the
arts themselves; for example, a composer may not shrink from
having the public hear his "love letter in tones," while a poet
may feel sensitive about having everyone read his "letter in
words." When the object of the love is mankind the sensitiveness
is changed only in degree.

But the message of Thoreau, though his fervency may be incon-
stant and his human appeal not always direct, is, both in thought
and spirit, as universal as that of any man who ever wrote or sang
—as universal as it is nontemporaneous—as universal as it is
free from the measure of history, as "solitude is free from the
measure of the miles of space that intervene between man and
his fellows." In spite of the fact that Henry James (who knows
almost everything) says that "Thoreau is more than provincial—
that he is parochial," let us repeat that Henry Thoreau, in respect
to thought, sentiment, imagination, and soul, in respect to every
element except that of place of physical being—a thing that means
so much to some—is as universal as any personality in literature.
That he said upon being shown a specimen grass from Iceland
that the same species could be found in Concord is evidence of
his universality, not of his parochialism. He was so universal that
he did not need to travel around the world to *prove* it. "I have

more of God, they more of the road." "It is not worth while to go around the world to count the cats in Zanzibar." With Marcus Aurelius, if he had seen the present he had seen all, from eternity and all time forever.

Thoreau's susceptibility to natural sounds was probably greater than that of many practical musicians. True, this appeal is mainly through the sensational element which Herbert Spencer thinks the predominant beauty of music. Thoreau seems able to weave from this source some perfect transcendental symphonies. Strains from the Orient get the best of some of the modern French music but not of Thoreau. He seems more interested *in* than influenced *by* Oriental philosophy. He admires its ways of resignation and self-contemplation but he doesn't contemplate himself in the same way. He often quotes from the Eastern scriptures passages which were they his own he would probably omit, *i.e.,* the Vedas say "all intelligences awake with the morning." This seems unworthy of "accompanying the undulations of celestial music" found on this same page, in which an "ode to morning" is sung —"the awakening to newly acquired forces and aspirations from within to a higher life than we fell asleep from . . . for *all* memorable events transpire in the morning time and in the morning atmosphere." Thus it is not the whole tone scale of the Orient but the scale of a Walden morning—"music in single strains," as Emerson says, which inspired many of the polyphonies and harmonies that come to us through his poetry. Who can be forever melancholy "with Aeolian music like this"?

This is but one of many ways in which Thoreau looked to Nature for his greatest inspirations. In her he found an analogy to the Fundamental of Transcendentalism. The "innate goodness" of Nature is or can be a moral influence; Mother Nature, if man will but let her, will keep him straight—straight spiritually and so morally and even mentally. If he will take her as a companion, and teacher, and *not* as a duty or a creed, she will give him greater thrills and teach him greater truths than man can give or teach—she will reveal mysteries that mankind has long concealed. It was the soul of Nature not natural history that Thoreau was after. A naturalist's mind is one predominantly scientific, more interested in the relation of a flower to other flowers than its relation to any philosophy or anyone's philosophy. A transcendent love of Nature and writing "Rhus glabra" after sumach doesn't necessarily make a naturalist. It would seem that although thorough in observation (not very thorough according to Mr. Burroughs) and with a keen perception of the specific, a naturalist—inherently—was exactly what Thoreau was *not*. He seems rather to let Nature put him under her microscope than to hold her under his. He was too fond of Nature to practice vivisection upon her. He would have found that painful, "for was he not a part with her?" But he had this trait of a naturalist, which is usually foreign to poets, even great ones; he observed acutely even things that did not particularly interest him—a useful natural gift rather than a virtue.

The study of Nature may tend to make one dogmatic, but the love of Nature surely does not. Thoreau no more than Emerson could be said to have compounded doctrines. His thinking was too broad for that. If Thoreau's was a religion of Nature, as some say—and by that they mean that through Nature's influence man is brought to a deeper contemplation, to a more spiritual self-scrutiny, and thus closer to God—it had apparently no definite doctrines. Some of his theories regarding natural and social phenomena and his experiments in the art of living are certainly not doctrinal in form, and if they are in substance it didn't disturb Thoreau and it needn't us. . . . "In proportion as he simplifies his life the laws of the universe will appear less complex and solitude will not be solitude, nor poverty poverty, nor weakness weakness. If you have built castles in the air your work need not be lost; that is where they should be, now put the foundations under them." . . . "Then we will love with the license of a higher order of beings." Is that a doctrine? Perhaps. At any rate, between the lines of some such passage as this lie some of the fountain heads that water the spiritual fields of his philosophy and the seeds from which they are sown (if indeed his whole philosophy is but one spiritual garden). His experiments, social and economic, are a part of its cultivation and for the harvest—and its transmutation, he trusts to moments of inspiration—"only what is thought, said, and done at a certain rare coincidence is good."

Thoreau's experiment at Walden was, broadly speaking, one of these moments. It stands out in the casual and popular opinion as a kind of adventure—harmless and amusing to some, significant and important to others; but its significance lies in the fact that in trying to practice an ideal he prepared his mind so that it could better bring others "into the Walden-state-of-mind." He did not ask for a literal approval, or in fact for any approval. "I would not stand between any man and his genius." He would have no one adopt his manner of life, unless in doing so he adopts his own—besides, by that time "I may have found a better one." But if he preached hard he practiced harder what he preached—harder than most men. Throughout *Walden* a text that he is always pounding out is "Time." Time for inside work out-of-doors; preferably out-of-doors, "though you perhaps may have some pleasant, thrilling, glorious hours, even in a poor house." Wherever the place—time there must be. Time to show the unnecessariness of necessities which clog up time. Time to contemplate the value of man to the universe, of the universe to man, man's excuse for being. Time *from* the demands of social conventions. Time *from* too much labor for some, which means too much to eat, too much to wear, too much material, too much materialism for others. Time *from* the "hurry and waste of life." Time *from* the "St. Vitus Dance." *But,* on the other side of the ledger, time *for* learning that "there is no safety in stupidity alone." Time *for* introspection. Time *for* reality. Time *for* expansion. Time *for* practicing the art, of living the art of living. Thoreau has been criticized for practicing his policy of expansion by living in a vacuum—but he peopled that vacuum with a race of beings and established a social order there, surpassing any of the precepts in social or political history. ". . . for he put some things behind and passed an invisible boundary; new, universal, and more liberal laws were around and within him, the old laws were expanded and interpreted in a more liberal sense and he lived with the license of a higher order"—a community in which "God was the only President" and "Thoreau not Webster was His Orator." It is hard to believe that Thoreau really refused to believe that there was any other life but his own, though he probably did think that there was not any other life besides his own. Living for society may not always be best accomplished by living *with* society. "Is there any virtue in a man's skin that you must touch it?" and the "rubbing of elbows may not bring men's minds closer together"; or if he were talking through a "worst seller" (magazine) that "had to put it over" he might say, "forty thousand souls at a ball game does not, necessarily, make baseball the highest expression of spiritual emotion." Thoreau, however, is no cynic, either in character or thought, though in a side glance at himself, he may have held out to be one; a "cynic in independence," possibly because of his rule laid down that "self-culture admits of no compromise."

It is conceivable that though some of his philosophy and a good deal of his personality, in some of its manifestations, have outward colors that do not seem to harmonize, the true and intimate relations they bear each other are not affected. This peculiarity, frequently seen in his attitude towards social-economic problems, is perhaps more emphasized in some of his personal outbursts. "I love my friends very much, but I find that it is of no use to go to see them. I hate them commonly when I am near." It is easier to see what he means than it is to forgive him for saying it. The cause of this apparent lack of harmony between philosophy and personality, as far as they can be separated, may have been due to his refusal "to keep the very delicate balance" which Mr. Van Doren in his *Critical Study of Thoreau* says "it is necessary for a great and good man to keep between his public and private lives, between his own personality and the whole outside universe of personalities." Somehow one feels that if he had kept this balance he would have lost "hitting power." Again, it seems that something of the above depends upon the degree of greatness or goodness. A very great and especially a very good man has no separate private and public life. His own personality though not identical with outside personalities is so clear or can be so clear to them that it appears identical, and as the world progresses towards its inevitable perfection this appearance becomes more and more a reality. For the same reason that all great men now agree, in principle but not in detail, in so far as words are able to communicate agreement, on the great fundamental truths. Someone says: "Be specific—what great fundamentals?" Freedom over slavery; the natural over the artificial; beauty over ugliness; the spiritual over the material; the goodness of man; the Godness of man; God; with all other kindred truths that have been growing in expression through the ages, eras, and civilizations, innate things which once seemed foreign to the soul of humankind. All great men—there are millions of them now— agree on these. Around the relative and the absolute value of an attribute, or quality, or whatever it may be called, is where the fight is. The relative not *from* the absolute—but *of* it, always *of* it. Geniuses—and there are millions of them—differ as to *what* is beautiful and *what* is ugly, as to *what* is right and *what* is wrong —there are many interpretations of God—but they all agree that beauty is better than ugliness and right is better than wrong, and that there is a God—all are one when they reach the essence. Every analysis of a criticism or quality of Thoreau invariably leads back and stands us against the great problems of life and eternity. It is a fair indication of the greatness of his problems and ideals.

The unsympathetic treatment accorded Thoreau on account of the false colors that his personality apparently gave to some of his important ideas and virtues, might be lessened if it were more constantly remembered that a command of his to-day is but a mood of yesterday and a contradiction to-morrow. He is too volatile to paint, much less to catalogue. If Thoreau did not oversay he said nothing. He says so himself. "I desire to speak somewhere without bounds like a man in a waking moment to men in their waking moments . . . for I am convinced that I cannot exaggerate enough even to lay a foundation for a true expression."

For all that, it is not safe to think that he should *never* be taken
literally, as for instance in the sentence above. His extravagance
at times involves him but Thoreau never rejoices in it as Meredith
seems to. He struggles against it and seems as much ashamed of
being involved as the latter seems of not being. He seldom gets
into the situation of Meredith—timidly wandering around with
no clothes after stepping out of one of his involvedensities. This
habit may be a part of the novelists' license, for perhaps their
inspiration is less original and less natural than that of the poets,
as traits of human weakness are unnatural to or "not an innate
part with human nature." Perhaps if they (novelists) had broader
sources for their inspiration they would hardly need licenses and
perhaps they would hardly become novelists. For the same reason
that Shakespeare might have been greater if he hadn't written
plays. Some say that a true composer will never write an opera
because a truly brave man will not take a drink to keep up his
courage; which is not the same thing as saying that Shakespeare
is not the greatest figure in all literature; in fact, it is an attempt
to say that many novels, most operas, all Shakespeares, and all
brave men and women (rum or no rum) are among the noblest
blessings with which God has endowed mankind—because, not
being perfect, they are perfect examples pointing to that perfection which nothing yet has attained.

Thoreau's mysticism at times throws him into elusive moods—
but an elusiveness held by a thread to something concrete and
specific, for he had too much integrity of mind for any other
kind. In these moments it is easier to follow his thought than to
follow him. Indeed, if he were always easy to follow, after one
had caught up with him, one might find that it was not Thoreau.

It is, however, with no mystic rod that he strikes at institutional
life. Here again is felt the influence of the great transcendental
doctrine of "innate goodness" in human nature—a reflection of
the like in nature; a philosophic part which, by the way, was a
more direct inheritance in Thoreau than in his brother transcendentalists. For besides what he received from a native Unitarianism
a good part must have descended to him through his Huguenot

blood from the "eighteenth-century French philosophy." We trace a reason here for his lack of interest in "the church." For if revealed religion is the path between God and man's spiritual part—a kind of formal causeway—Thoreau's highly developed spiritual life felt, apparently unconsciously, less need of it than most men. But he might have been more charitable towards those who do need it (and most of us do) if he had been more conscious of his freedom. Those who look to-day for the cause of a seeming deterioration in the influence of the church may find it in a wider development of this feeling of Thoreau's; that the need is less because there is more of the spirit of Christianity in the world to-day. Another cause for his attitude towards the church as an institution is one always too common among "the narrow minds" to have influenced Thoreau. He could have been more generous. He took the arc for the circle, the exception for the rule, the solitary bad example for the many good ones. His persistent emphasis on the value of "example" may excuse this lower viewpoint. "The silent influence of the example of one sincere life . . . has benefited society more than all the projects devised for its salvation." He has little patience for the unpracticing preacher. "In some countries a hunting parson is no uncommon sight. Such a one might make a good shepherd dog but is far from being a good shepherd." It would have been interesting to have seen him handle the speculating parson, who takes a good salary—more per annum than all the disciples had to sustain their bodies during their whole lives—from a metropolitan religious corporation for "speculating" on Sunday about the beauty of poverty, who preaches: "Take no thought (for your life) what ye shall eat or what ye shall drink nor yet what ye shall put on . . . lay not up for yourself treasure upon earth . . . take up thy cross and follow me"; who on Monday becomes a "speculating" disciple of another god, and by questionable investments, successful enough to get into the "press," seeks to lay up a treasure of a million dollars for his old age, as if a million dollars could keep such a man out of the poor-house. Thoreau might observe that this one good example of Christian degeneracy undoes all the acts of regeneracy of a thousand humble five-hundred-dollar country parsons; that it out-influences the "unconscious influence" of a dozen Dr. Bushnells if there be that many; that the repentance of this man who did not "fall from grace" because he never fell into it—that this unnecessary repentance might save this man's own soul but not necessarily the souls of the million headline readers; that repentance would put this preacher right with the powers that be in this world—and the next. Thoreau might pass a remark upon this man's intimacy with God "as if he had a monopoly of the subject"—an intimacy that perhaps kept him from asking God exactly what his Son meant by the "camel," the "needle"—to say nothing of the "rich man." Thoreau might have wondered how this man *nailed down* the last plank in *his* bridge to salvation, by rising to sublime heights of patriotism, in *his* war against materialism; but would even Thoreau be so unfeeling as to suggest to this exhorter that *his* salvation might be clinched "if he would sacrifice his income" (not himself) and come-in to a real Salvation Army, or that the final triumph, the supreme happiness in casting aside this mere $10,000 or $20,000 every year must be denied him—for was he not captain of the ship—must he not stick to his passengers (in the first cabin—the very first cabin)—not that the *ship* was sinking but that *he* was . . . we will go no further. Even Thoreau would not demand sacrifice for sacrifice sake—no, not even from Nature.

Property from the standpoint of its influence in checking natural self-expansion and from the standpoint of personal and inherent right is another institution that comes in for straight and cross-arm jabs, now to the stomach, now to the head, but seldom sparring for breath. For does he not say that "wherever a man goes, men will pursue him with their dirty institutions"? The influence of property, as he saw it, on morality or immorality and how through this it may or should influence "government" is seen by the following: "I am convinced that if all men were to live as simply as I did, then thieving and robbery would be unknown. These take place only in communities where some have got more than is sufficient while others have not enough—

Nec bella fuerunt,
Fagimus astabat dum
Scyphus ante dapes—

You who govern public affairs, what need have you to employ punishments? Have virtue and the people will be virtuous." If Thoreau had made the first sentence read: "If all men were *like* me and were to live as simply," etc., everyone would agree with him. We may wonder here how he would account for some of the degenerate types we are told about in some of our backwoods and mountain regions. Possibly by assuming that they are an instance of perversion of the species. That the little civilizing their forbears experienced rendered these people more susceptible to the physical than to the spiritual influence of nature; in other words if they had been purer naturists, as the Aztecs for example, they would have been purer men. Instead of turning to any theory of ours or of Thoreau for the true explanation of this condition— which is a kind of pseudo-naturalism—for its true diagnosis and permanent cure, are we not far more certain to find it in the radiant look of humility, love, and hope in the strong faces of those inspired souls who are devoting their lives with no little sacrifice to these outcasts of civilization and nature. In truth, may not mankind find the solution of its eternal problem—find it after and beyond the last, most perfect system of wealth distribution which science can ever devise—after and beyond the last sublime echo of the greatest socialistic symphonies—after and beyond every transcendent thought and expression in the simple example of these Christ-inspired souls—be they Pagan, Gentile, Jew, or angel.

However, underlying the practical or impractical suggestions implied in the quotation above, which is from the last paragraph of Thoreau's *Village*, is the same transcendental theme of "innate goodness." For this reason there must be no limitation except that which will free mankind from limitation, and from a perversion of this "innate" possession. And "property" may be one of the causes of this perversion—property in the two relations cited above. It is conceivable that Thoreau, to the consternation of

the richest members of the Bolsheviki and Bourgeois, would propose a policy of liberation, a policy of a limited personal property
right, on the ground that congestion of personal property tends
to limit the progress of the soul (as well as the progress of the
stomach)—letting the economic noise thereupon take care of itself—for dissonances are becoming beautiful—and do not the
same waters that roar in a storm take care of the eventual calm?
That this limit of property be determined not by the *voice* of the
majority but by the *brain* of the majority under a government
limited to no national boundaries. "The government of the world
I live in is not framed in after-dinner conversation"—around a
table in a capital city, for there is no capital—a government of
principles not parties; of a few fundamental truths and not of
many political expediencies. A government conducted by virtuous
leaders, for it will be led by all, for all are virtuous, as then their
"innate virtue" will no more be perverted by unnatural institutions. This will not be a millennium but a practical and possible
application of uncommon common sense. For is it not sense,
common or otherwise, for Nature to want to hand back the earth
to those to whom it belongs—that is, to those who have to live on
it? Is it not sense, that the average brains like the average
stomachs will act rightly if they have an equal amount of the
right kind of food to act upon and universal education is on the
way with the right kind of food? Is it not sense then that all
grown men and women (for *all* are necessary to work out the
divine "law of averages") shall have a *direct* not an *indirect* say
about the things that go on in this world?

Some of these attitudes, ungenerous or radical, generous or conservative (as you will), towards institutions dear to many, have
no doubt given impressions unfavorable to Thoreau's thought and
personality. One hears him called, by some who ought to know
what they say and some who ought not, a crabbed, cold-hearted,
sour-faced Yankee—a kind of a visionary sore-head—a cross-
grained, egotistic recluse—even non-hearted. But it is easier to
make a statement than prove a reputation. Thoreau may be some
of these things to those who make no distinction between these

qualities and the manner which often comes as a kind of by-product of an intense devotion to a principle or ideal. He was rude and unfriendly at times but shyness probably had something to do with that. In spite of a certain self-possession he was diffident in most company, but, though he may have been subject to those spells when words do not rise and the mind seems wrapped in a kind of dull cloth which everyone dumbly stares at, instead of looking through—he would easily get off a rejoinder upon occasion. When a party of visitors came to Walden and some one asked Thoreau if he found it lonely there, he replied: "Only by your help." A remark characteristic, true, rude, if not witty. The writer remembers hearing a school-teacher in English literature dismiss Thoreau (and a half hour lesson, in which time all of *Walden*—its surface—was sailed over) by saying that this author (he called everyone "author" from Solomon down to Dr. Parkhurst) "was a kind of a crank who styled himself a hermit-naturalist and who idled about the woods because he didn't want to work." Some such stuff is a common conception, though not as common as it used to be. If this teacher had had more brains, it would have been a lie. The word *idled* is the hopeless part of this criticism, or rather of this uncritical remark. To ask this kind of a man, who plays all the "choice gems from celebrated composers" literally, always literally, and always with the loud pedal, who plays all hymns, wrong notes, right notes, games, people, and jokes literally, and with the loud pedal, who will die literally and with the loud pedal—to ask this man to smile even faintly at Thoreau's humor is like casting a pearl before a coal baron. Emerson implies that there is one thing a genius must have to be a *genius* and that is "mother wit." . . . "Doctor Johnson, Milton, Chaucer, and Burns had it. Aunt Mary Moody Emerson has it and can write scrap letters. Who has it need never write anything but scraps. Henry Thoreau has it." His humor though a part of this wit is not always as spontaneous, for it is sometimes pun shape (so is Charles Lamb's)—but it is nevertheless a kind that can serenely transport us and which we can enjoy without disturbing our neighbors. If there are those who think him cold-

hearted and with but little human sympathy, let them read his
letters to Emerson's little daughter, or hear Dr. Emerson tell
about the Thoreau home life and the stories of his boyhood—the
ministrations to a runaway slave; or let them ask old Sam Staples,
the Concord sheriff about him. That he "was fond of a few intimate friends, but cared not one fig for people in the mass," is a
statement made in a school history and which is superficially
true. He cared too much for the masses—too much to let his
personality be "massed"; too much to be unable to realize the
futility of wearing his heart on his sleeve but not of wearing his
path to the shore of "Walden" for future masses to walk over and
perchance find the way to themselves. Some near-satirists are fond
of telling us that Thoreau came so close to Nature that she killed
him before he had discovered her whole secret. They remind us
that he died with consumption but forget that he lived with consumption. And without using much charity, this can be made to
excuse many of his irascible and uncongenial moods. You to
whom that gaunt face seems forbidding—look into the eyes! If
he seems "dry and priggish" to you, Mr. Stevenson, "with little
of that large unconscious geniality of the world's heroes," follow
him some spring morning to Baker Farm, as he "rambles through
pine groves . . . like temples, or like fleets at sea, full-rigged,
with wavy boughs and rippling with light so soft and green and
shady that the Druids would have forsaken their oaks to worship
in them." Follow him to "the cedar wood beyond Flint's Pond,
where the trees covered with hoary blue berries, spiring higher
and higher, are fit to stand before Valhalla." Follow him, but not
too closely, for you may see little, if you do—"as he walks in so
pure and bright a light gilding its withered grass and leaves so
softly and serenely bright that he thinks he has never bathed in
such a golden flood." Follow him as "he saunters towards the
holy land till one day the sun shall shine more brightly than ever
it has done, perchance shine into your minds and hearts and light
up your whole lives with a great awakening, light as warm and
serene and golden as on a bankside in autumn." Follow him
through the golden flood to the shore of that "holy land," where

he lies dying as men say—dying as bravely as he lived. You may be near when his stern old aunt in the duty of her Puritan conscience asks him: "Have you made your peace with God?" and you may see his kindly smile as he replies, "I did not know that we had ever quarreled." Moments like these reflect more nobility and equanimity perhaps than geniality—qualities, however, more serviceable to world's heroes.

The personal trait that one who has affection for Thoreau may find worst is a combative streak, in which he too often takes refuge. "An obstinate elusiveness," almost a "contrary cussedness," as if he would say, which he didn't: "If a truth about something is not as I think it ought to be, I'll make it what I think, and it *will* be the truth—but if you agree with me, then I begin to think it may not be the truth." The causes of these unpleasant colors (rather than characteristics) are too easily attributed to a lack of human sympathy or to the assumption that they are at least symbols of that lack instead of to a supersensitiveness, magnified at times by ill health and at times by a subconsciousness of the futility of actually living out his ideals in this life. It has been said that his brave hopes were unrealized anywhere in his career —but it is certain that they started to be realized on or about May 6, 1862, and we doubt if 1920 will end their fulfillment or his career. But there were many in Concord who knew that within their village there was a tree of wondrous growth, the shadow of which—alas, too frequently—was the only part they were allowed to touch. Emerson was one of these. He was not only deeply conscious of Thoreau's rare gifts but in the *Woodland Notes* pays a tribute to a side of his friend that many others missed. Emerson knew that Thoreau's sensibilities too often veiled his nobilities, that a self-cultivated stoicism ever fortified with sarcasm, none the less securely because it seemed voluntary, covered a warmth of feeling. "His great heart, him a hermit made." A breadth of heart not easily measured, found only in the highest type of sentimentalists, the type which does not perpetually discriminate in favor of mankind. Emerson has much of this sentiment and touches it when he sings of Nature as "the incarnation of a thought," when he generously visualizes Thoreau, "standing at the Walden shore invoking the vision of a thought as it drifts heavenward into an incarnation of Nature." There is a Godlike patience in Nature—in her mists, her trees, her mountains—as if she had a more abiding faith and a clearer vision than man of the resurrection and immortality!

There comes to memory an old yellow-papered composition of school-boy days whose peroration closed with "Poor Thoreau; he communed with nature for forty odd years, and then died." "The forty odd years"—we'll still grant that part, but he is over a hundred now, and maybe, Mr. Lowell, he is more lovable, kindlier, and more radiant with human sympathy to-day, than, perchance, you were fifty years ago. It may be that he is a far stronger, a far greater, an incalculably greater force in the moral and spiritual fibre of his fellow-countrymen throughout the world to-day than you dreamed of fifty years ago. You, James Russell Lowells! You, Robert Louis Stevensons! You, Mark Van Dorens! with your literary perception, your power of illumination, your brilliancy of expression, yea, and with your love of sincerity, you know your Thoreau, but not my Thoreau—that reassuring and true friend, who stood by me one "low" day, when the sun had gone down, long, long before sunset. You may know something of the affection that heart yearned for but knew it a duty not to grasp; you may know something of the great human passions which stirred that soul—too deep for animate expression—you may know all of this, all there is to know about Thoreau, but you know him not, unless you love him! . . .

LEO STOLLER

✪

The Union of Principle and Expediency

I

Thoreau's early approach to nature . . . had contained two antagonistic elements. The first, its limit mysticism, was associated with the utopian phase of his opposition to the economic order. The second, its limit pure science, expressed that aspect of his personality which spontaneously accepted this order. During the years at Walden, when this polarity first became undeniably evident, the second element was carried in Thoreau's investigations of the pond, and these studies he continued and extended in his remaining years.[1] But as the vehicle for his general intellectual development they were succeeded by his research in forestry.

Thoreau's investigation of forest trees began, as did his scientific botany in general, about 1850 (XV, 157),* during the period when his approach to nature was still dominated by the

1. For an account of Thoreau's study of limnology, see Edward S. Deevey, Jr., "A Re-examination of Thoreau's *Walden,*" *Quarterly Journal of Biology,* XVII (March 1942), 1–11.
* Parenthetical page references are to the 1906 Walden Edition of Thoreau's writings [ed.].

Reprinted from *After Walden: Thoreau's Changing Views On Economic Man,* pp. 72–94, 104–107, by Leo Stoller, with the permission of the publishers, Stanford University Press. © 1957 by the Board of Trustees of the Leland Stanford Junior University.

search for an extra-societal ideal. It is not surprising, therefore, that he can be observed projecting into trees the characteristics of the utopian order and of the heroic aspirant man about whom it was to have centered. Idealization of the tree at the expense of man, combined with regret for a lost youth and with yearning for a society not to be found in industrializing America, is threaded all through the *Journals* of the eighteen-fifties.

At the end of 1851, for example, Thoreau watched from a hillside while two men cut down a pine below. The tree "towered up a hundred feet . . . one of the tallest probably in the town-ship and straight as an arrow," aspiring to perfection as should each man, and it fell "as softly as a feather, folding its green mantle about it like a warrior, as if, tired of standing, it embraced the earth with silent joy, returning its elements to the dust again." Those who had felled it were "diminutive manikins," gnawing through its bole "like beavers or insects" (IX, 162f.). The pine, wrote Thoreau a few months later, "seems the emblem of my life; it stands for the west, the wild" (IX, 452).

The best example of this projection, witnessing the persistence of the unrewarded seeker, occurs in the first days of 1856, when there was cut down on the Boston Road in Concord a venerable elm whose rings showed it to have sprung up some one hundred and thirty years earlier, a half-century before the township fired its rifles against the British. Thoreau had first measured this tree —the Davis Elm—in 1852 (X, 90). When it began to creak in the winter storms three years later and Mrs. Davis feared for her roof, he visited daily to watch the preparations for the felling. He looked into his histories and botanies for descriptions of other giants of the species and compared this tree in his *Journal* with the surviving notable elms of Concord. To a Thoreau increasingly aware of his own aging and changing, the great elm represented the lost preindustrial township whose idealization had been an element in his lost youth. "Another link that bound us to the past is broken," he exclaimed. "It has passed away together with the clergy of the old school and the stage-coach which used to

rattle beneath it. . . . How much of old Concord falls with it!"
(XIV, 131)

In the elms he recovered symbolically the human heroes who
had long been absent from his native town: not the hacks of
political parties, but the nonjoining men of principle whom he
once thought to have glimpsed in Nathaniel Peabody Rogers.
"They attend no caucus," he wrote shortly after the felling of
the Davis Elm, "they make no compromise, they use no policy.
Their one principle is growth. They combine a true radicalism
with a true conservatism. Their radicalism is not cutting away of
roots, but an infinite multiplication and extension of them under
all surrounding institutions. They take a firmer hold on the earth
that they may rise higher into the heavens. . . . Their conservatism is a dead but solid heartwood, which is the pivot and
firm column of support to all this growth, appropriating nothing
to itself, but forever by its support assisting to extend the area
of their radicalism. Half a century after they are dead at the core,
they are preserved by radical reforms" (XIV, 140f.).

Standing within the Thoreau who composed these sentimental
epitaphs on an idealism beyond his practice was the man who
surveyed wood lots for auction to lumber dealers and calculated
their yield in salable cords. After the woodcutters had felled the
pine, Thoreau went down into the valley and estimated it: "It
was about four feet in diameter where it was sawed, about one
hundred feet long" (IX, 163). The venerable elm too he looked
at with his other, his commercial eye: "Supposing the first fifteen
feet to average six feet in diameter, they would contain more than
three cords and a foot of wood, but probably not more than three
cords" (XIV, 132).

Thoreau thus witnessed the accelerating destruction of New
England's forests from contradictory aspects. The indispensability
of nature to a just man striving for self-culture rather than profit
he had long accepted as an absolute principle. But to begin with,
he had so far yielded to expediency as to become an important
instrument in the very destruction which he necessarily regretted.

The first survey recorded in his "Field Notes" was the division of
Isaac Watts's woodland,[2] where twenty-five years earlier, as a
child unconsciously absorbing the influences of nature, he had
"played horse in the paths of a thick wood and roasted apples
and potatoes in an old pigeon-place and gathered fruit at the
pie-apple tree" (VIII, 88). Shortly after he laid them out the
lots were auctioned, and then the trees were cut down. And one
after another in the early fifties, alternating with house lots and
farms and an occasional road and once even a design for a machine, the surveys of woodland appear in his record: Ralph
Waldo Emerson's lot in March of 1850, Cyrus Stow's the same
month, a second of Emerson's in October, three for Nathan
Brooks, Cyrus Stow again, and James B. Wood in November; in
1851 two more for Cyrus Stow and single lots for John Hosmer,
Reuben Brown, and Samuel Barrett—a new element making itself felt in his relation to the forest.[3] "To-day," he writes in 1850
of a field where he had once been blackberrying, "I was aware
that I walked in a pitch pine wood, which ere long, perchance, I
may survey and lot off for a wood auction" (VIII, 89).

Nor did Thoreau view his role as a destructive agent wholly
with aversion. He protested vigorously against the deforestation
of his native Middlesex County, exclaiming in one place, "The
very willow-rows lopped every three years for fuel or powder,
and every sizable pine and oak, or other forest tree, cut down
within the memory of man! As if individual speculators were to
be allowed to export the clouds out of the sky, or the stars out
of the firmament, one by one." [4] What is perhaps more significant,

2. "Field Notes of Surveys," p. 1.
3. The rest of the record may be found in the "Field Notes of Surveys,"
where all the surveys mentioned here are listed. Thoreau completed a plan
of a "lead-pipe machine" for George Loring on September 15, 1852, charg-
ing him twelve dollars and apparently receiving only five ("Field Notes,"
pp. 87, 149). What appears to be a sketch of this machine is now in the
Concord Free Public Library on a sheet later used in the January 1853
survey of the land of John Le Grosse.
4. This passage is from "Chesuncook" (III, 170) and was thus not published until 1858, but I have assumed that it represents a sentiment of 1853,
the year of the trip to Maine described in that essay. The "powder" is a

he pondered the evil effects of this deforestation on his own life
and by implication on the lives of others. Once in 1850 he con-
siders this problem symbolically, writing of "simple brooks"
which were dammed up and thus "taught to use their influence
to destroy the primitive forests on their borders" and which now
"for penalty . . . flow in shrunken channels" (VIII, 82). Two
years later he is more explicitly personal. "The woods I walked
in in my youth are cut off," he writes. "Is it not time that I ceased
to sing?" (IX, 345f.)

But this same year brings a question of an opposite order:
"These woods! Why do I not feel their being cut more sorely?
Does it not affect me nearly?" (IX, 224) And although he goes
on to say, "I shall go to Walden less frequently," he is unable
to hold to his resolution. Not a week later he walks to the pond
again, seeking a compensation for the lost woodland. Earlier he
had visited the hill on which Watts's trees had once stood and
found it "a pleasant surprise . . . to see, instead of dense ranks
of trees almost impermeable to light, distant well-known blue
mountains in the horizon and a . . . white village over an expanded open country" (VIII, 88). So now he finds that though
the Walden woods are being cut off, it is "not all loss," for it
makes "some new and unexpected prospects" (IX, 253).

Among these prospects was the sight of the woodcutters: "the
logger's team, his oxen on the ice chewing the cud, the long pine
tree, stripped of its branches, chained upon his sled, resting on
a stout cross-bar or log and trailing behind, the smoke of his
fire curling up blue amid the trees, the sound of the axe and of
the teamsters' voices" (IX, 253). Despite his love of the forest
and his desire to see it preserved, Thoreau was drawn extraordi-
narily to the woodcutter and the lumberer. It was an old attraction going back at least as far as the Walden years, when he was
celebrating that "true Homeric" man the wood-chopper Therien
(II, 159), an element of the general tug of the primitive which
the younger Thoreau had felt so intensely and which the older

reference to the use of willows at the Acton powder mill, for a record of
which see VIII, 410.

man never entirely lost. What especially satisfied him as he observed the felling of the Walden woods was that it brought to Concord—barely over the horizon from metropolitan Boston—the wild flavor of Maine and New Hampshire (IX, 253).

When Thoreau in 1853 voyaged to Maine for the second time, he fell in with men whose job was to find cuttable timber, and in "Chesuncook" he described their "solitary and adventurous life" with relish: "They search for timber over a given section, climbing hills and often high trees to look off; explore the streams by which it is to be driven, and the like; spend five or six weeks in the woods, they two alone, a hundred miles or more from any town, roaming about, and sleeping on the ground where night overtakes them, depending chiefly on the provisions they carry with them, though they do not decline what game they come across. . . . They work ever with a gun as well as an axe, let their beards grow, and live without neighbors . . . far within a wilderness."

The life he was thus drawn to was that of men who participated in the ravaging of the forests, and Thoreau tried to confront its evil consequences by ending his essay with a plea for conservation. But there remained the echo of the counterpoint: "I have often wished since that I was with them" (III, 112).

The significance of Thoreau's silvical investigations is that they led to a reconciliation of these contradictory strains in his attitude to the forest. His discovery of the mechanism of succession pointed to a system of forest management which would yield lumber and profit to satisfy man's grosser instincts and at the same time preserve nature for the disciplining of his spirit.

II

The succession of forest trees had been observed by New Englanders for many years before Henry Thoreau became a botanist. As far back as 1796 the Rev. Timothy Dwight (later to become president of Yale University) traversed in one of his many journeys a plain of yellow pines over part of which these trees had been cut down and succeeded by oaks. "Such a change in forest vegetation is not uncommon," he noted, "and will hereafter be made a subject of inquiry" [5]—and so in time it was.

Dwight himself knew that the spontaneous succession which he had observed could be the means for making the New England forests, as he expressed it, "in a sense ever-living." [6] For he had noticed, or perhaps read somewhere, that the forest floor itself provided optimum conditions for the germination and growth of the seeds of forest trees. These seeds would not do well on a sunlit field or if planted in earth. Covered by the fallen leaves, however, they were not only sheltered from hungry rodents but were allowed to rest on the surface of a loose, light, waterholding soil and to spring up under the protecting shade of the woodland. "In this manner, and by a process totally superior to any contrived by the human mind," concluded the pious Dwight, "forests are furnished by the Author of nature with the means of perpetual self-restoration." [7]

The conditions which would encourage research in natural succession were not present, however, in Dwight's America. In 1795 the Society of Arts and Manufactures in the State of New York did indeed publish a report on the "best mode of preserving and increasing the growth of timber." [8] But more typical was the discussion of forest lands in Tench Coxe's *A View of the United States of America,* issued a year earlier.[9] Although Coxe was sufficiently foresighted to warn that it would be unwise for Americans to "neglect the due preservation of their timber," [10] his chief concern was to show how their vast forests might be used to supply exports to Europe and thus earn money for investment in industry while at the same time freeing more earth for farm-

5. *Travels in New-England and New-York,* 4 vols. (London, 1823), I, 270.

6. *Ibid.,* I, 81.

7. *Ibid.,* I, 80.

8. Quoted in Bernhard E. Fernow, *A Brief History of Forestry in Europe, the United States and Other Countries* (Toronto, 1907), p. 402.

9. (Philadelphia, 1794), pp. 450–457.

10. *Ibid.,* p. 457.

ing. Instead of rules for conservation, he therefore provided his readers with instructions on how to clear forest lands and with lists of the manufactures employing wood.

Even as late as 1851, a writer in a government report on agriculture apologized for discussing French attempts to use fertilizers in forests with the remark that this question had an interest in France which could "hardly be understood in America," where the difficulty was "rather to clear the ground of its woody growth than to stimulate it to greater fruitfulness." [11]

The successive availability of great wooded regions in the West, combined with the development of railroads to transport lumber from forest and mill, kept silviculture from being a national concern in our country until near the end of the nineteenth century.[12]

That Henry Thoreau (among others) thus anticipated national developments by several decades was due first of all to his being so much a New Englander. The deforestation whose economic effect is the parent of silviculture was in the normal course of events felt first in the region where towns and industries had existed longest. Thoreau's surveying gave him a vantage point from which he could hardly fail to notice it, and his belief in man's need for nature, combined with a commercial instinct educated in the wood-using pencil manufacture, heightened the sensitivity of his observation. It was this foundation, involving both his livelihood and philosophy, that made it possible for him to use his knowledge of biology in order to arrive at an understanding of the mechanism of succession.

Like other biologists of his day, Thoreau was interested in the significance of the distribution of plants and animals and in the relevant subject of the dispersion of seeds. As early as the summer of 1850, when his disciplined study of botany was just beginning (XV, 157), he remarked on a little pitch pine which

11. "Cultivating Forests," in *Report of the Commissioner of Patents for the Year 1851, Part II: Agriculture* (Washington, D.C., 1852), p. 53.

12. Fernow, *Brief History of Forestry,* p. 403. Herbert A. Smith, "The Early Forestry Movement in the United States," *Agricultural History,* XII (October 1938), 326.

grew in his yard although he did not know of another such tree "within half a mile" (VIII, 41). The following year he began to pay careful attention to the methods by which the seed of such a tree might have been planted.

In May he was reading about Jimson weed in a materia medica but, instead of noting down its medicinal properties, copied into his journal the quotation that it "emigrates with great facility, and often springs up in the ballast of ships, and in earth carried from one country to another" (VIII, 219). Two months later, finding the plant on the Massachusetts seacoast, he felt as if he was "on the highway of the world, at sight of this cosmopolite and veteran traveller" (VIII, 343). Back in Concord in the fall he noticed "the downy seeds of the groundsel . . . taking their flight" (VIII, 490), picked the barbed beggar-ticks from his clothing (IX, 65), and freed the dense-packed milkweed seeds to watch their graceful voyaging (IX, 17–23). "By all methods," he wrote, nature distributes plants, "whether by the balloon, or parachute, or hook, or barbed spear . . . or mere lightness which the winds can waft" (IX, 65).

Thoreau did not realize at this time that there was a connection between the dispersion of seed and the succession of forests. He was perhaps dimly aware of the latter, for he began to count rings on the stumps of great trees as if to reconstruct the primitive woodland which had almost entirely vanished from Concord, and he remarked at one point, "How foreign is the yellow pine to the green woods"—and asked, "What business has it here?" (VIII, 29) But his perception was limited by the accepted opinion that the way to produce mature forests was to plant them from seed. Thus in the fall of 1851 he noticed a few of the primitive oaks in a pasture ("great ornaments" he thought them), noticed too that no young oaks were replacing them, and wondered if there would be any a century later, but concluded, "One day they will be planted, methinks, and nature reinstated to some extent" (VIII, 461f.).

In April of 1852 Thoreau still talked of planting forests, but now in connection with an observation which was to lead in a new direction. He noticed that recently-fallen acorns lying among the dead leaves had been sprouting, the rootlet "already turning toward the bowels of the earth, already thinking of the tempests which it is destined as an oak to withstand, if it escapes worm and squirrel." If you would "make a forest," he advised, "pick these up and plant them" (IX, 481).

Eight months later Thoreau observed the sprouting of chestnuts under similar conditions and realized that he had learned how new forests are planted by nature. The nuts which had fallen that year were already "partially mixed with the mould, as it were, under the decaying and mouldy leaves," where they had "all the moisture and manure" they needed and were "concealed from squirrels" (X, 434f.). Having thus established for himself what Timothy Dwight had known at least a generation earlier, Thoreau had now to determine why it was that the seeds which sprouted successfully in a forest were not those which had fallen from its trees but were of different species that might be growing only at a distance.

Early in 1853, continuing his study of the dissemination of chestnuts, he found little piles of these nuts near the galleries of meadow mice. By March he was ready to conclude that mice and squirrels stored many nuts away in "secure, sufficiently dry and sufficiently moist places" (XI, 9) to allow them to sprout and that thus "new groves of chestnuts" were being born (XI, 30). After "chestnuts" Thoreau added in parentheses the query "and of oaks?" He knew then that what he had learned about chestnuts might also be true of these other species, which are involved in succession patterns with pines and which were among those which Thoreau wished to have preserved.

For almost three years Thoreau allowed this knowledge to rest in his mind and *Journal* unexploited. He continued to be interested in the dispersion of seed, particularly in the way squirrels cut down pine cones and opened their scales.[13] He also observed with a regret that now approached anguish the accelerating destruction of Concord's remaining forests. "Our woods," he

13. XIII, 214, 227f., 447.

wrote in early spring of 1855, "are now so reduced that the chopping of this winter has been a cutting to the quick" (XIII, 231). And in December: "Now I hear, half a mile off, the hollow sound of woodchopping, the work of short winter days begun, which is gradually laying bare and impoverishing our landscape. In two or three thicker woods which I have visited this season, I was driven away by this ominous sound" (XIV, 48).

On April 28, 1856, the hitherto unrelated pieces of information lying dormant in Thoreau's mind were precipitated into a synthesis. The immediate impulse, preserved in the *Journal,* was a comment by a man who seems to have been helping Thoreau survey a farm.[14] "Observing the young pitch pines by the road south of Loring's lot that was so heavily wooded, George Hubbard remarked that if they were cut down oaks would spring up, and sure enough, looking across the road to where Loring's white pines recently stood so densely, the ground was all covered with oaks." His mind alerted, Thoreau immediately instructed himself in his *Journal* to "look at the site of some thick pine woods which I remember"—woods which he had very likely surveyed for cutting himself—"and see what has sprung up" (XIV, 315). Some ten days later he recorded one such observation which confirmed Hubbard's remark (XIV, 329), and before another week had passed he formulated an hypothesis to explain what he had seen.

If after a dense pine wood is cut down the trees which spring up are not pine but oak and other hardwoods, it is because the seeds of these hardwoods have been transported to the pines from distant groves by animals and have sprouted under their shade, ready to shoot up when the pines are felled. It may appear to some that the acorns must have lain dormant in the soil since the day that this land had been occupied by oaks, "but if you look through a thick pine wood," wrote Thoreau, "you will detect many little oaks, birches, etc., sprung probably from seeds carried into the thicket by squirrels, etc., and blown thither, but

14. On this day Thoreau was surveying for Samuel Staples, the constable who had jailed him in 1846 ("Field Notes of Surveys," p. 106).

which are overshadowed and choked by the pines. This planting under the shelter of the pines may be carried on annually, and the plants annually die, but when the pines are cleared off, the oaks, etc., having got just the start they want, and now secured favorable conditions, immediately spring up to trees" (XIV, 334f.).

Thoreau did not seriously test this hypothesis until September 24, 1857. That morning he noticed a squirrel burying something under a hemlock, and digging after the animal found two hickory nuts under about an inch and a half of soil. "This, then," he wrote, reaffirming his conclusion of 1853, "is the way forests are planted. This nut must have been brought twenty rods at least and was buried at just the right depth. If the squirrel is killed, or neglects its deposit, a hickory springs up" (XVI, 40). That afternoon, incited by this incident perhaps, Thoreau visited a "very dense and handsome white pine grove" and found on its floor, "as often as every five feet, a little oak, three to twelve inches high." "I was surprised," he confessed to himself, "to find my own theory so perfectly proved" (XVI, 40f.).

It was this theory, supported more firmly by other observations, that Thoreau presented to an audience of Middlesex County farmers on September 20, 1860, in his lecture "The Succession of Forest Trees." The only element in it new to science—and he claimed no more—was that which derived from Thoreau's studies of the dispersion of seed. The other essential components had already been described by the botanist George B. Emerson in 1846.[15]

In the development of Thoreau's social philosophy, this explanation of the mechanism of succession was important less for itself than for its consequences. Immediately after Thoreau formulated his hypothesis in 1856, he recorded a conversation which shows him to have been thinking about the implications of an understanding of succession for the management of wood lots. He had been speaking to the successful farmer John Hosmer

15. *A Report on the Trees and Shrubs Growing Naturally in the Forests of Massachusetts* (Boston, 1846), pp. 19, 28–30.

about the wood lot pointed out by Hubbard, on which the pines were being succeeded by shrub oak, an economically useless growth. Hosmer's opinion was that its new owner would never see "any decent wood there as long as he lives." But he went on to tell Thoreau about a similar experience of his own whose significance he perhaps did not fully understand. He had had "a lot of pine in Sudbury, which being cut, shrub oak came up. He cut and burned and raised rye, and the next year (it being surrounded by pine woods on three sides) a dense growth of pine sprang up." What Hosmer had done without prevision was to take advantage of the mechanism of succession to get a growth of salable pine instead of profitless shrub oak. "If you cut the shrub oak soon," generalized Thoreau, "probably pines or birches, maples or other trees which have light seeds, will spring next, because squirrels, etc., will not be likely to carry acorns into open land" (XIV, 363).

By 1856, then, Thoreau had groped his way to the threshold of a fundamentally modern forestry, which, as a recent authority has stated, is "primarily a matter of continuous management of existing forests, with dependence chiefly on natural reproduction, not tree planting, for replacement of the stand." [16] Using his knowledge of the natural laws of the forest community, Thoreau saw the possibility of a management which would both encourage the growth of profitable timber and minimize the time during which forest land was not covered by trees. In the period of intense labor which followed his lecture on succession and which was cut short only by the onset of his fatal illness, Henry Thoreau systematically investigated the forest on the basis of this principle.[17]

One line of his research sought to deepen his understanding

16. Smith, "The Early Forestry Movement in the United States," p. 328. A similar definition is given by the pioneer American forester Gifford Pinchot in *Breaking New Ground* (New York, 1947), p. 1.

17. For other comments on this period, see Deevey, "A Re-examination of Thoreau's *Walden*," p. 8f., and Kathryn Whitford, "Thoreau and the Woodlots of Concord," *New England Quarterly,* XXIII (September 1950), 294ff.

of the different patterns of succession. He turned from the pine-oak sequence to study the succession of white pines to pitch pines.[18] Moreover, since his pure pine wood succeeded by pure oak was an abstraction from which actual forests differed owing both to natural complexities and the unplanned management of their owners, Thoreau began to acquaint himself with the ways in which succession took place in woods of mixed species and uneven densities.[19]

Related to this subject were his speculations on the environmental demands of a species which determined where it might best flourish and what other species it might succeed. "It is an interesting inquiry," he wrote, to determine "which species shall grow on a given tract." Certainly the soil was involved, for massed red maples and swamp white oaks were quite common in wet places, lacking in uplands, but allowances must also be made for minute variations in the light and warmth available under different stands.[20] In these speculations, Thoreau arrived at the modern idea of the climax: that "in the natural state of things, when sufficient time is given, trees will be found occupying the places most suitable to each," so that the forest is generally "in a transition state to a settled and normal condition" (XX, 218).

Each of Thoreau's investigations of silvics—another that might be mentioned is his study of the rate of growth of various trees, especially pitch pines, to determine the most profitable age for cutting[21]—was adding to the foundation for a modern forest management and thus increasing the possibility of a union between satisfactory profits and the preservation of nature. However, for an understanding of the relation between Thoreau's forestry and his attitude to the economic order, the most significant point is perhaps that on the relative value of trees which

18. See for example XX, 258, 268, 280.
19. See for example XX, 140, 152, 183, 255, 271, 280.
20. XX, 134, 143, 258. See also XX, 147, 181.
21. See for example XX, 175f., 185f., 190, 193f., 197, 203–207, 232–239, 251.

originally sprouted from stumps and trees which originally sprang from seed.

When Timothy Dwight recognized that succession might be employed to make New England's forests "ever-living," he also described another method which his countrymen thought would achieve the same end. "When a field of wood is, in the language of our farmers, cut clean," wrote Dwight, that is, "when every tree is cut down, . . . vigorous shoots sprout from every stump, and having their nourishment supplied by the roots of the former tree, grow with a thrift and rapidity never seen in stems derived from the seeds. Good ground will thus yield a growth, amply sufficient for fuel, once in fourteen years." [22] In Thoreau's time as in Dwight's, it was chiefly this procedure, technically known as the coppice method, that was relied on to produce new woods around Concord.

Thoreau's investigation of the coppice method sprang from his suspicion that it led to the destruction of an indispensable portion of nature. Shortly after he delivered his lecture on succession, he recorded his feeling that "the noblest trees and those which it took the longest to produce, and which are the longest-lived," such as chestnuts, oaks, and perhaps hickories, "are the first to become extinct under our present system and the hardest to reproduce" (XX, 135). Repeated clear-cutting and growth from sprouts was destroying "our noblest hardwood forests" (XX, 200) and replacing them "by pines and birches, of feebler growth than the primitive pines and birches, for want of a change of soil" (XX, 135).

This hypothesis Thoreau could test only with the rigor available to a natural historian, not with that of the scientific technician, but he applied himself to essentially the same problems singled out by his better-equipped successors.[23] He observed young shoots sprouted from stumps which had in turn sprouted from other stumps still outlined by their sides, and wished to

22. *Travels in New-England and New-York,* I, 80.
23. Ralph C. Hawley, *The Practice of Silviculture,* 5th ed. (New York, 1946), pp. 176–187.

know how long such regeneration could continue.[24] He specu-
lated on whether old trunks would produce sprouts as readily
as younger ones and whether sprouting was influenced by the
season at which the tree was cut.[25] He thought that sprout trees
would succumb to disease sooner than seedlings, being merely
extensions of trunks and roots of a previous generation and
thus old before their time.[26] He knew that sprouts grew more
rapidly than seedlings, but suspected that their trunks were
shaky, that with both trees and men "you must grow slowly to
last long." [27]

Sickness prevented Thoreau from completing his studies; at
the time he caught the cold which first became bronchitis and
then became his death, he was still examining chestnut sprouts
circled round the parent stump (XX, 290). But the direction of
his investigations is clear to see: the coppice method might yield
a quick turnover, but it did not produce the best trees; fuel perhaps, but not wide boards and noble symbols of heroism and
aspiration.[28] To grow these one must start from seed, and the
seed of oak and chestnut grew best under other trees.

The groves of chestnut which once enriched the Concord
landscape had been eaten up in railroad sleepers, planks, and
wooden rails, and there was danger in Thoreau's day that the
species would become extinct.[29] Farmers complained that they
could find no seedlings to transplant. But in his exploration of
the undergrowth beneath other species Thoreau found many
young chestnuts, probably planted by squirrels. They were especially plentiful under pines.[30] It followed then that they might
be allowed to grow under the shelter of other trees until strong

24. XX, 93f., 105, 168f., 223, 256, 268f.
25. XX, 157, 165, 169, 177, 211, 212f., 276f.
26. XX, 145, 190f.
27. XX, 191. See also XX, 217.
28. Recent forestry is in essential argreement; see Whitford, "Thoreau
and the Woodlots of Concord," p. 304f., and Hawley, *The Practice of
Silviculture,* p. 184f.
29. Thoreau was thinking of its extinction by man; it has since been
made scarce by the chestnut blight.
30. XX, 137f., 188f.

enough to withstand transplanting. Moreover, they might even succeed to the covering species if the latter were properly removed. "Thus it appears," concluded Thoreau, "that by a judicious letting Nature alone merely we might recover our chestnut wood in the course of a century" (XX, 138).

In a similar way the township might recover its old oak wood. Thoreau did not find beneath the older trees many young oaks ready to shoot up if given space and sunlight but noticed them in great numbers under pines.[31] In the vicinity of Concord, he concluded, "the pine woods are a natural nursery of oaks" (XX, 139), establishing themselves on unoccupied or exhausted lands and preparing the soil for their more demanding successors (XX, 130, 150). But the seedling oaks flourished beneath the dense pines only from six to ten years. After that they needed a wider prospect and might be transplanted to open ground or favored by first cutting branches off the pines and at the proper time felling the cover altogether to leave the oaks in control of the plot (XX, 139f.). The owner who planned to cut a fine oak wood and wished his descendants to enjoy its equal "should be considering how to favor the growth of pines" (XX, 213), to which the new oaks would succeed in their turn.

Whatever the inadequacies of Thoreau's pioneering approximation of forest realities in Massachusetts,[32] his underlying principle was a sound one. He came back always to succession, the natural laws whose operation led the forest by stages toward the climax. Only by taking advantage of these could man grow trees to serve both lower ends and higher.

But the owners of Concord wood lots were for the most part ignorant of natural laws, shallow empirical men who could better see the immediate dollar than the many that might be scientifically planned for. Thoreau was disgusted by their improvident practices in the woodland. A foresighted husbandman, he held,

31. XX, 139f., 144f., 150, 180–183, 249f.
32. Deevey, for example, suggests that he "overemphasized the reversibility of plant succession" ("A Re-examination of Thoreau's *Walden*," p. 8).

examines the ground beneath his trees to "ascertain what kind of wood is about to take the place of the old and how abundantly, in order that he may act understandingly and determine if it is best to clear the land or not" (XX, 94). But again and again he discovered his neighbors ignoring nature's preparations for a new crop and violating the forest's laws to their own ultimate disadvantage. The most common malpractice involved the cutting or burning of seedling trees left on newly cut land.

Sometimes a farmer who used his plow or bushwhack on the young pines annually invading his field finally decided to give up and allow nature to present him with a wood lot. One such owner, writes Thoreau, "blind to his own interests," plowed the little trees under "and got a few beans for his pains," but the pines "grew while he slept" and were "so thick and promising" that he at length "concluded not to cut his own fingers any more, *i.e.,* not further than up to the last joint," and allowed the trees to form a border to his planting. But "they would have covered the half or perhaps the whole of his barren field before this, if he had let them" (XX, 128).

Other farmers refused to give in. One, felling his pines but unable to see beyond grass, repeatedly cut down the hickories which had succeeded them and got, in a few years, not a valuable young wood lot but a sterile field on which the succession cycle would have to begin anew with birches and other first growth (XX, 94). A second, cutting dense pine, burned over the land, killed the many seedling oaks that had been nursed in the grove, and planted rye, a procedure which could yield only "starved pasture" in the end. "What a fool!" exclaimed Thoreau on seeing what he had done. "He has got his dollars for the pine timber, and now he wishes to get his bushels of grain and finger the dollars that they will bring; and then, Nature, you may have your way again. Let us purchase a mass for his soul. A greediness that defeats its own ends" (XX, 131f.).[33]

33. Other examples of mismanagement will be found in XX, 126–128, 132f., 145f., 150f., 176f., 187f., 198. An example of proper manage-

But what was to be done to bring such men's actions into correspondence with the laws of nature? The answer toward which Thoreau took a first step in the fall of 1860 is a commonplace of our day, but it is not usually associated with the author of "Civil Disobedience." Commenting on the last-mentioned farmer, who had ruined his one chance of getting oaks in order to profit from a little rye, Thoreau wrote: "I am chagrined for him. That he should call himself an agriculturalist! He needs to have a guardian placed over him. A forest-warden should be appointed by the town. Overseers of poor husbandmen" (XX, 131). Convinced that the individual involved was unable to see beyond the sale of his next harvest to a source of profit that would also give the whole community a grove of trees serving higher ends than money, Thoreau was willing to restrict the area reserved for the action of the man's private conscience.

Thoreau's conclusion was inevitable from his premises. When he accepted a profit-directed economy as impersonally dictated necessity he did not cease to insist that acquisition should be subordinated to the higher end of self-culture. Morality—to use the word broadly—had always been more important to him than possessions, and it continued to be so. Within the narrow limits of forest management he experimented, as he had done at the pond, in the relation between the order of production and the higher order of morality, attempting once again to discover how the two might be made congruent. But his beginnings of a solution within this narrow field necessarily came into conflict with minds educated to venality, and he was forced, like others both before him and after, to advocate control of the material acquisition of the individual in favor of the spiritual appropriation of the many. To achieve this control, Thoreau turned to the instrument of the many nearest to hand and most proportionate to the task: the peaceful processes of government. In another as-

---

ment is described in XX, 191f., where Thoreau shows how a farmer took advantage of white pine and pitch pine succession relations to produce "a valuable and salable woodland."

pect of this general problem, Negro slavery, the peaceful instruments of the majority would in his opinion prove inadequate, and Thoreau would become a supporter of a government at war.

III

The conflict between the material acquisition of the one and the spiritual appropriation of the many is the key to Thoreau's advocacy of conservation, which complements his research in forestry and carries his social thought to government ownership.

A little more than four years before he built his hut on Emerson's lake frontage at Walden, Thoreau had attempted to rent or buy some farmland on which to declare his independence. When he failed from poverty he fell back defiantly on the contention that the spiritual farming which really interested him could be carried on without occupancy. "What have I to do with plows?" he asked. "I cut another furrow than you see" (VII, 245).

Looking back on this or a similar experience in the summer of 1851, he was still able to say to himself that though he had failed to buy a certain plot "for want of money," he had harvested there annually nonetheless—"in my own fashion" (VIII, 439). But the previous winter he had already recognized that the end of such free spiritual appropriation of nature was coming into sight. "I trust," he had written, "that the walkers of the present day are conscious of the blessings which they enjoy in the comparative freedom with which they can ramble over the country . . . , anticipating with compassion that future day when possibly it will be partitioned off into so-called pleasure-grounds, where only a few may enjoy the narrow and exclusive pleasure which is compatible with ownership,—when walking over the surface of God's earth shall be construed to mean trespassing on some gentleman's grounds, when fences shall be multiplied and man traps and other engines invented to confine men to the public road" (VIII, 156f.).

For Thoreau and his frequent companion Channing the "evil

days" (V, 216) of that suburbanized future had already begun to arrive, and the lengthening, branching fences diverted their walks toward the pine barrens, swamps, and streams. "The river is my own highway," wrote Thoreau in the spring of 1852, "the only wild and unfenced part of the world hereabouts" (X, 77). Ten months later he repeated the statement with a significant addition: "In relation to the river, I find my natural rights least infringed on. It is an extensive 'common' still left. Certain savage liberties still prevail in the oldest and most civilized countries" (XI, 45f.).

Access to nature was thus an inherent right of mankind which had been respected, he believed, in more primitive societies but was being progressively eroded by civilization. "Among the Indians," he wrote in a late manuscript, "the earth & its productions generally were common & free to all the tribe, like the air & water —but among us who have supplanted the Indians, the public retain only a small yard or common in the middle of the village, with perhaps a grave-yard beside it, & the right of way, by sufferance, by a particular narrow route, which is annually becoming narrower, from one such yard to another." He was "not overflowing with respect and gratitude" to the men who had thus laid out New England's villages, "for I think," he declared, "that a 'prentice hand liberated from Old English prejudices could have done much better in this new world. If they were in earnest seeking thus far away 'freedom to worship God,' as some assure us —why did they not secure a little more of it, when it was so cheap? At the same time that they built meeting-houses why did they not preserve from desecration & destruction far grander temples not made with hands?" [34]

To make up for the failure of the original settlers, Thoreau advocated conservation. The "natural features which make a township handsome" should be preserved for the public and not surrendered to individuals: "a river, with its waterfalls and mead-

34. From "Portion of Holograph Journal, 1860–1861," now in the Henry W. and Albert A. Berg Collection of the New York Public Library, by whose permission it is here quoted.

ows, a lake, a hill, a cliff or individual rocks, a forest, and ancient trees standing singly"—as many as possible of the "precious natural objects of rare beauty" (XX, 304f.). This radical principle of conservation Thoreau applied concretely in three distinct areas: original wilderness unchanged by man, humanized nature shaped by its role in the economy, and wholly domesticated nature along streets and roads.

The rationale behind Thoreau's desire to preserve samples of wilderness parallels the extended metaphor in "Walking." Primitive nature unmodified by man is needed as "a resource and background, the raw material of all our civilization." The poet, for example, both for "strength" and for "beauty," must periodically "travel the logger's path and the Indian's trail, to drink at some new and more bracing fountain of the Muses, far in the recesses of the wilderness" (III, 172f.).

Thoreau found the closest approach to original nature in Maine, and he concluded the account of his second trip to that territory with a request for "national preserves," presumably owned by the federal government but how acquired he does not say, "in which the bear and panther, and some even of the hunter race, may still exist, and not be 'civilized off the face of the earth'" (III, 173).[35] Similarly, the last pages of his journal include a statement that the top of New Hampshire's Mt. Washington, then in dispute between two individuals, "should not be private property" at all but be left "unappropriated," together with its approaches, so that access to its inspirations would not depend on the generosity of private owners (XX, 305).

The wild, however, was not the poet's true home but only its essential supplement. It was humanized nature that provided the only adequate natural environment for civilized man. Thoreau first realized this fact (as was pointed out earlier in these pages) on his trip to Mt. Katahdin in the summer of 1846. He stated

35. It is chiefly these words which lead Paul H. Oehser ("Pioneers in Conservation: Footnote to the History of an Idea," *Nature Magazine*, XXXVIII [April 1945], 189) to consider Thoreau as "perhaps . . . America's first real conservationist."

it most explicitly, however, in "Chesuncook," published in 1858 but recounting the experiences of his trip to Maine five years earlier.

Despite the impulse whose satisfaction demanded the wilderness, Thoreau found it "a relief" to get back from Maine to the "smooth but still varied landscape" around Concord, for it was this, and not primitive nature, that a civilized man needed for his "permanent residence." Placed in the original forest, such a man must eventually pine, "like a cultivated plant which clasps its fibres about a crude and undissolved mass of peat." He needed the frontier farmers and the lumbermen to tame the wilderness and prepare a nature on which civilization could sustain itself. Poets in particular, such at least as "compose the mass of any literature," though they needed breaths of a stronger air, were inspired chiefly by "the partially cultivated country" rather than by the wild and could not thrive unless the "logger and pioneer" had first "humanized Nature" for them.

But nature was not to be subdued too far, not to the point of "elaborately and willfully wealth-constructed parks and gardens." Perhaps, thought Thoreau, it was such fields and woods as lay about Concord, "with the primitive swamps scattered here and there in their midst, but not prevailing over them," that were "the perfection of parks and groves, gardens, arbors, paths, vistas, and landscapes"—"the common which each village possesses, its true paradise" (III, 171f.). "Each town," he wrote the year after the publication of "Chesuncook," "should have a park, or rather a primitive forest, of five hundred or a thousand acres, where a stick should never be cut for fuel, a common possession forever, for instruction and recreation" (XVIII, 387).

Had the original settlers of Concord been sufficiently foresighted, thought Thoreau, they might easily have reserved such a "true paradise" for the townspeople. "All Walden Wood," he wrote in 1859, "might have been preserved for our park forever, with Walden in its midst, and the Easterbrooks Country, an unoccupied area of some four square miles, might have been our huckleberry-field" (XVIII, 387). The town's first planners,

he added in the late manuscript quoted from earlier, should also
have "made the river available as a common possession forever.
The town collectively should at least have done as much as an
individual of taste who owns an equal area commonly does in
England. Indeed," he continued, "not only the channel, but one
or both banks of every river should be a public highway—for a
river is not useful merely to float on. In this case, one bank might
have been reserved as a public walk & the trees that adorned it
have been protected, and frequent avenues have been provided
leading to it from the main street."

But though the conservation of parks, rivers, and river banks
was the responsibility of "the town collectively," Thoreau did
not rely on the power of local government to regain the lands
which had been surrendered to private ownership. Instead, re-
ducing one tradition of American agrarianism to philanthropy,
he fell back on inheritance. After the 1859 *Journal* passage on
Walden Wood and the Easterbrooks Country, he went on to say:
"If any owners of these tracts are about to leave the world without natural heirs who need or deserve to be specially remembered, they will do wisely to abandon their possession to all, and
not will them to some individual who perhaps has enough already" (XVIII, 387).

Elsewhere, however, Thoreau does speak of a "committee appointed to see that the beauty of the town received no detriment"
(XX, 304), and when he incorporates this statement into the
late manuscript we have quoted from he seems to be thinking
of some governmental privilege such as eminent domain. Before
it he writes that he does not consider a man "fit to be the founder
of a state or even of a town" who does not preserve its best natural features for public use, and immediately after it: "If here is
the largest boulder in the country, then it should not belong to
an individual nor be made into doorsteps." Action by the local
government to appropriate boulders, river banks, hilltops, seems
to be a natural extension of its other activities. "There are a few
hopeful signs," writes Thoreau in the manuscript. "There is the
growing library—& then the town does set trees along the high-

way—but does not the broad landscape itself deserve attention?"

The action of the selectmen in having trees set along the highway was praised by Thoreau more than once, both in his *Journal* and in his lecture "Autumnal Tints." Within towns and between towns he wanted mankind to move beneath branches. "Let us have a good many maples and hickories and scarlet oaks," he demanded. "A village is not complete, unless it have these trees to mark the season in it" (V, 276). When he entered Massachusetts after an excursion to New Hampshire in 1858, he was happy to get away from the "long bleak or sunny roads" of the Granite State and take advantage of the shade trees planted by the older Bay State. But he was still not satisfied. A farmer apparently ran over when he made a fire by the roadside. "What barbarians we are!" he exclaimed to himself. "The convenience of the traveller is very little consulted. He merely has the privilege of crossing somebody's farm by a particular narrow and maybe unpleasant path." The sides of a road, like the banks of a river, "should belong to mankind inalienably." The road itself "should be of ample width and adorned with trees expressly for the use of the traveller," and "there should be broad recesses in it, especially at springs and watering-places, where he can turn out and rest, or camp if he will" (XVII, 55). . . .

IV

Thoreau's demand for public conservation, whether of wilderness tracts, large parks, or rows of trees, can be adequately explained by the two concepts already referred to: man's need for both wild and humanized nature, and the tendency of private owners to exclude other people from their lands. But his rationale included a third element incompletely integrated with the others and perhaps more significant.

Its starting point is the tendency of private owners not only to fence mankind off from nature but actually to destroy nature. In Concord (as we have already seen) Thoreau witnessed the destruction of humanized nature by men who cut their wood lots without providing for the succession of a new stand. In Maine he encountered a similar shortsighted destruction of the wild forest.

On his trip to Mount Katahdin, made during the Walden experiment and dominated (as has been shown) by its ideology, Thoreau was not yet ready to be self-consciously aware of the need for conservation. But he gathered ample evidence preparing the way for the later conclusion. Though he himself gave instructions for cutting and burning timber in order to prepare land for cultivation (III, 15), he was distressed by the sight of a hundred acres newly felled and still smoking and by its implication: "the whole of that solid and interminable forest . . . doomed to be gradually devoured thus by fire, like shavings, and no man be warmed by it" (III, 18f.). He also saw much of lumbering on this trip, noticed the fire-breeding carelessness with which the lumberers treated the forest after the best white pine had been taken out (III, 45), and concluded that the ambition of mankind in Maine seemed to be "to drive the forest all out of the country, from every solitary beaver swamp and mountain-side, as soon as possible" (III, 5f.).

Thoreau's trip to Chesuncook Lake in 1853 provided additional evidence of this destructivity. But when he came to write it up—the account was not published, as has been noted, until 1858—he was ready to contrast the motive which led to the ravaging of the forest with another which led to its preservation.

Talking shop with the lumbermen, watching his companions kill a moose, Thoreau learned "how base or coarse are the motives which commonly carry men into the wilderness." Neither lumberman nor professional hunter was anything more than mercenary. The first tried to find cuttable timber—as much as he could possibly get out; the second tried to kill moose—as many as he could possibly skin. But "there is a higher law affecting our relation to pines as well as to men," declared Thoreau. Pine boards and moose hides have their "petty and accidental" functions, "for everything may serve a lower as well as a higher use." But the living pine "is no more lumber than man is, and to be made into boards and houses is no more its true and highest use than the truest use of a man is to be cut down and made into manure." It is not the man who performs economic functions upon the pines—cuts them, planes them, or distills their turpentine—who makes the "truest use" of them but rather the poet, "who loves them as his own shadow in the air, and lets them stand." "It is the living spirit of the tree," wrote Thoreau, "not its spirit of turpentine, with which I sympathize and which heals my cuts" (III, 133–135).

This exposition of the two opposing categories in their abstract and artistically polarized forms, like the similar one in his two late lectures, should not be mistaken for the totality of Thoreau's opinion. He did not mean to starve the community's body while feeding its soul. It has already been pointed out that the nature which he considered to be man's proper environment was not the wilderness but humanized nature, in which lumbermen, hunters, and frontier farmers had already been active. The properly managed wood lots which his silviculture made possible were not untouchable sacred groves but large stands which continued to provide lumber without ever being wholly cut down. Humanized nature might feed man's economy without starving his soul. Activities aimed solely at profit, however, served nothing but the economy. The sinfulness of the lumberman and professional hunter did not lie either in changing trees into boards or moose into hides but in that search for money which led them to cut and kill without rule whenever they could do so.

In the last years of his short life, Thoreau came to believe that the destruction of nature and the primacy of the material motive were in his own time inextricably bound up with private property, and opposition to the latter became an element in the rationale behind his advocacy of conservation. The best expression of this late and undeveloped addition to his thinking is in the manuscript lecture quoted from earlier, in a passage developed from *Journal* entries of the summers of 1858 (XVII, 78f.) and 1860 (XX, 56f.).

The other components of Thoreau's philosophy of conservation did not exclude the possibility of a man's extracting spiritual sustenance from a nature which he neither owned nor shared in as public property but to which its holder gave him access. The new component made it difficult for Thoreau to enjoy any part of nature which had been privately acquired for the purpose of making money. It was as though the higher uses of nature could no longer be grafted on lower ones associated with acquisition and private property.

"What sort of a country," he asks, "is that where the huckleberry fields are private property?" And he answers: "When I pass such fields on the highway, my heart sinks within me, I see a blight on the land. Nature is under a veil there. I make haste away from the accursed spot. Nothing could deform her fair face more. I cannot think of it ever after but as the place where fair & palatable berries are converted into money, where the huckleberry is desecrated." In a further development of this idea, he writes: "As long as the berries are free to all comers they are beautiful, though they may be few and small, but tell me that this is a blueberry swamp which somebody has hired, & I shall not want even to look at it." [51]

It is after this passage that Thoreau goes on to speak of the common property in nature enjoyed by the Indians and to advocate conservation in order to make up for the failure of the original settlers of New England. But he also carries the idea one step further to reach the extreme point in his critique of the industrial economy. "It is true," he writes, "we have as good a right to make berries private property, as to make wild grass & trees such —it is not worse than a thousand other practices which custom has sanctioned—but that is the worst of it, for it suggests how bad the rest are, and to what result civilisation & division of labor naturally tend, to make all things venal." [52]

The idea approached in this passage—the incompatibility between an economy of private property and aims higher than

51. From "Notes on Fruits," now in the Henry W. and Albert A. Berg Collection of the New York Public Library, by whose permission it is here quoted.
52. *Ibid.*

acquisition—Thoreau did not develop further. But it provides the final evidence about Thoreau's view of the coupled opposites, relation to spirit and relation to body and economy. It was the first which was absolute. In the union of principle and expediency it was the lower which was always to be accommodated to the higher.

RAYMOND D. GOZZI

✪

"Some Aspects of Thoreau's Personality"

Those who knew Thoreau personally have found nothing so surprising as the cult which has grown up about him or so difficult of a rational explanation (G. W. Cooke, "The Two Thoreaus," *The Independent,* XLVIII [December 10, 1896], 3).

When we speak of a peculiarity in a man or a nation, we think to describe only one part; but it is not so. It pervades all. Some parts may be further removed than others from this center, but not a particle so remote as not to be shined on or shaded by it (*The Journal of Henry D. Thoreau,* I, 16 [December 12, 1837]).

Few pictures of Thoreau exist that were made during his lifetime. Mark Van Doren's careful scrutiny of two of them resulted in this highly perceptive description:

The Rowse crayon [1854, Frontispiece of Volume I of the *Journal*] and the Worcester daguerreotype [1856, Frontispiece of *A Week*] both show a face by no means simple to describe—contemptuous yet sensi-

Reprinted from Raymond D. Gozzi's *"Tropes and Figures: A Psychological Study of Henry David Thoreau"* (Doctoral Dissertation, New York University, 1957), pp. 93–123, by permission of Raymond D. Gozzi. It is available on microfilm: Order #57–2490, University Microfilms, Ann Arbor, Michigan. This selection and the one following have been edited slightly by Professor Gozzi for this book.

tive, aglint with irony yet dissolved in the pains of self, cold yet sensuous, alert yet lonely.[1]

The man described in these words does not, I believe, clearly appear in any of the biographies. I like to think that the ensuing analysis of Thoreau's personality, though of limited scope, is consistent with and supported by Van Doren's observations.

Thoreau was about medium height, with short legs and long trunk. His nose was very prominent and his chin very receded; in 1857, five years before his death, he grew a full beard. Emerson once told C. J. Woodbury, "Henry was homely in appearance, a rugged stone hewn from the cliff. I believe it accorded to all men to be moderately homely; but he surpassed sex. He had a beautiful smile and an earnest look. . . ." [2]

Habitually he kept his grey-blue eyes on the ground, rarely looking people in their faces.[3] His hands, Channing writes, he tended to keep "clasped behind him, or held closely at his side, the fingers made into a fist." [4] Channing also reports that Thoreau kept his mouth "pursed" and had a "wary, transitory air," giving an impression of "active earnestness, as if he had no moment to waste" (p. 25).

This element of tension is also emphasized by G. W. Curtis in an interesting sketch of an 1861 meeting he had with Thoreau.

He seated himself, maintaining the same habitual erect posture, which made it seem impossible that he could ever lounge or slouch, and which made Hawthorne speak of him as "cast iron," and immediately began to talk in a strain familiar to his friends. It was a staccato style of speech, every word coming separately and distinctly, as if preserving the same cool isolation in the sentence that the speaker did in Society; but the words were singularly apt and choice, and Thoreau

1. *Henry David Thoreau* (Boston, 1916), p. 6.

2. *Talks with Ralph Waldo Emerson* (New York, 1890), p. 79.

3. *Journal* (Boston, 1906), referred to hereinafter as J, III, 115–116 (November 14, 1851). Moncure Conway found an "intellectual furtiveness" in Thoreau ("Thoreau," *Fraser's Magazine*, LXXIII (April 1866), 461.

4. *Thoreau: The Poet-Naturalist* (Boston, 1873), pp. 10–11.

had always something to say. . . . His manner and matter both reproved trifling, but in the most impersonal manner. It was like the reproof of a statue of a god. There seemed never to be any loosening of the intellectual tension, and a call from Thoreau in the highest sense "meant business." [5]

This description by Curtis is pretty much of a military man—and Thoreau seemed military to many people. Young boys used to call him "Trainer Thoreau" (after the soldiers, who were called "Trainers") because of his "soldier-like carriage." [6] But there was really deeper reason for this name, and it was no doubt largely the power of impersonally reproving that Curtis noted. In the Thoreaus' school there was no flogging, yet Edward Emerson reports a former student as saying that he never saw "so absolutely military discipline. How it was done I scarcely know. Even the incorrigible were brought into line." [7] Alcott wrote in his *Journals* (Boston, 1938), p. 315, "He is rightly named *Thorough, Through,* the pervading *Thor,* the sturdy sensibility and force in things." After what must have been a particularly exasperating experience with Thoreau, Emerson jotted this in his *Journal*:

Henry is military. He seemed stubborn and implacable; always manly and wise, but rarely sweet. One would say that, as Webster could not speak without an antagonist, so Henry does not feel himself except in opposition. He wants a fallacy to expose, a blunder to pillory, requires a little sense of victory, a roll of the drums, to call his powers into full exercise (VIII, 375 [June 14, 1853]).

In a list that Emerson made up in which he equates various great men of the past to his contemporary friends, we find Plato associated with Alcott, Swedenborg with Jones Very—and Napoleon with Thoreau (Emerson J, VIII, 62 [October 19–November 17,

5. "Editor's Easy Chair," *Harper's,* XXV (February 1869), 415.
6. G. F. Hoar, *Autobiography of Seventy Years* (New York, 1905), p. 70.
7. *Henry Thoreau as Remembered by a Young Friend* (Boston, 1917), p. 22. In his essay on Thoreau, R. W. Emerson remarks, ". . . and what accusing silences, and what searching and irresistible speeches, battering down all defences, his companions can remember!"

1849]). Sanborn too, who knew Thoreau well, says he was "pugnacious" and "never quite gave up" a belligerent attitude.[8] Thoreau himself once wrote, "I have a deep sympathy with war, it so apes the gait and bearing of the soul." [9] "The soul" is, of course, his soul.

When confined by sickness to his house for several days once, he wrote the following:

I have been conscious of a certain softness to which I am commonly otherwise a stranger, in which the gates were loosened to some emotions; and if I were to become a confirmed invalid, I see how some sympathy with mankind and society might spring up. Yet what is my softness good for, even to tears. It is not I, but nature in me. I laughed at myself the other day to think that I cried while reading a pathetic story. . . . The tears were merely a phenomenon of the bowels. . . . I found that I had some bowels, but then it was because my bowels were out of order (J, III, 106 [November 11, 1851]).

This passage is of special interest because it suggests that Thoreau's hardness, aggressiveness, and determined anti-sociableness were of the nature of a reaction-formation to precisely the opposite qualities. He feared these opposite qualities; they were dangerous to him and he mocks them as being phenomena "of the bowels." These opposite qualities were brought to the fore when, it is to be presumed, he received especially loving care while ill at home. The danger they held for him was that they undermined the defense systems which he had set up and which now helped constitute his "every-day personality."

Thoreau was indeed "commonly" a stranger to softness, as he himself noted. His eyes were "sincere, but capable of a twinkle, and again of austerity, but not of softness," remembered Edward Emerson.[10] Yet, on occasion, he could express tenderness and pity.

8. Introduction to Thoreau's *Sir Walter Raleigh* (Boston, 1905), p. 9.
9. J, I, 156 (June 30, 1840). Other pages in this first *Journal*, particularly pp. 97–106, offer much on bravery and warriors. These and other passages were probably collected to form "The Service," first titled "The Brave Man."
10. *Henry Thoreau as Remembered by a Young Friend*, p. 2.

He showed tenderness toward his dying father, toward the woman of the "Sister" manuscripts, sometimes when writing about friends and dying friendships. Pity he showed mainly toward slaves, some poor Irish (notably Little Johnny Riordan), and dying animals. Alcott wrote in his *Journal* once that Thoreau "took refuge under a brusque and somewhat defiant manner—at heart [he was] as diffident and fine-strung" as Emerson and Hawthorne.[11]

"At heart," I think we must agree, Thoreau had depths of softness, but I also feel sure that the prevailing image he offers is of aggression. "Thoreau is military"—in our language, loaded with aggression. Violence creeps into many of his sentences, is evident in the curtness of his judgments; it gave his personality pungency and today helps save many of his moralisms from oblivion—he seems more modern than he is.

The main vehicle of Thoreau's aggression was words. Writing of the captured John Brown, Thoreau says, "He could afford to lose his Sharpe's rifles, while he retained his faculty of speech, —a Sharpe's rifle of infinitely surer and longer range" (J, XII, 414 [October 21, 1859]). Thoreau's Sharpe's rifle was loaded with wit—"Henry Thoreau has it," noted Emerson one day when writing about "Mother Wit" (Emerson J, VIII, 414 [September 8, 1853]). Thoreau "liked to do his thinking out loud, and expected that you would be an auditor rather than a companion." [12] In this connection, Alcott provides us with observations of Thoreau with his "disciples." Ricketson, he says, is a disciple, "though not in the absolute way he has Blake of Worcester, whose love for his genius partakes of the exceeding tenderness of women. . . . But Ricketson is himself, and plays the manly part in the matter, defending himself against the master's twistiness and tough 'thoroughcraft' with spirit and ability." [13] The implication here is that Thoreau steadily sought domination, using wit as his means to

11. *The Journals of Bronson Alcott* (Boston, 1938), p. 415 (July 19, 1870). Stressing Thoreau's basic tenderness is Robert Francis, in "Thoreau's Mask of Serenity," *Forum,* CVI (January 1947), 76.

12. Hoar, p. 72.

13. *Journals,* p. 298 (April 3, 1857).

force subservience by others. Emerson on at least one occasion felt shattered by Thoreau's aggressive wit (Emerson J, VII, 498 [August 1848]). Alcott, a tremendous talker who could not be pinned down, as Thoreau noted, found Thoreau's thoughts "invigorating" and his company "tonic, never insipid." [14] He seems never to have recorded being troubled by Thoreau's aggressive wit.

Alcott too was relatively unbothered by Thoreau's egoism, finding him only "a little over-confident and somewhat stiffly individual, perhaps. . . ." [15] To Whitman, however, Thoreau had "a very aggravated case of superciliousness." [16] And Henry James, Sr. makes the most extreme statement. He says Thoreau

was literally the most childlike, unconscious and unblushing egotist it has ever been my fortune to encounter in the ranks of manhood; so that, if he happened to visit you on a Sunday morning, as like as not you would soon find yourself intoning subaudible phrases to the meticulous skill which had at last succeeded in visibly marrying such sheer and mountainous self-esteem with such harmless and beautiful force of outward demeanor. . . . I have . . . honestly tried to read them [Thoreau's books] but owing, I suppose, to prejudice derived from personal contacts with him, their wit always seemed more or less spoiled, to my taste, by intention, and even their sagacity seemed painfully aggressive and alarming; so I relinquished my task without any edifying result.[17]

Looking from the outside, James saw a "mountainous ego" and aggressive wit; looking from the inside, Thoreau probably saw only a justifiable self-reliance and an earnestness to speak the truth in the best words.

An awareness that Thoreau was colossally egoistic is, I think, important in helping us to understand him. His egoism, strong before, was probably reinforced by his acceptance of Emerson's

14. *Journals,* p. 257 (November 5, 1851).
15. *Journals,* p. 250 (June 9, 1851).
16. Henry Seidel Canby, *Thoreau* (Boston, 1939), p. 417, quoting Traubel, *With Walt Whitman in Camden* (New York, 1906), I, 202.
17. Letter of James to the Boston *Herald,* April 24, 1881, quoted by Austin Warren, *The Elder Henry James* (New York, 1934), pp. 182–183.

doctrines, with their tincture of philosophic idealism and their powerful assertion of self-reliance. In Thoreau's early twenties he was writing essays and letters that reveal an imperious certainty, an intimidating assurance, that is astonishing. His genius, tension, aggressiveness, and wit help explain this, and so does his egoism or narcissism. In addition I think Thoreau lacked a sense of humor. He was witty, punned much, and laughed a good deal too (according to Channing), but had little sense of humor in the phrase's popular meaning when applied to persons. He could not laugh at himself—really criticize and make little of a mood or insight because of its partiality, its aggressive self-assertion to the exclusion of other realities. His ego and militancy could not brook it. In this humorless stance, what he gained in power and pungency he lost in humanity.[18]

Thoreau was so deadly earnest in his thinking partly because, as a passage we will now study suggests, thinking was his main outlet for aggression and one of his important means of defense against castration-anxiety. Through thinking, he says here, one achieves omnipotence and safety. Writing to Blake on September 26, 1859, about eight months after his father's death (which led, I think, to the climax of Thoreau's life), he says he is serving King Admetus ("confound him")—*i.e.,* he is taking care of the family business and hates it. (Thoreau often seems unconsciously to associate King Admetus and his father.) Too much effort is required to run things and also have thoughts: "You've got to carry on two farms at once,—the farm on the earth and the farm in your mind." The thinker is a kind of superior father, he next implicitly asserts: "It is easy enough to maintain a family, or a state, but it is hard to maintain these children of your brain. . . ." The thinker is also a kind of superior soldier, one who cannot be

18. Bradford Torrey, who spent several years editing Thoreau's *Journals,* notes that Thoreau's life "might have been smoother for him had he been less exacting in his idealism, more tolerant of imperfection in others and in himself, had he taken his studies, and even his spiritual aspirations, a grain or two less seriously." Torrey also remarks on "something like priggishness" in Thoreau. See "Thoreau as a Diarist," *Atlantic Monthly,* CXV (January 1905), 5–18.

defeated. Thoughts can "overrun a country," they can "send their bullets home to heaven's door."

You *fail* in your thoughts, or you *prevail* in your thoughts only. Provided you *think* well, the heavens falling, or the earth gaping, will be the music for you to march by. No foe can ever see you, or you him; you cannot so much as *think* of him. Swords have no edges, bullets no penetration for such a contest. In your mind must be a liquor which will dissolve the world whenever it is dropt in it. There is no universal solvent but this, and all things together cannot saturate it. It will hold the universe in solution, and yet be as translucent as ever. The vast machine may indeed roll over our toes, and we not know it, but it would rebound and be staved to pieces like an empty barrel, if it should strike fair and square on the least angular of a man's thoughts (*Familiar Letters*, pp. 356–357).

Thoughts are here imaged as violence-doers that can conquer countries and every fate—invisible foes, swords, and bullets. Thought can dissolve all things. The universe may "roll over our toes" (displaced castration image), but any thought we have could destroy it. Thus, to Thoreau, thoughts were the route to safety from danger, the means to destroy the foe who might well roll over his toes when he was not thinking—he, who had cut off "a good part" of one of his own toes in childhood.

In various ways, Thoreau, as a personality, never matured. He liked to play with children, to do things for them, to show them the ways of nature. To them he seemed "the best kind of older brother," [19] or "a glorious boy." [20] He had the adolescent's perfervid intellectualization, which seems to minister to day-dreams, as Anna Freud points out, and helps control instinctual pressures.[21] Note the underlying sexual imagery in this passage, as well as Thoreau's first thought of himself as a "youth" (he was thirty-four years old then): "Can a youth, a man, do more

19. Edward Emerson, p. v.
20. Storms Higginson, quoted in S. A. Jones, *Pertaining to Thoreau* (Detroit, 1901), p. 121. Franklin B. Sanborn, *The Life of Henry David Thoreau* (Boston, 1917), p. 169, says Thoreau always retained "a strain of . . . juvenility."
21. *The Ego and the Mechanisms of Defense* (New York, 1946), p. 181.

wisely than to go where his life is to be found, . . . We are surrounded by a rich and fertile mystery. May we not probe it, pry
into it, employ ourselves about it, a little?" (J, II, 471 [September
7, 1851]).

Thoreau's extreme idealization of friendship is adolescent, and
so is his attitude toward love. He never did break away from
home, always remaining the well-domesticated son. For all his
asceticism (in itself frequently found among the emotionally immature), he sought his own varieties of pleasure—nature walks,
camping, reading, writing—with the avidity of the young, allow-
ing little interference with them. Even in the matter of self-
support, an area in which he tended to be meticulous, he was to
some degree willing to be the one provided for by affectionate
elders. At the age of twenty-four, with his neighbors doubtless
the Emersons, he wrote: "I will depend upon the extravagance of
my neighbors for my luxuries, for they will take care to pamper
me if I will be overfed" (J, I, 309 [January 2, 1842]).

The above quotation is also a beautiful example of Thoreau's
rationalizing in full flight. "Extravagance," "luxuries," "pamper,"
"overfed"—with these words he makes it hard for us (and himself?) to see that he is just saying, "I will accept good things from
others." As a rationalizer Thoreau has already been accorded a
place in Karl Menninger's popular book, *The Human Mind* (New
York, 1949). Menninger uses as one of his examples of rationalization Thoreau's response to his accidentally setting the woods
on fire when on an April 1844 outing with his friend Edward
Hoar, who was still at Harvard. (The woods, Thoreau asserts,
belonged more to him than to their merely legal owners, etc.,
etc.—see J, II, 21–40, dated "1850," and *Walden,* the "House-
warming" chapter.) Another example in which Thoreau asserts
his control over a situation he actually did not control, is in the
Journals for April 4, 1854. He was employed at the time as a
surveyor by Mr. Hoar (Edward Hoar's father) to do some work
in Carlisle. Apparently Mr. Hoar drove him back to Concord on
this day.

I rode with my employer a dozen miles today, keeping a profound silence almost all the way as the most simple and natural course. I treated him simply as if he had bronchitis and could not speak, just as I would a sick man, a crazy man, or an idiot. The disease was only an unconquerable stiffness in a well-meaning and sensible man (J, VI, 185).

Not till we come to the last sentence do we realize as most probable that *Thoreau* was treated stiffly—apparently he had tried to be conversational at the start of the journey—and not the opposite.[22]

Several critics have noted Thoreau's rationalizing power and do not see it as being indulged in only occasionally. In Mark Van Doren's study (p. 66) we find, "He who wept at twenty to stay in Concord affected thereafter to scorn locality. He who evaded the crisis in which most youths choose professions was thereafter a loud despiser of professions 'on principle.' " And Joseph Wood Krutch feels that Thoreau's "intellectual convictions were rationalizations of his needs and desires." To Krutch, Thoreau's "principal achievement was not the creation of a system but the creation of himself," and in the literary creation of that image rationalization was highly important.[23] It has been said that artists "transform their individual conflicts and complexes onto a vast screen of a social group, a nation, or humanity." [24] Thoreau was aided in his transformations-into-art by his almost incredible power of rationalization. His lack of humor helped too.

The literary image of himself that Thoreau made for himself and posterity is a compound of the reigning ideals of Western civilization, given further depth by some ideals of the East. Espe-

22. It seems likely that Mr. Hoar excited Thoreau's April 16, 1854, withering outburst against one of his "ridiculously stately neighbors" (J, VI, 199–200).

23. *Henry David Thoreau* (New York, 1948), p. 11. Canby (p. 23), referring to "Civil Disobedience," says, "Thoreau was a great rationalizer of his emotions when the time came to philosophize them."

24. G. Bychowski, "From Catharsis to Work of Art," *Psychoanalysis and Culture* (New York, 1951), p. 395.

cially as the writer of *Walden* and a number of essays (and most Thoreau readers go no further), has Thoreau established a literary image of himself in the public mind. This image corresponds, I believe, with Thoreau's ego-ideal; it is Thoreau as he wished himself to be—and as, to a certain extent, he was.

What is *Walden* as an ego-document? What is its dream of the "I"? *Walden* is a country-poem, emphatically *not* saccharine-bucolic, in which Thoreau celebrates himself—his ways of life and his views. Surveying the world, he finds it wanting. True values he says are found in having relation to nature, in subjectivity, in art, in observation, and in intellectuality. He displays himself as the man who steadily achieves these values and enjoys high freedom, living the life of individualism and self-reliance. He is a man pure, hard, clear, wild and yet controlled and cultured, saturnine and yet sweet, self-indulgent and yet ascetic. He is a farmer-poet, fisherman-flutist, scientist-artist, naturalist-mystic, doer-thinker. He is vigorously alive, sensitive, triumphant. Anxiety, dread, tedium, despair—even merely ordinary "out-of-sorts-ness"—are pretty well banished from this image; they are facts of *others'* lives. Above all, Thoreau is the aggressive and wise critic of life, the man not hornswoggled by reality, the man stepping clear of the traps that catch and destroy others. He avoids cant, detests "show," lives simply, thinks incisively. Appreciative heir to the best of the past, he creatively exploits the Now for a rich fulfillment.

The difference between this image, fashioned out of interior need and limned by a brilliant pen, and the real Thoreau does not need to be specially developed here, for this difference is implicitly indicated by many phases of my study. But we may note here that Thoreau received, from an admiring reader of *Walden,* a letter in which the reader asked to be permitted to see him. This was Thoreau's reply:

You may rely on it that you have the best of me in my books, and that I am not worth seeing personally, the stuttering, blundering clod-hopper that I am. Even poetry, you know, is in one sense an infinite brag and exaggeration. Not that I do not stand on all that I have written,—but what am I to the truth I feebly utter? (Letter to C. H. Greene, February 11, 1856 [*Familiar Letters,* p. 410])

Thoreau stands by his message but not his image of himself.

An insight into a psychological area of Thoreau as yet not discussed is afforded by a letter to Blake dated April 10, 1853. On the whole, in his writings Thoreau gives the impression of a strong and integrated ego, but he here shows an atomized, disintegrated, depersonalized ego that reminds one of Dostoevski's *Notes from the Underground.* In the Thoreau canon only the passage he wrote about the top of Mt. Ktaadn, quoted later in the "Mother-Nature" chapter, is comparable to the following:

["You are" is understood] Another kind of spiritual football,—really nameless, handleless, homeless, like myself,—a mere arena for thoughts and feelings; definite enough outwardly, indefinite more than enough inwardly. But I do not know why we should be styled "masters" or "misters"; we come so near to being anything or nothing, and seeing that we are mastered, and not wholly sorry to be mastered, by the least phenomenon. It seems to me that we are the mere creatures of thought,—one of the lowest forms of intellectual life, we men,—as the sunfish is of animal life. As yet our thoughts have acquired no definiteness nor solidity; they are purely molluscous, not vertebrate; and the height of our existence is to float upward in an ocean where the sun shines,—appearing only like a vast soup or chowder to the eyes of the immortal navigators. It is wonderful that I can be here, and you there, and that we can correspond, and do many other things, when, in fact, there is so little of us, either or both, anywhere. In a few minutes, I expect, this slight film or dash of vapor that I am will be what is called asleep,—resting: forsooth from what? Hard work? and thought? The hard work of the dandelion down, which floats over the meadow all day; the hard work of a pismire that labors to raise a hillock all day, and even by moonlight. Suddenly I can come forward into the utmost apparent distinctness, and speak with a sort of emphasis to you; and the next moment I am so faint an entity, and make so slight an impression, that nobody can find the traces of me. I try to hunt myself up and find the little of me that is discoverable is falling asleep, and then I assist and tuck it up. How can *I* starve or feed? Can *I* be said to sleep? There is not enough of me even for that. If you hear a noise,—'tain't I,—'tain't I,—as the dog says with the tin-kettle tied to his tail. I read of something happening to another the other day: how happens it that nothing ever happens to me? A dande-lion down that never alights,—settles,—blown off by a boy to see if his mother wanted him,—some divine boy in the upper pastures.

Well, if there really is another such a meteor sojourning in these spaces, I would like to ask you if you know whose estate this is that we are on? For my part I enjoy it well enough, what with the wild apples and the scenery; but I shouldn't wonder if the owner set his dog on me next . . . (*Familiar Letters*, pp. 217–218).

By way of analyzing this extraordinary letter—at the end of which, by the way, Thoreau felt he had to add, "I trust you realize what an exaggerator I am"—we may say that as a whole it shows a weakening of "the feel" of reality, a loss of the sense of the "I," and tremendous unconscious anxiety from Oedipal sources. Specifically, there is much to note. He feels he is a "spiritual foot-ball"—i.e., perhaps kicked around, mentally, and often "in the air." He is "nameless, handleless." Here we may remember that Thoreau changed his own name from David Henry to Henry David, and he had almost a mania about names, trying to learn the names of everything in nature and himself bestowing names upon places that had no name before.[25] He is "homeless." His response to the threat of being homeless—when his mother told him he could leave the family home and become a peddler—was a burst of tears. He is not a "master" but rather is mastered. He is like a sunfish and the best he can achieve is to be as food for the "immortal navigators." Now we must remember the poem "Tell Me Ye Wise Ones" with its lines "We walk mid great rela-tions feet,/What they let fall alone we eat," and we should be aware that Thoreau's father sometimes apparently figured as the Eater in Thoreau's unconscious. Proceeding, we find that Thoreau metaphorically calls himself a "slight film or dash of vapor." He occasionally used the word "mist" in such ways as to suggest that to his unconscious it was related to women, love, and death. The "dash of vapor" soon sleeps, resting from its hard work, that

25. Channing, p. 47, says that Thoreau "wanted names" for everything.

of "the dandelion down, which floats over the meadow all day." A game of Thoreau's childhood consisted of blowing off the down of a dandelion, with these words accompanying each blow, "Your mother wants you," followed by, "She doesn't want you" (J, IV, 79–80). While, of course, in the game, "Your mother wants you" means only she wants you to come home instead of playing away from home, to the unconscious this phrase and its negative could easily mean "Mother loves you" or "Mother does not love you." Thoreau's floating "over the meadow all day" like a dandelion down—his main daily activity—was unconsciously an effort to keep close to Mother, as we shall see in the "Mother-Nature" chapter following.

Next we find him telling how he is a distinct entity at times and soon after cannot be found—he loses his sense of the "I." This depersonalization probably had its source, as it often does, as defense against "the fear of organ change or loss" [26]—*i.e.,* in the case of Thoreau, very likely castration fear. The Oedipal context also supports this suggestion that castration fear may have led to this defense, whereby the "I," which so deeply fears, loses reality and thus is protected from the fear. Further, the image of the dog with the tin kettle tied to his tail, which follows next in the passage, supports it. The dog is, to Thoreau, in a castration situation, and says, " 'tain't I,—'tain't I."

The person to whom "nothing ever happens" is, psychoanalysis suggests, unconsciously homoerotic. The Oedipal source of Thoreau's homoerotism is revealed in the next sentence, where Thoreau returns to his earlier image of the dandelion down "blown off by a boy to see if his mother wanted him." And the final sentences of the passage, with their imagery of being on someone else's property and in danger of attack, carry out the Oedipal theme.

This passage, as I previously mentioned, is almost unique in Thoreau. In only one other place does he give such clear evidence of depersonalized feelings; in few other places does he depart so far from the ego-image of himself as a person and writer which

26. Edward Glover, *Psycho-Analysis* (London, 1949), p. 226.

achieved sharpest focus in a number of places in the *Journal,*
in the short essays, and in *Walden.*

Thoreau had such a passion for freedom, and his writing
powers make him seem so psychically mobile (for he had in full
measure the artist's power of dipping into the unconscious), that
we tend not to see him also as a compulsive personality. And yet,
were there no other evidence, the fourteen volumes of his *Journal*
alone clearly show how compulsive he was. Much of the *Journal*
consists precisely of "a continual coining of the present moment"
such as Emerson noted of Thoreau's conversation on a particular
day.[27] Such coinages even the literary genius of Thoreau could not
make into fine art much of the time. And though it must be
admitted that this sort of obsessive notation of present reality
can afford the basis of good science (actually doing so, to a
certain extent, for Thoreau), nevertheless it is obsessive.

Emerson provides us with a vignette on Thoreau as a compulsive type:

It is curious that Thoreau goes to a house to say with little preface
what he has just read or observed, delivers it in lump, is quite inatten-
tive to any comment or thought which any of the company offer on
the matter, nay, is merely interrupted by it, and when he has finished
his report departs with precipitation (Emerson J, IX, 34 [April 26,
1856]).[28]

Thoreau shows in numerous ways the characteristics of a compulsive, obsessional personality. He was "scrupulous, neat, pedan-
tic, meticulous, formal, punctual, and in ethical matters strict to
the point of asceticism." [29] He had a tendency to isolate ideas from

27. Emerson's *Journal,* V, 515 (May 8, 1844). Rev. John Weiss, a
classmate at Harvard, noted Thoreau "spoke with that deliberation from
which there seemed as little escape as from the pressure of the atmosphere."
("Thoreau," *Christian Examiner* [July 1865], quoted in S. A. Jones, *Pertaining to Thoreau,* p. 143.)

28. Thoreau as an obsessive talker also appears in W. S. Robinson,
"Warrington" Pen-Portraits (Boston, 1877), p. 68: "He was a great talker,
sitting with his head bent over, and carrying on the 'conversation' all by
himself."

29. B. Lewin, "Obsessional Neurosis," in S. Lorand, *Psychoanalysis
Today* (New York, 1936), p. 204.

affects arising from painful situations;[30] this is best indicated when he says, "Of acute sorrow I suppose I know comparatively little. My saddest and most genuine sorrows are apt to be but transient regrets. The place of sorrow is supplied, perchance, by a certain hard and proportionately barren indifference." [31] "Erotized thinking," generally masked by symbols, is widespread in his writings, as are evidences of reaction formations of "conscientiousness, pity and cleanliness." [32] That "lowermost layer of hysterical symptoms" that Freud noted as present in compulsives may be seen in Thoreau's development of lockjaw symptoms at the time of his brother's death.

A final reason for thinking of Thoreau as an obsessional personality is that he shows elements of unconscious libidinal regression to what is termed the "anal-sadistic" level.[33] Such regression is typical of obsessional neurotics. Perhaps the most dramatic evidence of this regression in Thoreau is provided by his interest in and literary descriptions of sand-and-clay banks having an excrementitious appearance. His interest in these banks (especially the one in the "Deep Cut" dug for the Fitchburg Railroad near Walden Pond) was great; for most of the years of the 1850's there are *Journal* entries on them. He made notes reminding himself to view them, and the view he found invigorating, rejuvenating. As examples, here are a few of his *Journal* comments:

The flowing clay on the east side is still richer today. I know of nothing so purgative of winter fumes and indigestion (J, III, 235 [January 26, 1852]).

I see where the banks have deposited great heaps, many cartloads, of clayey sand, as if they had relieved themselves of their winter's indiges-

30. Freud, *The Problem of Anxiety* (New York, 1936), pp. 71, 146.
31. Letter to Blake, May 2, 1848 (*Familiar Letters*, p. 168).
32. Channing, p. 261, says Thoreau was "intensely nice in his personal" life. Freud, pp. 60, 68.
33. His attitude is expressed in several *Journal* passages: "What have we to boast of? We are made the very sewers, the cloacae of nature" (J, II, 9 [1850]). "The roses in the front yard do not atone for the sink and pigsty and jakes in the rear" (J, IV, 133 [June 23, 1852]). See also J, IV, 15 (May 4, 1852).

tions, and it is not easy to see where they came from (J, III, 343 [March 9, 1852]).

I see the sand flowing in the Cut and hear the harp [sound made by the wind and the telegraph wire] at the same time. Who shall say that the primitive forces are not still at work? Nature has not lost her pristine vigor, neither has he who sees this (J, III, 348 [March 12, 1852]).

The sand foliage is now in its prime (J, VI, 147 [March 1, 1854]).

Still cold and blustering. I came to see the sand and subsoil in the Deep Cut, as I would to see a spring flower, some redness in the cheek of Earth (J, VIII, 232 [March 30, 1856]).

But the fullest and most interesting of his accounts, which draws from his *Journal* entries for December 31, 1851, and March 2, 1854, is in the "Spring" chapter of *Walden*. Below is quoted a part of this *Walden* account.

Few phenomena gave me more delight than to observe the forms which thawing sand and clay assume in flowing down the sides of a deep cut on the railroad through which I passed on my way to the village. . . . When the frost comes out in the spring, and even in a thawing day in the winter, the sand begins to flow down the slopes like lava, sometimes bursting out through the snow and overflowing it where no sand was to be seen before. Innumerable little streams over-lap and interlace one with another, exhibiting a sort of hybrid product, which obeys half way the law of currents, and half way that of vegetables. As it flows it takes the forms of sappy leaves or vines, making heaps of pulpy sprays a foot or more in depth, and resembling, as you look down on them, the laciniated, lobed, and imbricated thalluses of some lichens; or you are reminded of coral, of leopards' paws or birds' feet, of brains or lungs or bowels, and excrements of all kinds . . . The whole cut impressed me as if it were a cave with its stalactites laid open to the light. The various shades of the sand are singularly rich and agreeable, embracing the different iron colors, brown, gray, yellowish, and reddish . . .
The whole bank, which is from twenty to forty feet high, is some-times overlaid with a mass of this kind of foliage, or sandy rupture,

for a quarter of a mile on one or both sides, the produce of one spring day. What makes this sand foliage remarkable is its springing into existence thus suddenly. When I see on the one side the inert bank,— for the sun acts on one side first,—and on the other this luxuriant foliage, the creation of an hour, I am affected as if in a peculiar sense I stood in the laboratory of the Artist who made the world and me,— had come to where he was still at work, sporting on this bank, and with excess of energy strewing his fresh designs about. I feel as if I were nearer to the vitals of the globe, for this sandy over-flow is something such a foliaceous mass as the vitals of the animal body . . .

You see here perchance how blood-vessels are formed. If you look closely you observe that first there pushes forward from the thawing mass a stream of softened sand with a drop-like point, like the ball of a finger, feeling its way slowly and blindly downward, until at last with more heat and pressure, as the sun gets higher, the most fluid portion, in its effort to obey the law to which the most inert part also yields, separates from the latter and forms for itself a meandering channel or artery within that, in which is seen a little silvery stream glancing like lightning from one stage of pulpy leaves or branches to another, and ever and anon swallowed up in the sand . . . What is man but a mass of thawing clay? The ball of the human finger is but a drop congealed. The fingers and toes flow to their extent from the flowing mass of the body. Who knows what the human body would expand and grow to under a more genial heaven?

Thoreau then fancifully accounts for the growth of certain parts of the human body—the hand, the ear, the lip, the nose, the chin, the cheeks.

Thus it seemed that this one hillside illustrated the principle of all the operations of Nature. The Maker of this earth but patented a leaf. What Champollion will decipher this hieroglyphic for us, that we may turn over a new leaf at last? This phenomenon is more exhilarating to me than the luxuriance and fertility of vineyards. True, it is somewhat excrementitious in its character, and there is no end to the heaps of liver, lights, and bowels, as if the globe were turned wrong side outward; but this suggests at least that Nature has some bowels, and there again is mother of humanity.

In writing the literary descriptions that he combined and added

to in order to form the above passage, Thoreau was roughly in
the position of a person taking a Rorschach test, who must tell
what he "sees" in certain inkblots. What one "sees" in inkblots—
or running sand-and-clay banks—is a function of his psychological make-up. I had the above passage read, keeping hidden the
fact that Thoreau was its author, by two separate persons trained
in Rorschach-test interpretation. Each was asked to comment on
the psyche of the author. I quote the comment of one:

The creative genius who is closer to nature than to man. His unconscious drives are strong and his anal aggressive tendencies are
in conflict with his fine sensitivity. His creative power is the sub-
limation of these trends ordered by a need for exhibitionism, which
is, in turn, channelled into poetic self-expression.

The interpretation of the second Rorschach tester was substan-
tially the same.

Was Thoreau a happy man?—several critics have posed this
question. Canby (p. 104) thinks that "most of the time Thoreau
was happy," while Ethel Seybold, in *Thoreau: The Quest and
the Classics* (New Haven, 1951), p. 68, feels it necessary to remark, "Thoreau's expressions of personal unhappiness have received less attention than they deserve." Each of these critics,
it seems to me, is right. Thoreau had many sources of satisfaction
—study, nature, short trips, friends, writing—which suited his
temperament. As a whole, his life does not appear to have been
one of "quiet desperation." Yet there was more pain, sorrow, and
even quiet desperation in his life than is generally recognized. The
main sources of his unhappiness I judge to have been his failure
to achieve any wholly satisfactory friendship, his alienation from
the townspeople of Concord, and his occasional subjection by
destructive unconscious forces. Physical sickness should also be
added to the list.

On the subject of friendship, let it here be sufficient to quote
one *Journal* entry as expressive of the unhappiness he often felt
for lack of friends: "Woe to him who wants a companion, for he

is unfit to be the companion even of himself" (J, II, 33 [1850]).

By the town of Concord generally, Thoreau was given "a hard time." It is true that he was respected and in varying degrees liked by the other writers of Concord, residing permanently or off and on—Emerson, Alcott, Channing, Hawthorne. This holds true for at least parts of the families of some of the solid folk too, the Hoars and Hosmers particularly come to mind. But, still, he did not "belong" to the town's people as he did to its fauna and flora.

Canby (p. 10) observes that of the Concord "Social Club," which was "perhaps indicative of such social discrimination as existed in the upper register," Emerson was a member, but not Thoreau or Alcott. Now I do not know if Thoreau was ever asked to join and refused the invitation—this is possible—but I do know he does some indirect sniping at the club in his later years.[34] And Channing, in some vague sentences, seems to imply that the "upper crust" did not esteem Thoreau:

With these plain ways, no person was usually easier misapplied [placed in the wrong social status?] by the cultivated class than Thoreau. Some of those afflicted [by snobbery?] about him have started with the falsetto of humming a void estimate on his life, his manners, sentiments, and all that in him was (p. 31).

To many of the ordinary people of Concord he was a loafer, a misfit, an object of amusement,[35] or, worse, an object of suspicion or hatred. In the *Journal* for June 22, 1840, he writes: "Nothing can shock a truly brave man but dullness. One can tolerate many things. What mean these sly, suspicious looks, as if you were an odd fish, a piece of crockery-ware to be tenderly handled?" (J, I, 148) At the time he and Edward Hoar accidentally set many acres of woods on fire, Concordians were very angry with him. Canby (p. 211) says Thoreau was saved from prosecution because he was with the son of an eminent family, and for a long

34. See J, XII, 13 (March 4, 1859) and J, XIV, 261 (November 23, 1860) especially; the indirect chiding and lecture of the second entry continue on November 24, 26, and 28.

35. J. K. Hosmer, *The Last Leaf* (New York, 1912), p. 235. Thoreau noted that the town regarded him as a loafer in J, IV, 253 (July 24, 1852).

time afterwards Thoreau was taunted with the words "burnt woods."

Thoreau tells of three episodes in which he was watched or taunted while on his nature walks.[36] Of the three, the episode occurring on October 20, 1858, is perhaps the most interesting because of its clear revelation of his ego-defenses at work. The passage essentially goes like this:

As I approached the pond, I saw a hind in a potato-field (digging potatoes), who stood stock-still for ten minutes to gaze at me in mute astonishment, till I had sunk into the woods . . . and when I emerged again, there he was, motionless still, on the same spot, with his eye on me . . . I must hasten away or he'll lose his day. I was as indifferent to his eye-shot as a tree walking, for I am used to such things . . . He stirs the earth; I stir him . . . But he shall not spoil my day . . . Talk of reaping machines! I did not go into that field at all. I did not meddle with the potatoes. He was the only crop I gathered at a glance. Perchance he thought, "I harvest potatoes; he harvests me!" (J, XI, 230–231)

From the contemptuous word "hind"—very unusual in his work—through his solicitude for the farmer's losing his day, from his assertion of indifference through his calling the farmer a reaping machine, and finally from his assertion of innocence through his ascription to the farmer of the fantastic "perchance" thought at the end, we see Thoreau defending his ego from the hurt it had received.

As a generalization with exceptions, it is true that "There is no doubt about it, the neighbors didn't like Thoreau . . . But there is no doubt either that Thoreau didn't like the neighbors."[37] Their lives and ways were too different for mutual appreciation. While he asserted his independence of them and difference from them, still he was wounded by them. "I must confess I have felt mean enough when asked how I was to act on society . . ." (J, I,

36. J, III, 199–200 (January 17, 1852); J, V, 92–93 (April 4, 1853); J, XI, 230–231 (October 20, 1858).

37. Raymond Adams, "Thoreau and His Neighbors," *Thoreau Society Bulletin*, No. 44 (Summer 1953), 1.

350 [March 26, 1842]). His townspeople's response to him was no psychological support; on the contrary, they made up a destructive human environment. Toward this environment he would retaliate in phrases like this: "Society, man, has no prize to offer me that can tempt me; not one" (J, III, 461 [April 24, 1852]). But there were deeper, Oedipal and pre-Oedipal sources of his attitude of alienation and hostility—sources that were the basic cause of the town's feeling toward him. These sources were the same ones that made him a solitary, limited his powers (but not his dreams) of friendship, created the ebb tides in his feeling of well-being, and in fact influenced—as they filtered through his genetic inheritance—every aspect of his life.

Thoreau once wrote to his sister Helen, "To speak or do anything that shall concern mankind, one must speak and act as if well, or from that grain of health which he has left." [38] On the whole, he follows his own advice, and his writings are known for their vigor and confidence. Whatever moods of deepest negation he may have had, he either did not write or could not write during them, so nothing much can be known of them. But that he was the object of substantial self-destructive forces there can be no question. It could be posited from the fact that he was very neurotic; it can be proved from much that he tells us.

38. October 18, 1843. Harding, "Correspondence," p. 294.

★

"Mother-Nature"

Forgive my English plainness of speech. Your love for, and intimate acquaintance with, nature is ancillary to some affection you have not yet discovered (Letter of Thomas Cholmondeley to Thoreau, December 16, 1856).

I am engaged to Concord and my own private pursuits by 10,000 ties, and it would be suicide to rend them (Letter of Thoreau to Ricketson, September 23, 1856).

Sometimes a mortal feels in himself Nature, not his Father but his Mother stirs within him, and he becomes immortal with her immortality. From time to time she claims kindredship with us, and some globule from her veins steals up into our own (*A Week on the Concord and Merrimack Rivers,* p. 404).

No certain explanation can be provided for Thoreau's devoted feeling for nature. But a psychological point of view can offer at least a suggestive explanation of this central fact of his life.

Thoreau's love of nature apparently was, in his unconscious, at once an expression of his fixation on his mother and his defense against that fixation, as well as against fear of loss of love. His

Reprinted from Raymond D. Gozzi's *"Tropes and Figures: A Psychological Study of Henry David Thoreau"* (Doctoral Dissertation, New York University, 1957), pp. 229–250, by permission of Raymond D. Gozzi.

touching poem of separation and loss, "Sic Vita," and the episode of his crying when his mother told him he could leave home to make his fortune, suggest how much he feared to lose his mother's love. Mother-nature seems to have been the material-spiritual object which he could steadily love without suffering rebuff. Nature was, psychologically, his particular Virgin Mother.

In his *New Introductory Lectures* ([New York, 1933], p. 190), Freud tells of how an unnamed famous man said to him, ". . . I have never had any sexual feeling for my mother," and how he replied, "But there's no need at all for you to have been conscious of it, such processes are unconscious in grown-up people." This answer satisfied the "famous man." Supposing, for the sake of convenience, that it satisfies (at least as an hypothesis) my readers, I shall proceed.

Thoreau's response to nature was not like other men's—let us realize that clearly at the start. Of course, a few other people are comparable to him in respect to nature-love; but they are few indeed compared to the vast number who can hardly imagine why nature should be adored, who find it pleasant enough, even exhilarating and inspiring on occasion, yes, but who do not exist with it as a main center of emotional polarity. Thoreau affirmed, "All nature is my bride" (J, IX, 337 [April 22, 1857]). But men in general choose real brides, not nature.

Thoreau was taking his own advice, "Dwell as near as possible to the channel in which your life flows," when he spent his free time with nature.[1] And in this he was an epicure of epicures. Nature provided him with the steady source of pleasure that their families, work, food, drink, and ordinary recreation provide for other men.

In a healthy state . . . I find myself in perfect connection with nature, and the perception, or remembrance even, of any natural phenomenon is attended with gentle pleasurable excitement. . . . Each man's necessary path . . . is the way to the deepest joys he is sus-

---

1. *Journal* (Boston, 1906), referred to hereinafter as J, V, 16–17 (March 10, 1853).

ceptible of; though he converses only with moles and fungi and dis-
graces his relatives, it is of no matter if he knows what is steel to
his flint (J, X, 188 [November 18, 1857]).

I see that my neighbors look with compassion on me, that they think
it is a mean and unfortunate destiny which makes me to walk in
these fields and sail on this river alone. But so long as I find here
the only real elysium, I cannot hesitate in my choice (J, IX, 121
[October 18, 1856]).

Nature was his source of joy, of "gentle pleasurable excitement,"
it set off the sparks in him, it was the steel for his particular flint.
As for the disgrace to his relatives, that hurt was felt no doubt
mainly by his mother—and this helped mask the unconscious
meaning of his nature-love as well as provide an outlet for hostility
for her.

    At the risk of laboring it, the point that Thoreau's love of
nature was a function of his own psychology must be stressed.
Channing (p. 15) thought Thoreau had a peculiar interest in the
place of his birth—"Concord . . . The phrase local associations,
or the delightful word home, do not explain his absorbing love
for a town with few picturesque attractions beside its river."
The best that Channing has to offer by way of explanation is to
say the "materials" for Thoreau's work were there—"no better
place for his business." Perhaps true enough, but why was nature
his business? What was the source of the "peculiar interest"?

    Thoreau found in nature, among other things, the emotional
fulfillment and health he failed to derive from ordinary human
relations.[2] "You who complain that I am cold," he said, "find
nature cold. To me she is warm" (J, II, 147 [December 21,
1851]). "In society you will not find health, but in nature."[3] He

---

    2. Robert Francis stresses this point, that frustrated human relation-
ships made Thoreau need nature as a refuge, in "Thoreau's Mask of
Serenity," *Forum,* CVII (January 1947), 72–77.
    3. "The Natural History of Massachusetts," *Writings,* IV, p. 105. Mon-
cure Conway, who walked in the woods with Thoreau, noted his face
"shone with a light I had not seen in the village" ("Thoreau," *Fraser's
Magazine,* LXXIII [April 1866], 462).

wrote, "My pulse must beat with Nature" [4]—when it did not, he felt unquiet, taxed, separated from what he found normalizing and health-giving.

Open all your pores and bathe in all the tides of Nature, in all her streams and oceans, at all seasons. Miasma and infection are from within, not without . . . Drink of each season's influence as of a vial, a true panacea of all remedies mixed for your especial use . . . For all Nature is doing her best each moment to make us well. Do not resist her. With the least inclination to be well, we should not be sick . . . Why, "nature" is but another name for health. . . . (J, V, 394–395 [August 23, 1853]).[5]

Nature here is a sort of feminine hound of heaven seeking us out to make us drink of her health-giving resources; it is like a mother feeding and caring for her sick child.

That nature appears like a mother to the human race in general is certified by the widespread use of the phrase "mother Nature." But with Thoreau "mother Nature" was more than a simple image having slight psychological implications; with him mother-nature was in a significant way a substitutive image for his mother, and as such it gave rise to a host of attitudes toward nature that are alien to the ordinary person, who is not so oriented.

The fact that Mrs. Thoreau was a nature-lover was probably a determining cause of his unconscious choice of nature as a symbol for her. Freud tells us that Little Hans (subject of a famous study) was helped in choosing a horse as a symbol for his father by the fact that the father played "horsie" with the child.[6] Neither Little Hans nor Thoreau was aware that he had displaced to something else emotions relating to a parent.

4. J, II, 268 (June 22, 1851).
5. This passage, by the way, follows some paragraphs in which Thoreau tells of seeing a poke stem grove and the excitement it caused in him. (These paragraphs, slightly altered, he incorporated in "Autumnal Tints.") It seems that nature here afforded him some release from castration-anxiety.
6. *The Problem of Anxiety*, p. 42. See also "Analysis of a Phobia of a Five-Year-Old Boy," in Freud's *Collected Papers* (New York, 1924), III, 149–288.

We cannot, of course, equate Mrs. Thoreau and Thoreau's image of nature more than very roughly. Thoreau's literary and scientific image was constituted of a good deal more than his image of his mother; reality entered in, as well as wish-fulfillment (to have a *better* mother) and other elements. Still, at times Mrs. Thoreau seems to appear behind some of Thoreau's statements about nature. Here, for instance, we may be seeing the strict superego of his mother:

I would meet the morning and evening on very sincere ground . . . Something like this is the secret charm of Nature's demeanor toward us, strict conscientiousness and disregard of us when we have ceased to have regard for ourselves. She can never offend us. How true she is!—and never swerves. In her most genial moment her laws are as steadfastly and relentlessly fulfilled . . . as in her sternest moments (J, I, 191 [February 3, 1841]).

The mother that he was so emotionally dependent on that he could not leave home appears reflected in these lines from his poem "Nature":

> For I had rather be thy child
> And pupil in the forest wild
> Than be the king of men elsewhere
> And most sovereign slave of care
> To have one moment of thy dawn
> Than share the city's year forlorn.
> Some still work give me to do
> Only be it near to you
> (*Collected Poems of Henry Thoreau*,
> ed. Carl Bode [Chicago, 1943], p. 216).[7]

A south wind on January 8, 1842, melts, he says, both the snow and him, and it perfumes the air:

Then is she my mother earth. I derive a real vigor from the scent of the gale wafted over the naked ground, as from strong meats, and

7. The conventional rhetoric here should not lead us to think this is mere "literary convention"; the personal validity of these sentiments is supported by the facts of his life.

realize again how man is the pensioner of Nature. We are always conciliated and cheered when we are fed by [such] an influence, and our needs are felt to be part of the domestic economy of Nature (J, I, 315).

When he feared he was not to be part of the "domestic economy," he cried. His home, too, was a "pension," [8] and he a pensioner who paid for food and lodging.

Mrs. Thoreau as the aggressive, rejecting, hostile mother appears to have some part in Thoreau's famous passage describing his feelings while alone near the summit of Mt. Ktaadn. He has the sense of having gone when he should not go, and nature, like a "stepmother," sternly chides him:

It is vast, Titanic, and such as man never inhabits. Some part of the beholder, even some vital part, seems to escape through the loose grating of his ribs as he descends. He is more lone than you can imagine. There is less of substantial thought and fair understanding in him than in the plains where men inhabit. His reason is dispersed and shadowy, more thin and subtile, like the air. Vast, Titanic, inhuman Nature has got him at disadvantage, caught him alone, and pilfers him of some of his divine faculty. She does not smile on him as in the plains. She seems to say sternly, Why came ye here before your time. This ground is not prepared for you. Is it not enough that I smile in the valleys? . . . I cannot pity nor fondle thee here, but forever relentlessly drive thee hence to where I *am* kind. Why seek me where I have not called thee, and then complain because you find me but a stepmother? Shouldst thou freeze or starve, or shudder thy life away, here is no shrine, nor altar, nor any access to my ear . . . The tops of mountains are among the unfinished parts of the globe, whither it is a slight insult to the gods to climb and pry into their secrets, and try their effect on our humanity. Only daring and insolent men, perchance, go there. Simple races and savages do not climb mountains,—their tops are sacred and mysterious tracts never visited by them (*Maine Woods,* pp. 70–72).

8. Thoreau several times writes of Nature's halls being swept and preparations being made for a new occupant. See J, VII, 204 (February 21, 1855) and *A Week,* p. 335.

A few pages later in the same book he writes more about Nature "vast and drear and inhuman"—

It was Matter, vast, terrific,—not his Mother Earth that we have heard of, not for him to tread on or be buried in,—no, it were being too familiar even to let his bones lie there,—the home, this, of Necessity and Fate. There was clearly felt the presence of a force not bound to be kind to man. It was a place for heathenism and superstitious rites (*Maine Woods,* pp. 77–78).

This is the "other side" of Mother Nature, when she is not really a mother—but represents Matter, the basic stuff "of what God saw fit to make this world." Thinking of Matter, Thoreau then writes:

I stand in awe of my body, this matter to which I am bound has become so strange to me. I fear not spirits, ghosts, of which I am one,—*that* my body might,—but I fear bodies, I tremble to meet them. What is this Titan that has possession of me? Talk of mysteries! Think of our life in nature,—daily to be shown matter, to come in contact with it,—rocks, trees, wind on our cheeks! the *solid* earth! the *actual* world! the *common sense! Contact! Contact! Who* are we? *where* are we?

This passage reminds one of that quoted in the "Personality" chapter above in showing loss of sense of reality and depersonalization. And like it, it may well have had an acute attack of castration-anxiety as perhaps its main cause. Thoreau was doing something that he sensed deep down was forbidden. Anxiety pervades his picture. Anxiety gives him the feeling that "some part of the beholder, even some vital part, seems to escape between the loose grating of his ribs";[9] that his "reason is dispersed." Anxiety puts the words into Mother-Nature's chiding mouth, gives him his sense of alienation from his body.

What is forbidden—to cause such anxiety—about climbing the highest mountain in Maine? Of course, only that which Thoreau's

9. The lungs seem to be suggested here, though it could also be the heart. If it was the lungs he was thinking of, here is a possible connection between his anxiety and his tuberculosis.

unconscious said was forbidden. Again hypothesizing the Oedipus complex gives us a path to understanding. To Thoreau's unconscious, I suggest, climbing so high was like taking possession of Mother Nature, challenging the father.[10] Because of his anxiety his conscious feeling is that the reverse has occurred: a Titan has "possession" of him. Thus, while symbolically filling the masculine role, he is forced into fantasying himself in a feminine role. Linked to Matter-Mother-Nature, unkind mother-nature, he loses through (unconscious) castration-anxiety his faculty of reason and ordinary sense of reality, falling into a depersonalized state. The mountaintop was "a place for heathenism and superstitious rites" because the whole venture of climbing to it called out archaic impulses and fears.

My understanding is that Thoreau never did climb to the very top of Mt. Ktaadn but turned back before he reached the final summit.

Mother-nature is never imaged again as being quite so hostile as here in Thoreau's works. But several animal images he uses show the hostile side did come to his mind at times. Nature he once called an "old she-wolf" [11] and several times, in varied forms, "the great leopard mother." [12]

Darwin's nature, as represented in Tennyson's phrase, "red in

10. In her very interesting essay, Fannie Eckstorm wrote that Thoreau "knew the traditions of the place [Mt. Ktaadn], the awe and veneration with which the Indians regarded it as the dwelling place of Pamola, their god of thunder, who was angry at any invasion of his home and resented it in fogs and sudden storms." She sees Thoreau as "invading the throne of Pamola the Thunderer as Prometheus harried Zeus of his lightnings" ("Thoreau's 'Maine Woods,'" *Atlantic Monthly,* CII [August 1908], 249).

11. Quoted in Channing, p. 94.

12. J, XII, 97 (March 28, 1859). See also "Walking," *Writings,* V, 237, where he uses an image involving a leopard for nature. In *The Maine Woods,* pp. 203–204, he senses a hostile force in the woods which he fantasies as an "invisible glutton" ready, ape-like, "to drop from the trees and gnaw at the heart of the solitary hunter. . . ."

Nature also figures as a hen who "broods us" (J, II, 372 [August 5, 1851]). A similar image may be found in *The Moon,* p. 36. The appearance of the ground once led Thoreau to ask, "Is the earth in her monthly courses?" (J, IV, 288 [August 8, 1852]). Nature figures as a cow in rut on May 20, 1856 (J, VIII, 349).

tooth and claw," hardly figures in Thoreau's writing. Once, however, telling of a still-alive turtle that had been half gouged out by, probably, a bird with a very powerful beak, he exclaimed: "Such is Nature, who gave one creature a taste or yearning for another's entrails as its favorite tidbit!!" (J, XIII, 346–347 [June 11, 1860]) The two exclamation points he uses here—and only rarely elsewhere—well enough indicate how unusual this thought was to him. Nature was primarily his comforter, not disturber.[13]

Among nature's comforting psychological uses to Thoreau was the oral satisfaction it provided. Some of his images suggest that, to one of his deepest levels, nature was the equivalent of milk, representative to the infant of food and love. Thinking one day of what his business in life was, Thoreau expressed himself this way: "I make it my business to extract from Nature whatever nutriment she can furnish me, though at the risk of endless iteration. I milk the sky and the earth" (J, V, 478 [November 3, 1853]). Another time, thinking not of nature but of his life's difficulties and loneliness, he wrote:

The world is a cow that is hard to milk,—life does not come so easy, —and oh, how thinly it is watered ere we get it! But the young bantling calf, he will get at it. There is no way so direct. This is to earn one's living by the sweat of his brow. It is a little like joining a community, this life, to such a hermit as I am. . . .[14]

And "our life without love," he felt, "is like coke and ashes,— like the cocoanut in which the milk is dried up" (J, I, 348 [March 25, 1842]). Nature provided him with most of the "milk" he got.

Nature as a source of fantasied oral satisfaction also appears in some nonlactial images. One day, in *The Maine Woods* (p. 143), he tells us, "For my dessert, I took a large slice of the Chesuncook woods, and took a hearty draught of its waters with all my senses."

13. Robert Francis (*loc. cit.*) thinks Thoreau never really acknowledged the evil in nature, needing it kind and good.

14. Letter to Emerson,, November 14, 1847. "The Correspondence of Henry David Thoreau," ed. Walter Harding, Doctoral Dissertation (Rutgers University, 1950), pp. 372–373.

He as an "eater" of nature appears in his *Journals* several times. On January 31, 1854, he writes, "I go a-budding like a partridge"; later in this same entry we see, "If you would know what are my winter thoughts, look for them in the partridge's crop" (J, VI, 88–89). On December 12, 1851, he bursts out with, "Ah, dear nature, the mere remembrance, after a short forgetfulness, of the pine woods! I come to it as a hungry man to a crust of bread" (J, III, 133).[15]

Thoreau had various fantasies about eating woodchucks, the sap of trees, and other items, and he experimented with eating unusual plants.

An astonishing passage was written by Thoreau on August 17, 1851, which I quote in full:

Ah, the very brooks seem fuller of reflections than they were! Ah, such provoking sybylline sentences they are! The shallowest is all at once unfathomable. How can that depth be fathomed where a man may see himself reflected? The rill I stopped to drink at I drink in more than I expected. I satisfy and still provoke the thirst of thirsts. Nut Meadow Brook where it crosses the road beyond Jenny Dugan's that was. I do not drink in vain. I mark that brook as if I had swallowed a water snake that would live in my stomach. I have swallowed something worth the while. The day is not what it was before I stooped to drink. Ah, I shall hear from that draught! It is not in vain that I have drunk. I have drunk an arrowhead. It flows from where all fountains rise.

How many ova have I swallowed? Who knows what will be hatched within me? There were some seeds of thought, methinks, floating in that water, which are expanding in me. The man must not drink of the running streams, the living waters, who is not prepared to have all nature reborn in him,—to suckle monsters. The snake in my stomach lifts his head to my mouth at the sound of running water. When was it that I swallowed a snake? I have got rid of the snake in my stomach. I drank of stagnant waters once. That accounts for it. I caught him by the throat and drew him out, and had a well day after all. Is there not such a thing as getting rid

15. See also J, XII, 67 (March 19, 1859).

of the snake which you have swallowed when young, when thought-
less you stooped and drank at stagnant waters, which has worried
you in your waking hours and in your sleep ever since, and appro-
priated the life that was yours? Then catch him boldly by the head
and draw him out, though you may think his tail be curled around
your vitals (J, II, 392–393).

If we accept all the metaphors here as Thoreau consciously
intended them, the passage is understandable enough, though
the author seems to have tried to do too much at one time with
his snake image. He tells us he got rid of the snake in his stomach
—of his inner disquietude—as a result of the psychological clari-
fication he experienced after enjoying the pure waters of Nut
Meadow Brook. He "had a well day after all." But when he
expands his thought to refer not to a day's ills but a life's—
here he does not get rid of the snake but only advises himself to
do so at all costs. To be observed also is his first using the snake
image to reflect something good ("I have swallowed something
worth the while"), and then reversing it as a symbol to make it
reflect something bad.

Basic to this passage is the unconscious idea that both good
and bad happen to us because of what we orally incorporate. We
can get rid of the bad by oral discharge. Also involved are the
childhood theory of sex that impregnation is oral and a feminine
identification—carried in the words "hatched," "reborn," and
"suckle," as well as in the idea of the snake living in his stomach.[16]

Several other times in Thoreau's *Journals* we find him very
exhilarated by something he has put in his mouth. Twice, at
least, berries had this effect on him. On July 11, 1852, he writes
of how he has been "inspired through the palate." "After I had

16. These strands of unconscious ideas, here separated, are mixed in
the complex whole of the passage, and I realize I have not gone far in
explaining it. To go a little further, I suggest that the snake as a breast-
phallic symbol at first implies good milk and release from castration-fear,
and then it implies bad milk and the source of castration-fear—which can
be eliminated by castration.

been eating these simple, wholesome, ambrosial fruits on this high hillside, I found my senses whetted, I was young again . . ." (J, IV, 219). And a passage in which he deifies Nature ("We pluck and eat in remembrance of Her. It is a sacrament, a communion. The not-forbidden fruits which no serpent tempts us to taste") is a reflection arising from his eating berries (J, V, 349 [July 30, 1853]). Were unconscious memories of feeding at the breast, berries equalling, to the unconscious, the nipple, stirred up, releasing euphoric feeling and the early sense of omnipotence that infants have? This would appear to be the explanation.[17]

The child at the breast is related to its mother very much as Thoreau was emotionally related to nature. "Henry talks about Nature," Canby (p. 90) quotes Madam Hoar, mother of Senator Hoar, as saying, "just as if she'd been born and brought up in Concord." He personalized nature, and, according to his friend Edward Hoar, he "seemed to infuse himself into her." [18] Alcott called Thoreau "a son of nature," adding, "He seems one with things, of Nature's essence and core . . . Perhaps he has the profoundest passion for it of any one living. . . ." [19] But these observations of his contemporaries merely support what any reader of Thoreau's works can see for himself—that Thoreau's emotional life was bound up with some deep image of nature.[20] This image of nature, I think, was a presentation acceptable to his ego of a deeper, unconscious image of his mother. In "Walking," Thoreau laments that "we are so early weaned from her [nature's] breast to society." This "wrong" he sought, unconsciously, to rectify during much of his life. Sanborn (1917) quotes Channing as saying of Thoreau, "He loved Nature in the lump. He had the filial feeling, the veneration of a son for his mother" (p. 341). In nature Thoreau found his mother again,

17. After being jailed by the state, Thoreau went on a huckleberrying party, he says.
18. Quoted in Edward Emerson, p. 118.
19. "The Forester," *Atlantic Monthly,* IX (April 1862), 158.
20. One of his most interesting statements expressing passion for nature may be found in J, III, 95 (November 7, 1851).

the mother of his infancy; he encompassed both with the same feeling, they became, in his emotion, identical.[21]

Just when Thoreau's passion for nature began cannot be determined precisely. Whatever the date, Thoreau tells us in the "Solitude" chapter of *Walden* of an experience that confirmed and settled him in this orientation of his emotions. Here is what he says:

I have never felt lonesome, or in the least oppressed by a sense of solitude, but once, and that was a few weeks after I came to the woods, when, for an hour, I doubted if the near neighborhood of man was not essential to a serene and healthy life. To be alone was something unpleasant. But I was at the same time conscious of a slight insanity in my mood, and seemed to foresee my recovery. In the midst of a gentle rain while these thoughts prevailed, I was suddenly sensible of such sweet and beneficent society in Nature, in the very pattering of the drops, and in every sound and sight around my house, an infinite and unaccountable friendliness all at once like an atmosphere sustaining me, as made the fancied advantages of human neighborhood insignificant, and I have never thought of them since. Every little pine needle expanded and swelled with sympathy and befriended me. I was so distinctly made aware of the presence of something kindred to me, even in scenes which we are accustomed to call wild and dreary, and also that the nearest of blood to me and humanest was not a person nor a villager, that I thought no place could ever be strange to me again.—

> "Mourning untimely consumes the sad;
> Few are their days in the land of the living,
> Beautiful daughter of Toscar."

In this passage we note that the event occurred "a few weeks" after Thoreau went to live by himself in the hut beside Walden Pond. The earliest excitement of taking up a new mode of life was over and the forces dragging him back to the old were asserting themselves. A time for coming to some sort of terms with his new reality had arrived. Thoreau felt "a slight insanity" in

21. This phrasing is adapted from Freud's *Delusion and Dream* (New York, 1919), p. 158.

his mood; the unconscious pressures on him were very great, threatening the control of his ego. Next we note that he says he foresaw his recovery; it appears that his mind knew its goal and was giving him an intimation of success in achieving a new psychic orientation. This orientation then is told of. Thoreau felt Nature's "sweet and beneficent society"; he felt "an infinite and unaccountable friendliness all at once like an atmosphere sustaining him"; he felt the "presence of something kindred" to him. Finally he states, ". . . the nearest of blood to me and humanest was not a person nor a villager"—it was the kindred Presence of Nature. This experience may well have been decisive in turning what Ellery Channing had predicted—to Thoreau dated March 5, 1845—in a letter would be a self-destructive period by Walden Pond into the constructive period it seems to have been.

After this experience in which important inner changes took place, the love and sense of relatedness his family, and friends, had supplied in insufficient measure to satisfy his needs were supplied in larger part than before by Nature's presence. Thoreau, characteristically exaggerating, asserts that the "advantages of human neighborhood" became "insignificant"; this was more true at the ecstatic moment than it actually later was. We know that he never did deprive himself—even while he lived by Walden Pond—of the "advantages of human neighborhood" for more than a few days at a time, he could be mournfully lonely, and he apparently gladly forgot the Presence of Nature when he could revel in the Presence of his Family in the months before his death.

Referring for a moment to the last sentence of the *Walden* passage, I bring up the strange contrast Thoreau makes in it: ". . . the nearest of blood to me and humanest was not a person nor a villager. . . ." What does he mean by "a person"? He may mean a human being as a separate entity, as against one as a social unit. I offer, however, that "a person" really means "a person dear to me"—he probably had in mind a member of the family or a close friend.

The quoted poem that finishes the paragraph is appropriate then, for several reasons. Most obviously, it ends the experience, which had to do with loneliness, by saying sadness leads to death; implicit is the adjuration to be joyful. And the means for being joyful though alone is now present; nature has just become a surrogate for loved people. The theme of joy is taken up in the next passage in the book, beginning, "Some of my pleasantest hours. . . ." Secondly, the poem fits in where it is because it acts as a kind of self-justification for the displacement of those who should not be displaced and who cannot be without guilt. In concluding comment about this poem, I observe that by using it, Thoreau identifies for the moment with a feminine figure, Malvina, daughter of Toscar, of the Ossianic poems.

In his book, J. W. Krutch made some statements that appear, on the whole, to support my understanding of this episode of Thoreau's life. Krutch spoke of Thoreau's effort to get into sympathetic relation with an intellectual group, including the Emerson household and Mrs. Emerson's sister, Mrs. Lucy Jackson Brown.

What drove him toward Walden was . . . not what is ordinarily called disappointment in love [for Mrs. Emerson or Mrs. Brown] nor anything much like it. Instead it was primarily the failure of sympathy between him and the only group with whom sympathy had seemed possible. There was no one except himself to whom he could turn (p. 67).

Krutch seems to me right in thinking of this situation as the cause of the trip. But Thoreau's need for a sympathetic relation and his inability to find one had their basic source in his inability to come to valid terms with himself in relation to his own family. Mrs. Emerson and Mrs. Brown served as mother-substitutes, but Henry's problem with his own mother was still there. After a short time at Walden Pond a third and more satisfactory mother-substitute, one that he had established as such long before, came to his aid—Mother Nature.

And although at times he lost his sense of relation to nature —once even being guilty of apostasy in a threnodic passage beginning, "We soon get through with Nature. She excites an expectation which she cannot satisfy" [22]—on the whole, Nature supported him well and long. It served him as completely as religion serves many people, as the following quotation shows:

To insure health, a man's relation to Nature must come very near to a personal one; he must be conscious of a friendliness in her; when human friends fail or die, she must stand in the gap for him. I cannot conceive of any life worth the name, unless there is a certain tender relation with Nature . . . I do not see that I can live tolerably without affection for Nature. If I feel no softening toward the rocks, what do they signify? (J, X, 252 [January 23, 1858])

Nature as his form of religion is also pointed up in his statement of what the phrase "Remember thy Creator in the days of thy youth" means. To him it means, "lay up a store of natural influences" (J, II, 330 [July 21, 1851]).

Nature served him as more than a practical alternative to religion; it provided him with that "prairie for outlaws" that released him from anxiety's inner constrictions and left his spirits "elastic and buoyant." [23] It provided him with his best material for the "perceptive 'taking in' " that is an oral component of all creative work.[24] And through its use as "tropes and symbols"— as well as flat scientific fact—he expressed a personality in both life and literature.

22. This passage continues: "The merest child which has rambled into a copsewood dreams of a wilderness so wild and strange and inexhaustible as Nature can never show him." He then decides the fault is in him, since he sees only what is in himself. In the past he knew real joy (J, VI, 293–294 [May 23, 1854]).

23. Storms Higginson, *Harvard Magazine* (May 1862), as reprinted in S. A. Jones, *Pertaining to Thoreau*, p. 120.

24. Daniel Schneider, *The Psychoanalyst and the Artist* (New York, 1950), p. 189.

✪

"Years of Decay and Disappointment?"

"The mass of men lead lives of quiet desperation. What is called resignation is confirmed desperation. A stereotyped but unconscious despair is concealed under what are called the games and amusements of mankind. There is no play in them, for this comes after work. But it is a characteristic of wisdom not to do desperate things."

This is not only Thoreau's most notorious statement; it is also his fundamental charge against his fellow men. He repeated it in his books and essays, in his letters, and, one gathers, in his talk. On the other hand, he never ceased to assert that men should live with faith, hope, and love, because, he said, life was full of promise: "Men esteem truth remote, in the outskirts of the system, behind the farthest star, before Adam and after the last man. In eternity there is indeed something true and sublime. But all these times and places and occasions are now and here. God, himself, culminates in the present moment, and will never be more divine in the lapse of all ages."

The whirligig of time brings in its revenges: some thoughtful critics claim that Thoreau himself lost faith in the years after Walden Pond, wasted his time in fruitless work, and declined into the confirmed desperation called resignation:

Reprinted from *The Thoreau Centennial,* ed. Walter Harding (Albany: State University of New York Press, 1964), pp. 53–64. Copyright © 1964 by State University of New York. The essay was originally entitled "Thoreau: Years of Decay and Disappointment?"

Thoreau, isolated in America, his wits straying through the endless and utterly formless reaches of a transcendental Journal did not end his literary career as happily as Flaubert and Stevenson, . . . and Pater . . . ended theirs. That [his] main product was nothing, and his main effort vain, his own Journal best betrays.[1]

The last decade of Thoreau's life was "a decade of increasingly frequent crises, the testimony of which was all too clear in the thirteen *Journals* of the years from 1850 to 1861. These *Journals* record the desperation of the spiritual seeker who has lost his communion.[2]

A consecutive reading of the last portions of the *Journal* conveys the intolerable anguish of his sense "that there hath passed away a glory from the earth." By 1850 . . . he was already frightened. . . . By 1852 the agony is becoming intense. . . . Hence the fury . . . in 1853. . . . This was whistling to keep courage up, but toward the end he could hardly whistle.[3]

In support of these statements, the critics point primarily to the thirteen volumes of the *Journals* from 1850 to 1861. In them, Thoreau regrets that he has lost the ecstasy of his younger days and complains that scientific observation prevents him from experiencing Nature with his whole being. The critics see him as unsettled, unhappy, and drawn in opposite directions. And, they add, the *Journal* reflects his sad plight indirectly. Pages and pages of identifications, and lists of flora and fauna, and innumerable measurements are very dull stuff, and he who made them but never used them must have been desperately aware that he could never use them and that his work was coming to nothing. In addition, some claim that his philosophy was so unsound that it must inevitably have brought him to spiritual and emotional bankruptcy; finally, even *Walden* is offered as evidence of unhappiness.

There are other judgments, however, by other thoughtful critics:

1. Mark Van Doren, *Henry David Thoreau, A Critical Study* (New York, 1916), pp. 84, 109.
2. Sherman Paul, *The Shores of America* (Urbana, 1958), p. 256.
3. Perry Miller, *Consciousness in Concord* (Boston, 1958), pp. 183–184.

Ecstasies were rare with him in these years, nostalgia for his more impressionable youth frequent, but the joy of free observation was constant. . . . For a man of his tastes, his temperament, and his philosophy, life had arranged itself ideally.[4]

The *Journal* is, after all, the most important part of the residuum of his life. . . . Here is a record of the use which he made of his time, of his sensibilities, and of his intelligence. And whatever the recording angel may think, whatever the posterity which remembers him may think, there seems to be no reasonable doubt that he himself regarded his life as a private success, however much it may have been a public failure. . . . there is no evidence that Thoreau ever found his life other than rewarding and sweet.[5]

My purpose is to show why I think these judgments right and the others wrong.

Of course, as he grew older, Thoreau found changes and losses as he compared the days of youth and of maturity; no reflective adult could fail to do so. William Butler Yeats, famous and admired, lamented at the age of forty-nine:

For some months now I have lived with my own youth and childhood . . . and I am sorrowful and disturbed . . . when I think of all the books I have read, and of the wise words I have heard spoken, and of the anxiety I have given to parents and grandparents, and of the hopes that I have had, all life weighed in the scales of my own life seems to me a preparation for something that never happens.[6]

Thoreau said: The youth gets together his materials to build a bridge to the moon . . . and at length the middle-aged man concludes to build a wood-shed with them (July 14, 1852).

Wordsworth regretted in his ode:

It is not now as it hath been of yore;
Turn wheresoe'er I may

4. Henry Seidel Canby, *Thoreau* (Boston, 1939), p. 333.
5. Joseph Wood Krutch, *Henry David Thoreau* (New York, 1948), pp. 145, 174.
6. *The Autobiographies of W. B. Yeats* (New York, 1938), p. 94.

By night or day,
The things which I have seen I now can see no more.

And Thoreau said, "I think that no experience which I have today comes up to, or is comparable with, the experiences of my boyhood . . . my life was ecstacy. In youth before I lost any of my senses, . . . I was alive" (July 16, 1851).

Thoreau watched his moods as narrowly as a cat does a mouse; he noted his moments of nostalgia; they recurred throughout the years. But they are only a minor theme, it seems to me, in the vast journal record of a full and satisfying life. And the complaint that observation and the gathering of scientific data kept him from true experience also recurs. There is no question that the complaint reflects a difficulty, a conflict. It was an inevitable difficulty that Thoreau's desire to know Concord and all its life drove him to and that he accepted in action. If he was to know Nature and her operations as he wanted to, he obviously recognized that subjective experience must be complemented by objective observation and records. He would not rest content with "sublimo-slipshod" appreciation; hence the long and frequent phenological lists; the measurements of snow depths, of rivers, and ponds; the counts of tree rings. But, no more than the nostalgia for his youth, does the occasional note of conflict between experience and observation seriously affect the impression—produced by myriad entries—of Thoreau forever searching and forever enjoying the search.

Consider how his regrets and complaints appear in the journal entries of the first six months of 1853:

March 23, 1853: Man cannot afford to be a naturalist, to look at Nature directly, but only with the side of his eye. . . . I feel that I am dissipated by so many observations. . . . I have almost a slight, dry headache. . . . O for a little Lethe!
March 30, 1853: Ah, those youthful days! are they never to return? . . . No worm or insect, quadruped or bird, confined [my] view, but the unbounded universe was [mine]. A bird is now become a mote in [my] eye.

We cannot deny the dissatisfaction here, nor the disappointment in his relations with Emerson which he also recorded at this time.

Other entries in March, 1853, suggest a struggle to keep his spirits up: "All enterprises must be self-supporting, must pay for themselves. . . . You must get your living by loving." "Not only narrow but rough is the way that leadeth to life everlasting." ". . . Life is a battle in which you are to show your pluck, and woe be to the coward . . . despair and postponement are cowardice and defeat. Men were born to succeed, not to fail." [7]

But these notes can hardly be said to dominate the 368 pages of entries from January 1 to June 30, 1853. The major impression, as everywhere in the *Journals* from 1850 to 1861, is a fully engrossed Thoreau, ceaselessly observing and inquiring: we have lists of, notes on, questions about, and carefully worked descriptions of, natural phenomena; miscellaneous information—historical, economic, literary, architectural, etc.; comments on the manners and morals of the day; and sometimes set-pieces such as the account of the explosion of the Acton powder mill. And often— far more often than expressions of regret—we find expressions of Thoreau's pleasure in his work and the world he inhabited.

In January he delighted in the "crystal palace" created by the ice-sheathed trees and shrubs; in the "perfect serenity and clarity and sonorousness in the earth" on a perfect winter morning; on another day he rejoiced in "an indescribably winter sky, pure and continent and clear, between emerald and amber, such as summer never sees!" [8]

In early March, after a day of riding about the country with a companion looking at farms, he commented: "I know of no more pleasing employment." On April 7th, eight days after one of his complaints about observations, he noted another side of the matter: "If you make the least correct observation of nature this

7. March 13 and 21.
8. For these and the undated entries of the following paragraph see, in the *Journals,* January 1, 3, 7, 20; March 8; May 9, 11, 17, 30; June 14, 15, 20, 22, 23.

year, you will have occasion to repeat it with illustrations the next, and the season and life itself is prolonged." On the same day he noted the beauty of the river at evening: "Nothing could be more elysian." In May he delighted in Alcott; and time and again he exclaimed at the loveliness of the earth: "How the air is saturated with sweetness on the causeways these willowy days," or ". . . that ineffable fragrance from the Wheeler meadow. . . . It is wafted from the garden of gardens," and "I was surprised, on turning around, to behold the serene and everlasting beauty of the world, it was so soothing . . . so much fairer, serener, more beautiful than my mood had been." And "The morning wind forever blows; the poem of the world is uninterrupted, but few are the ears that hear it." The same strain continues in June: "Here is home; the beauty of the world impresses you. There is a coolness in your mind as in a well. Life is too grand for supper." And, time after time, he states how his days are brightened by the beauty of wild roses, of water lilies, of a moonlit scene on the North River, by the songs of the blackbird or wood thrush, by the fragrance of the swamp pink.

These direct expressions of Thoreau's feelings in 1853 are characteristic of those in the whole *Journal*; I think they reveal a happy man.

There remain, however, several hypothetical propositions that are offered to support the interpretation that he was unhappy.

Great stretches of the *Journal*, it is said, are formless and tedious masses of facts gathered according to an unsound scientific method; Thoreau never used most of them and never could have; therefore, the collecting of them must have been wearying and carried on out of sheer resignation.

Well—what would any seeker's unsifted and unorganized data be but formless and tedious to read, especially if one came upon them in a journal such as Thoreau's? And since he was not, and did not aspire to be, a scientist like Agassiz, the criticism that his method was not strictly scientific is beside the point. He wanted to know all Concord in his own way as, for example, he knew the ponds.

He saw his raw facts for what they were; he explained to his friend Blake why he could not give a lecture in Worcester in 1856: "In fine, what I have is either too scattered or loosely arranged, or too light, or else is too scientific and matter of fact (I run a good deal into that of late) for so hungry a company. I am still a learner, not a teacher, feeding somewhat omnivorously, browsing both stalk and leaves; but I shall perhaps be enabled to speak with the more precision and authority by and by,—if philosophy and sentiment are not buried under a multitude of details." [9]

Before he died, he had time to speak with authority only on fragments of his knowledge: the succession of forest trees, autumnal tints, and wild apples. As Emerson said: "The scale on which his studies proceeded was so large as to require longevity, and we were the less prepared for his sudden disappearance." [10]

The statement that Thoreau had prepared "agonies of assimilation" for himself[11] and could hardly have created order out of the mass of facts he had gathered can be countered by a simple question: "If you had read only the *Journals* from 1837 to 1854, could you imagine *Walden* made from them?" Of course, the question proves no more than the statement it counters. "What might have been is an abstraction/Remaining a perpetual possibility/Only in a world of speculation." We must remember, however, that, in addition to dull notes and lists, the *Journal* contains innumerable passages of vintage Thoreau, testifying to the vibrant spirit that impelled his unremitting search. "A hunger and a thirst are elements in his happiness and make it something other than mere content. And it is hunger and thirst which are responsible for the excitement of his writing." [12] Above all, we must not attribute the limits of our creative imagination to Thoreau.

Nor should we accept the following argument:

9. *The Correspondence of Henry David Thoreau,* ed. Walter Harding and Carl Bode (New York, 1958), pp. 423–424.
10. "Biographical Sketch" in Henry D. Thoreau, *Excursions* (Boston, 1863), p. 33.
11. Paul, p. 114.
12. Krutch, p. 215.

(1) A Romantic egoist is bound to be unhappy.

(2) Thoreau was an extreme Romantic egoist.

(3) Therefore, Thoreau was bound to be unhappy.

Since I believe the facts contradict the conclusion of the syllogism, the argument might be dismissed out-of-hand; but I think something more should be said. This is no time to explore the major premise: that is, the humanists' judgment on the happiness of Romantic egoists. I would, however, question the minor premise: the judgment that Thoreau was so arrogant a Romantic egoist as to have been headed "as recklessly as Tamburlaine or Faust toward catastrophe,"[13] or that he "went a step beyond Emerson's mad (but manly) intellectual egoism,"[14] and was therefore doomed to despair. Against these statements I would place that of no less a critic of Romantic egoism than Paul Elmer More; he concluded his analysis of Thoreau and the German Romantic thinkers in this fashion: "The freedom of the romantic school was to the end that the whole emotional nature might develop; in Thoreau it was for the practice of a higher self-restraint. . . . And so, despite its provincialism and its tedium, the *Journal* of Thoreau is a document that New England may cherish proudly. . . . There remains this tonic example of a man who did actually and violently break through the prison walls of routine, and who yet kept a firm control of his career."[15]

Finally, *Walden* itself, one of the gayest of books, is offered as evidence of unhappiness. Professor Perry Miller characterizes the description of the thawing sandbank in "Spring" as "this ultimate—this derisive, tortured—irony at the end of *Walden*."[16] Since I cannot understand this reading, I cannot argue: in terms of the famous *New Yorker* cartoon, one of us sees broccoli, the other spinach. Or in more philosophical terms: *De gustibus et de coloribus non est disputandum.*

13. Miller, p. 34.

14. Van Doren, p. 34.

15. "Thoreau's Journal" in *Selected Shelburne Essays* (New York, 1935), pp. 114–116.

16. Miller, p. 127.

I can argue, however, against Professor Paul's use of *Walden* as evidence (supplementary to that of the *Journal*) of Thoreau's unhappiness after 1850.

He states that the experiment at Walden was effective and that Thoreau "renewed his faith by living there and by writing the *Week*." The cure was not lasting, however, and *Walden,* he continues, was "an attempt to drain the cup of inspiration to its last dregs. Whatever its public intention, its personal intention was therapeutic." [17]

The development of this point of view suffers from a serious error: it assumes that *Walden* did not finally get under way until after 1850, and it therefore offers as evidence of Thoreau's reaction to his alleged unhappiness in 1850–1854 a number of classic passages that he wrote in the first version of *Walden* in 1846–1847.

(1) The *Journals* from 1850 to 1861 "record the desperation of the spiritual seeker who has lost his communion and fully explain the sense of loss which Thoreau intended to convey in the allegorical passage in the hound, the bayhorse, and the turtle-dove."

(2) "To anticipate, not the sunrise and the dawn merely, but, if possible, Nature herself . . . expressed the enterprise of his years of decay."

(3) ". . . as his allusion to Hebe indicated, he was advising a cure for himself as well as his neighbors. Open all your pores to nature, live in all the seasons—these had been the injunctions of his years of decay."

(4) "With these losses [failure to achieve social influence, failure of the *Week* to sell] for his background, he described for the first time his purpose in going to Walden in a passage [trade with the Celestial Empire, "Economy,"] that brilliantly fused the imagery of self-reliance and spiritual recovery with that of commerce." [18]

But all four passages were in the Walden of 1846–1847; they

17. Paul, pp. 234, 294.
18. *Ibid.,* pp. 256, 321, 323, 327.

cannot be offered as evidence of Thoreau's reaction to despair and decay in 1850–1854.[19]

At the end of his explication of *Walden,* Professor Paul presents the ecstatic climax of what he calls the therapeutic—as well as literary—myth of rebirth that Thoreau's alleged unhappiness led him to create.

The ecstasy [of the passage on the thawing sand at the railroad cut] was not spontaneous or unconscious, but intellectual; it followed from his mature study of nature and his perception of law, an ecstatic praise of this guarantee in nature, but not the former ecstasy he was seeking . . . as an example of his conscious endeavor in nature it represented the intellectual basis from which the more successful symbols of ecstasy—the melting pond and the soaring hawk—were struck.[20]

He then summarizes paragraph thirteen, "The first sparrow of spring," and fourteen, "Walden is melting apace"; quotes almost all of fifteen, "The change from storm and winter to serene and mild"; summarizes the joys of the Golden Age; and presents the soaring, tumbling hawk, in paragraph twenty-two, as the final symbol of Thoreau's ultimate liberation.

But these "more successful symbols of ecstasy" were not born of despair in 1850–1854; nor were they struck off after the full development, in 1853–1854, of the long passage on the thawing sand. Thoreau wrote "The first sparrow of spring," "The change from storm and winter to serene and mild," and the description of the hawk in the *Walden* of 1846–1847.[21] He kept them for the published version of *Walden* and added other material later, not because he had to fend off despair, but because their ecstasy expressed his never failing belief in the promise of life, and also gave proof of its fulfillment.

In 1852–1853, Thoreau added the following passage to *Walden*: "I learned this, at least, by my experiment; that if

19. "The First Version of *Walden*," pp. 113, 114–115, 169, in J. Lyndon Shanley, *The Making of Walden* (Chicago, 1957).

20. Paul, pp. 349–351.

21. "The First Version," pp. 204–206.

one advances confidently in the direction of his dreams, and endeavors to live the life which he has imagined, he will meet with a success unexpected in common hours." I do not think Thoreau ever forgot the lesson he learned while living at Walden Pond. Those who knew him testified to his success. Immediately after Thoreau's death, a young Harvard student wrote:

He appeared to us more than all men to enjoy all life . . . for its intrinsic worth, taking great interest in everything connected with the welfare of the town, no less than delight in each changing aspect of Nature, with an instinctive love for every creature of her realm.

And his family told Mary Peabody Mann "they never could be sad in his presence for a moment; he had been the happiest person they had ever known, all through his life." [22]

And so, as he lay dying, Thoreau could say he was not aware that he and God had ever quarreled. We can regard this as flippant irreverence only if we take the lament of Job for the whole truth, and forget the happiness of the psalmist. Thoreau did not. He loved to quote: "Tomorrow to fresh woods and pastures new." As far as he was concerned, God had always given him "green pastures."

22. *Thoreau, Man of Concord,* ed. Walter Harding (New York, 1960), pp. 11–12, 114.

JOEL PORTE

✪

"A Purely Sensuous Life"

Thoreau's outlook was strongly dependent on the life of the five senses. Virtue for him was synonymous with the purity of the senses; and he defined health, both physical and mental, in exactly the same fashion: "In health all the senses receive enjoyment and each seeks its own gratification.—it is a pleasure to see, and to walk, and to hear—&c." [1] He was convinced that "to see the sun rise or go down every day would preserve us sane forever" (*Journal,* III, 208 [Boston, 1906], referred to hereinafter as J.; cf. J, VI, 329) and that true depression of spirits was impossible for the *pure* sensualist. "There can be no really black melan-choly to him who lives in the midst of nature and has still his senses" (J, I, 364). Predictably, Thoreau's over-all advice on living arose from the same source as his definitions of health and virtue:

We do not commonly live our life out and full; we do not fill all our pores with our blood; we do not inspire and expire fully and entirely enough, so that the wave, the comber, of each inspiration shall break upon our extremest shores, rolling till it meets the sand

1. In Perry Miller, *Consciousness in Concord* (Boston: Houghton Mifflin, 1958), p. 191.

---

which bounds us, and the sound of the surf come back to us. Might not a bellows assist us to breathe? That our breathing should create a wind in a calm day! We live but a fraction of our life. Why do we not let on the flood, raise the gates, and set all our wheels in motion? He that hath ears to hear, let him hear. Employ your senses (J, II, 251).

If the message is at first swallowed up in the turbulence of the metaphor, the simplicity of Thoreau's last sentence is admirably clear. He could, however, turn biblical exegete and deliver the same text in terms utterly familiar to New England ears (including his own):

Remember thy Creator in the days of thy youth; *i.e.*, lay up a store of natural influences. Sing while you may, before the evil days come. He that hath ears, let him hear. See, hear, smell, taste, etc., while these senses are fresh and pure (J, II, 330).

Unlike the Preacher, Thoreau did not advocate the fear of God as man's primary responsibility. "The whole duty of man," he wrote in 1840, "may be expressed in one line,— Make to yourself a perfect body" (J, I, 147). However Thoreau arranged his sermon, it always came out the same: "A man should feed his senses with the best that the land affords" (J, II, 496). And such magic words of the Transcendental movement as *genius* and *inspiration*—so frequently identified by Emerson and others with the Over-Soul and the eternal—were defined by Thoreau in his peculiarly mundane fashion:

What is called genius is the abundance of life or health, so that whatever addresses the senses, as the flavor of these berries, or the lowing of that cow . . . each sight and sound and scent and flavor,—intoxicates with a healthy intoxication (J, IV, 218).

We are forever brought back to the realm of the senses: "To perceive freshly, with fresh senses, is to be inspired" (J, VIII, 44). Thoreau simply thought of abstractions, when he thought of them at all, in terms of possible experience: "How much virtue there is in simply seeing! . . . We are as much as we see. Faith is sight and knowledge" (J, I, 247–248). His speculations were guided by the range of his five senses.

Indeed, so concerned was Thoreau with the senses that he was even loath to lump them together (except in a very special way) and devoted much space to precise anatomization of the particular virtues of each one, among which he almost always mentions its special affinity to the earth. Sight, for instance, which he once named the Brahmin caste of the five senses,[2] he could describe in a strikingly original metaphor: "If I am well, then I see well. The bulletins of health are twirled along my visual rays, like pasteboards on a kite string" (J, I, 266). In many references to the eye, he takes the opportunity to chastise subtly the Transcendental desire to see into the empyrean: "The eye must be firmly anchored to this earth which beholds birches and pines waving in the breeze in a certain light, a serene rippling light" (J, I, 351). He could even devise anatomical arguments to bolster his predilection for observing the commonplace:

Man's eye is so placed as to look straight forward on a level best, or rather down than up. His eye demands the sober colors of the earth for its daily diet. He does not look up at a great angle but with an effort (J, III, 387).

Smell, however, seems to have been as dear to his heart as vision, and in a *Journal* entry for 1852 he temporarily dethroned the latter in favor of the former, calling scent "a more primitive inquisition than the eye, more oracular and trustworthy. . . . By it I detect earthiness" (J, IV, 40). This it was—its sensitivity to earthiness—for which he chiefly valued his ability to smell: "I love the rank smells of the swamp, its decaying leaves" (J, IV, 305). And on March 18, 1853, he devoted a whole paragraph to announcing dramatically: "To-day first I smelled the earth" (J, V, 27). In another *Journal* entry he mixed smell and taste in a metaphor of perfect contentment: "As I go home by Hayden's I smell the burning meadow. I love the scent. It is my pipe. I smoke the earth" (J, VI, 439–440). Sensation was total experi-

2. *Ibid.,* p. 165.

ence for Thoreau; the scent of apples, he noted in 1853, "affects me like a performance, a poem, a thing done" (J, V, 328).

As with sight, smell, and taste, it is earthiness that Thoreau wants in his sound: "The creaking of the crickets seems at the very foundation of all sound. At last I cannot tell it from a ringing in my ears. . . . It reminds me that I am a denizen of the earth" (J, II, 306). The same is true of his sense of touch: "To the sane man the world is a musical instrument. The very touch affords an exquisite pleasure" (J, II, 269). For Thoreau man's grip on life is literally a tangible thing: "When I took the ether my consciousness amounted to this: I put my finger on myself in order to keep the place, otherwise I should never have returned to this world" (J, VIII, 142).

Thoreau is alive so long as he can feel himself in contact with the world; and it is just this desire for both specificity and totality of perception that allows him to lump his senses in the only way in which they will not lose their individuality—the unity of synesthesia:

The trees, seen dimly through the mist, suggest things which do not at all belong to the past, but are peculiar to my fresh New England life. It is as novel as green peas. The dew hangs everywhere upon the grass, and I breathe the rich, damp air in slices (J, I, 267).

The careful confusion here of sight, smell, taste, and touch suggests Keats; and in another *Journal* entry in which the senses are mixed, the Keatsian note is unmistakable:

As my eye rested on the blossom of the meadowsweet in a hedge, I heard the note of an autumnal cricket, and was penetrated with the sense of autumn. Was it sound? or was it form? or was it scent? or was it flavor? It is now the royal month of August. When I hear this sound, I am as dry as the rye which is everywhere cut and housed, though I am drunk with the season's wine (J, II, 370).

"O for a Life of Sensations rather than of Thoughts!" Keats wrote to Benjamin Bailey in 1817. "Oh, if I could be intoxicated on air and water!" Thoreau exclaimed to himself in 1850 (J, II,

72), anticipating by just a decade Emily Dickinson's "Inebriate of Air—am I—/And Debauchee of Dew." For all three, the drunkenness of pure sensation was synonymous with life, and the sobriety of a life without sense experience was but another name for the ever-threatening winter of death.

Indeed, Thoreau's intense annual distress at the approach of winter itself was not only the result of a symbolic anticipation of death; it was actually the time of year when the sources of life—the five senses—were least operative. Samuel Johnson was appalled at the thought that "we shall receive no letters in the grave";[3] Thoreau, one feels, was horrified because death was the end of sensation. (There, perhaps, we have one large difference, at least in literary terms, between the eighteenth and nineteenth centuries.) Thoreau's *Journal* entries for the beginning of winter are frequently bleak, such as this one for November 27, 1853: "Now a man will eat his heart, if ever, now while the earth is bare, barren and cheerless, and we have the coldness of winter without the variety of ice and snow" (J, V, 520). Four years later he dubbed that month "November Eat-heart":

Not only the fingers cease to do their office, but there is often a benumbing of the faculties generally. You can hardly screw up your courage to take a walk when all is thus tightly locked or frozen up and so little is to be seen in field or wood (J, X, 203).

March was equally bad: "I run about these cold and blustering days, on the whole perhaps the worst to bear in the year,—partly because they disappoint expectation—looking almost in vain for some animal or vegetable life stirring" (J, VII, 274). Two days later he concluded about both months that "he must have a great deal of life in him to draw upon, who can pick up a subsistence in November and March" (J, VII, 276). If it is true that character is most clearly exhibited in extreme conditions, Thoreau's entries for these marginal months should be particu-

3. *Boswell's Life of Johnson,* ed. G. Birkbeck Hill (Oxford, 1887), IV, 413.

larly revelatory; and indeed this is what we find. The entry for
November 13, 1851, for instance, seems a perfect illustration of
the Thoreauvian method literally laid bare:

A cold and dark afternoon, the sun being behind clouds in the west.
The landscape is barren of objects, the trees being leafless, and so
little light in the sky for variety. Such a day as will almost oblige a
man to eat his own heart. A day in which you must hold on to life
by your teeth. You can hardly ruck up any skin on Nature's bones.
The sap is down; she won't peel. Now is the time to cut timber for
yokes and ox-bows, leaving the tough bark on,—yokes for your own
neck. Finding yourself yoked to Matter and to Time. Truly a hard
day, hard times these! Not a mosquito left. Not an insect to hum.
Crickets gone into winter quarters. Friends long since gone there,
and you left to walk on frozen ground, with your hands in your
pockets. Ah, but is not this a glorious time for your deep inward
fires? And will not your green hickory and white oak burn clear in
this frosty air? Now is not your manhood taxed by the great Assessor?
Taxed for having a soul, a ratable soul. A day when you cannot
pluck a flower, cannot dig a parsnip, nor pull a turnip, for the frozen
ground! What do the thoughts find to live on? What avails you now
the fire you stole from heaven? Does not each thought become a
vulture to gnaw your vitals? (J, III, 110–111)

Thoreau is faced with a hard day, a day without sensations. He
carefully, even painfully, catalogs what there is available for
each sense and comes up with nothing. The landscape is barren,
the trees leafless, and the sky dark, so there is little to see; nature's
bones are skinless ("she won't peel"), and it is difficult to feel; as
for sound, the mosquitoes and crickets have deserted; and finally,
flowers, parsnips, and turnips are gone, now that the ground is
frozen, and there is nothing to smell or taste. In such a situation
he at least tries to fall back on the "deep inward fires" dear to the
hearts of all Transcendentalists, but he is forced to admit failure.
Reflection—which, to the Lockean philosopher, is all that exists
besides matter and sensation—is simply the mind turning back on
its own operations, so that each thought becomes "a vulture to
gnaw your vitals."

The desperate bleakness of Thoreau's life under such conditions is made clear by contrast with another day, in August of the same year, when the world was much different and there was abundant food for all his senses:

My heart leaps into my mouth at the sound of the wind in the woods. I, whose life was but yesterday so desultory and shallow, suddenly recover my spirits, my spirituality, through my hearing. . . . Ah, I would walk, I would sit and sleep, with natural piety! . . . For joy I could embrace the earth; I shall delight to be buried in it . . . now I have occasion to be grateful for the flood of life that is flowing over me. I am not so poor: I can smell the ripening apples; the very rills are deep; the autumnal flowers . . . feed my spirit, endear the earth to me, make me value myself and rejoice; the quivering of pigeons' wings reminds me of the tough fibre of the air which they rend. I thank you, God. I do not deserve anything, I am unworthy of the least regard; and yet I am made to rejoice. I am impure and worthless, and yet the world is gilded for my delight and holidays are prepared for me, and my path is strewn with flowers. . . . Ah, I would not tread on a cricket in whose song is such a revelation, so soothing and cheering to my ear! Oh, keep my senses pure! (J, II, 391–392)

The Wordsworthian echoes at the beginning of the passage are, of course, not accidental; but it is important to note the significant difference between the viewpoints of the two writers. For Wordsworth, since "nothing can bring back the hour/Of splendour in the grass, of glory in the flower," he must find his strength "in the faith that looks through death,/In years that bring the philosophic mind." But Thoreau has no desire to reconcile himself to the inevitable decay of his faculties; and the hardships of winter have taught him not to renounce his quest for sensation in preparation for death, but rather to await patiently the coming of spring. Wordsworth ends his "Ode" with a plea for philosophy; Thoreau can only beg: "Oh, keep my senses pure!"

Unlike Wordsworth, who believed the child blessed because of its still fresh intimations of immortality, Thoreau thought the child fortunate for reasons closer to Locke than to Plato: "The senses of children are unprofaned. Their whole body is one sense" (J, II, 291). In this *Journal* entry for 1851 we undoubtedly have the source of the notion which Thoreau uses to begin the chapter on "Solitude" in *Walden*: "This is a delicious evening, when the whole body is one sense, and imbibes delight through every pore. I go and come with a strange liberty in Nature, a part of herself" (*Writings,* II, 143 [Boston, 1906], referred to hereinafter as W).

For Thoreau the great thing was unity of perception. "This is a world," he wrote in 1851, "where there are flowers" (J, II, 401); but flowers are of many sorts: "Flowers are the different colors of the sunlight" (J, V, 185). In fact, in his *Journal* he writes of rainbows, fruit, birds, stars, and even whole days themselves as if they were all flowers.[4] He apparently liked to think of the entire world as one huge plant: "The heavens and the earth are one flower. The earth is the calyx, the heavens the corolla" (J, V, 225). Having envisioned all of nature as a single flower, Thoreau, like the Fabullus whom Catullus invited to dinner, could only pray that the gods would see fit to make him *totum nasum,* so that in one moment of perfect perception, he might sense the universe. . . .

Thoreau's preparation for his moments of mystical revelation, as we have already noticed, consisted entirely of a total immersion of his senses in the natural world. In religious or perhaps psychological terms, these preparatory acts seem sometimes to resemble a species of purification rite. There is an inordinate amount of bathing described in his *Journal,* and it often sounds particularly significant:

I bathe me in the river. I lie down where it is shallow, amid the weeds over its sandy bottom; but it seems shrunken and parched; I find it difficult to get *wet* through. I would fain be the channel of a mountain brook. I bathe, and in a few hours I bathe again, not remembering that I was wetted before (J, II, 335).

4. See J, IV, 128, 284–285, 306ff.; V, 247, 383; VI, 4; and VIII, 42.

Elsewhere he makes explicit the function of his bathing: "I am made more vigorous by my bath, am more *continent* of thought" (J, II, 435). But the bath not only helps him to contain his vigor; it also cleanses: "Open all your pores and bathe in all the tides of Nature, in all her streams and oceans, at all seasons. Miasma and infection are from within, not without" (J, V, 394). Yet, whatever need Thoreau may have felt to purify himself certainly merges, in his descriptions of bathing, with a sheer physical pleasure in the activity:

I had already bathed in Walden as I passed, but now I forgot that I had been wetted, and wanted to embrace and mingle myself with the water of Flint's Pond this warm afternoon, to get wet inwardly and deeply (J, II, 501).

"Bathing," he wrote on another occasion, "is an undescribed luxury. To feel the wind blow on your body, the water flow on you and lave you, is a rare physical enjoyment this hot day" (J, IV, 207). He could even bathe in the breeze when it was still too cold for the pond: "I love to sit in the wind on this hill and be blown on. We bathe thus first in air; then, when the air has warmed it, in water" (J, V, 159). And, finally, in the heat of full summer he would immerse himself completely:

What a luxury to bathe now! It is gloriously hot,—the first of this weather. I cannot get wet enough. I must let the water soak into me. When you come out, it is rapidly dried on you or absorbed into your body, and you want to go in again. I begin to inhabit the planet, and see how I may be naturalized at last (J, VI, 382–383).

The ultimate function of bathing was that it "naturalized" him, which was always the necessary preparation for his being "spiritualized." This is perhaps the point of an anecdote which he relates in *Walden*:

As I walked on the railroad causeway, I used to wonder at the halo of light around my shadow, and would fain fancy myself one of the elect. One who visited me declared that the shadows of some Irishmen before him had no halo about them, that it was only natives that were so distinguished (W, II, 224).

Apart from Thoreau's Yankee sense of humor (no Irishman could possibly be one of New England's "visible elect"!), the moral of the story seems to be that—unlike Benvenuto Cellini (a Catholic, like the Irishmen), for whom a similar experience was "basis enough for superstition"—Thoreau has been "so distinguished" for natural, rather than supernatural, reasons. Only someone who is "native to the universe" (J, II, 46) can have a truly religious experience. Thus in his *Journal* Thoreau describes his eating of berries as if it were the preparation for a spiritual vocation in nature: "We pluck and eat in remembrance of Her. It is a sacrament, a communion" (J, V, 331).

If we may allow ourselves to borrow St. Bernard's triadic scheme for the mystical apotheosis of the Reason, it is entirely possible to describe Thoreau's religious quest similarly, in terms of three levels of experience. To be sure, the categories will hardly stay put rigidly, and there is liable to be some haziness in the mid-range; but Thoreau himself seems clearly to delineate three stages of natural experience: "joy," "ecstasy," and what we might call the *epiphanic moment*. It was, it seems, mainly for the sake of this latter experience that Thoreau spent so many lonely days tramping in the woods; and it was the memory of these illuminated moments that carried him through the rigors of each winter, as he relates in one of his best poems, "Winter Memories":

> Within the circuit of this plodding life,
> There enter moments of an azure hue,
> Untarnished fair as is the violet
> Or anemone, when the spring strews them
> By some meandering rivulet, which make
> The best philosophy untrue that aims
> But to console man for his grievances.
> I have remembered, when the winter came,
> High in my chamber in the frosty nights,
> When in the still light of the cheerful moon,
> On every twig and rail and jutting spout,
> The icy spears were adding to their length

Against the arrows of the coming sun,
How in the shimmering noon of summer past
Some unrecorded beam slanted across
The upland pastures where the Johnswort grew . . .
(W, V, 103)

. . . Emerson misinterpreted when he wrote of Thoreau that "he knew the worth of the Imagination for the uplifting and consolation of human life, and liked to throw every thought into a symbol (Emerson, *Writings* [Boston, 1903], X, 475). Thoreau's precious moment has no symbolic reference; moreover, he disdains consolation and simply waits patiently for the repetition of his experience, as the closing lines of the poem make clear: "So by God's cheap economy made rich/To go upon my winter's task again." He can bear the hard New England winter because spring, and more "moments of an azure hue," are not far behind.

"Surely joy is the condition of life" (W, V, 106), he wrote in "The Natural History of Massachusetts" (where the poem discussed above also appears). What makes him condemn the "lives of quiet desperation" which most men lead is simply that they are joyless; and he advocates a return to nature because, for him, the natural world is the original source of joy:

When I took up a fragment of a walnut-shell this morning, I saw by its very grain and composition, its form and color, etc., that it was made for happiness. The most brutish and inanimate objects that are made suggest an everlasting and thorough satisfaction; they are the homes of content. Wood, earth, mould, etc., exist for joy (J, IX, 206–207).

These apparently brutish objects might leave stolid men unmoved, but they communicate their satisfaction to Thoreau. His animal contentment, which he describes in a letter to Blake as being "a good deal like that of the woodchucks," [5] often seems no more than a simple sense of physical well-being: "It is a bright, clear, warm November day. I feel blessed. I love my life. I warm toward all nature" (J, III, 86). Yet he admits that the precise

---

5. Thoreau, *Correspondence*, p. 222.

source of his joy is obscure, as when he describes his looking into a grove of pine trees: "I do not know exactly what it was that attracted my eye. I experienced a transient gladness, at any rate, at something which I saw" (J, III, 131). He is baffled by his own sentiments: "Why should it be so pleasing to look into a thick pine wood where the sunlight streams in and gilds it?" (J, III, 142). Nevertheless, he is willing to attribute his joy merely to the perfection of the natural world: "Methinks I am in better spirits and physical health now that melons are ripe. . . . The clouds do not entirely disperse, but, since it is decidedly fair and serene, I am contented" (J, IV, 332). And it is exactly this serene acceptance of his natural environment that constitutes Thoreau's inspirational message to his disciple H. G. O. Blake:

I am grateful for what I am & have. My thanksgiving is perpetual. It is surprising how contented one can be with nothing definite— only a sense of existance [sic]. Well anything for variety. I am ready to try this for the next 1000 years, & exhaust it. How sweet to think of! My extremities well charred, and my intellectual part too, so that there is no danger of worm or rot for a long while. My breath is sweet to me. O how I laugh when I think of my vague indefinite riches. No run on my bank can drain it—for my wealth is not possession but enjoyment.[6]

Yet, of course, since Thoreau's enjoyment was always dependent to a large extent on his physical vitality, the possibility of "drain" was a very real one. He would admit, in fact, in his *Journal,* to being a "torn fragment"; but he could add: ". . . not the less cheerfully we expand in a moist day and assume unexpected colors. We want not completeness but intensity of life" (J, IX, 378). And he would insist that we should "measure our lives by our joys. We have lived, not in proportion to the number of years that we have spent on the earth, but in proportion as we have enjoyed" (J, XIII, 159).

Not only was joy a sufficient end in itself; it could be a sign that something else was to follow: "No man ever makes a discovery,

6. *Ibid.,* p. 444.

ever . . . an observation of the least importance, but he is advertised of the fact by a joy that surprises him" (J, IV, 292). Thoreau's joy appears also to have been a kind of thanks-offering to the machinery of nature which prepared him for further experience: "I love and celebrate nature, even in detail, merely because I love the scenery of these interviews and translations" (J, IX, 209–210). Who or what, we may ask, was being "translated," if not Thoreau himself?

In a letter to Blake dated May 21, 1856, Thoreau insisted that it was the high importance of "translation" that made for his lack of sociability, not an intrinsic dislike of people:

As for the dispute about solitude & society any comparison is impertinent. It is an idling down on the plain at the base of a mountain instead of climbing steadily to its top. Of course you will be glad of all the society you can get to go up with. Will you go to glory with me? is the burden of the song. I love society so much that I swallowed it all at a gulp—i.e. all that came in my way. It is not that we love to be alone, but that we love to soar, and when we do soar, the company grows thinner & thinner till there is none at all. It is either the Tribune on the plain, a sermon on the mount, or a very private *extacy* still higher up.[7]

Of these three kinds of activity—plebeian affairs, Transcendentalism of the verbal-ethical sort, and "very private *extacy*"— Thoreau declares himself thoroughly committed to the last, an ecstasy which (unlike the shared rapture that John Donne describes in "The Ecstasy") is for him a solitary occupation. He had confided his preference to his journal in 1851:

My desire for knowledge is intermittent; but my desire to commune with the spirit of the universe, to be intoxicated even with the fumes, call it, of that divine nectar, to bear my head through atmospheres and over heights unknown to my feet, is perennial and constant (J, II, 150–151).

Thoreau tried to give a description of this experience—by his

7. *Ibid.*, p. 424.

own admission, a constant preoccupation—to the largest audience he ever reached, the readers of *Walden,* but those who have studied the *Journal* can only pronounce this "revery" a considerably toned-down public exhibition of yoga:

Sometimes, in a summer morning, having taken my accustomed bath, I sat in my sunny doorway from sunrise till noon, rapt in a revery, amidst the pines and hickories and sumachs, in undisturbed solitude and stillness, while the birds sang around or flitted noiseless through the house, until by the sun falling in at my west window, or the noise of some traveller's wagon on the distant highway, I was reminded of the lapse of time. I grew in those seasons like corn in the night, and they were far better than any work of the hands would have been. They were not time subtracted from my life, but so much over and above my usual allowance (W, II, 123–124).

Among other things, the measure of Thoreau's concession to his audience here is the use of an economic metaphor at the close of the description—that economic metaphor which constitutes the one pervasive deception in *Walden,* for, as he was to say of nature in a *Journal* entry for 1859, "her motive is not economy but satisfaction" (J, XII, 96). Moreover, Thoreau's self-parody in his description of the genesis of a "budding ecstasy" later in the book makes it plain that he thought it unwise to bare his soul completely in *Walden.* In this passage, he has just been disturbed by the visit of a "Poet" (presumably Ellery Channing):

Hermit alone. Let me see; where was I? Methinks I was nearly in this frame of mind; the world lay about this angle. Shall I go to heaven or a-fishing? If I should soon bring this meditation to an end, would another so sweet occasion be likely to offer? I was as near being resolved into the essence of things as ever I was in my life. I fear my thoughts will not come back to me. If it would do any good, I would whistle for them. When they make us an offer, is it wise to say, We will think of it? My thoughts have left no track, and I cannot find the path again. What was it that I was thinking of? It was a very hazy day. I will just try these three sentences of Confut-see; they may fetch that state about again. I know not whether it was the dumps or a budding ecstasy (W, II, 248–249).

In the *Journal* Thoreau never seems to have trouble distinguishing between the "dumps" and a "budding ecstasy." Furthermore, the latter state is rarely described as being inducible through reading—of Confucius or anybody else. It is shown, rather, to be the result of natural experience, particularly in connection with the sun, as in this "introduction" to an ecstasy in the *Journal* for 1841:

In the sunshine and the crowing of cocks I feel an illimitable holiness, which makes me bless God and myself. The warm sun casts his incessant gift at my feet as I walk along, unfolding his yellow worlds (J, I, 202).

The *rondo estatico* which follows completes the experience:

The eaves are running on the south side of the house; the titmouse lisps in the poplar; the bells are ringing for church; while the sun presides over all and makes his simple warmth more obvious than all else. What shall I do with this hour, so like time and yet so fit for eternity? . . . I lie out indistinct as a heath at noonday. I am evaporating and ascending into the sun (J, I, 203–204).

This kind of "translation" could also be effected by sound, to the divine powers of which Thoreau considered himself particularly sensitive. And in the privacy of his *Journal* he could describe the experience with considerably less inhibition than the public nature of *Walden* imposed:

The strains of the aeolian harp and of the wood thrush . . . lift us up in spite of ourselves. They intoxicate, they charm us. Where was that strain mixed into which this world was dropped but as a lump of sugar to sweeten the draught? I would be drunk, drunk, drunk, dead drunk to this world with it forever. He that hath ears, let him hear. The contact of sound with a human ear whose hearing is pure and unimpaired is coincident with an ecstasy. . . . It, as it were, takes me out of my body and gives me the freedom of all bodies and all nature. I leave my body in a trance and accompany the zephyr and the fragrance (J, VI, 39–40).

The reader of Thoreau with no sympathy for mystic states may be inclined to write off his descriptions of his ecstasies as simply hyperbole, or perhaps even affectation; but there is a good deal of evidence to show that neither explanation will suffice, that Thoreau was writing of something he knew. In the year of the passage quoted above (1853), he entered a paragraph of apparently etymological import in his *Journal*:

True words are those, as Trench says,—transport, rapture, ravishment, ecstasy. These are the words I want. This is the effect of music. I am rapt away by it, out of myself. These are truly poetical words. I am inspired, elevated, expanded. I am on the mount.[8]

It might at first seem curious that Thoreau, with all his insistence on the concrete and the factual, would approve of these abstract terms. One can only conclude that they must have signified some real experience to him. And, indeed, we find that the statement "I am on the mount" is at once one of Thoreau's favorite metaphors for his ecstatic moments and a literal description of one of the ways in which ecstasy could be attained.

"I am not taken up," Thoreau wrote in 1840, "like Moses, upon a mountain to learn the law, but lifted up in my seat here, in the warm sunshine and genial light" (J, I, 158). His refusal here to be identified with Moses upon Sinai was not to preclude, as we shall see, his associating himself with Moses upon Pisgah. Indeed, that was the very distinction he was making: unlike the other Transcendentalists, his concern was ecstasy—and ecstatic illumination—rather than ethics. Occasionally, to be sure, he could present the two possibilities without explicitly choosing:

Sometimes I come out suddenly upon a high plain, which seems to be the upper level and true surface of the earth, and by its very baldness aspires and lies up nearer to the stars,—a place where a decalogue might be let down or a saint translated (J, I, 186).

One assumes, knowing his attitude toward receiving the decalogue and his desire for "translation," that it was really the latter

8. J, IV, 466–467. Richard Chenevix Trench (1807–1886), English divine and philologist, originated the scheme for the Oxford English Dictionary.

he awaited. But he would claim to be happy to receive whatever came his way:

I only ask a clean seat. I will build my lodge on the southern slope of some hill, and take there the life the gods send me. Will it not be employment enough to accept gratefully all that is yielded me between sun and sun? (J, I, 244)

What the gods actually yielded Thoreau, however, was not very palpable, for of the "many a day spent on the hilltops waiting for the sky to fall, that I might catch something," he could only report that he "never caught much, only a little, manna-wise, that would dissolve again in the sun" (J, I, 435). But this was hardly important; he expected nothing palpable: "A greater baldness my life seeks, as the crest of some bare hill, which towns and cities do not afford. I want a directer relation with the sun" (J, I, 248). This latter-day follower of Apollo, relieved from time to time of the necessity of slaving for his Admetus, wanted only to re-establish contact with his master and, if not to receive an oracle, at least to be seized with sibylline rapture. Finally, of course, being "on the mount" was for Thoreau not simply a question of sublime sun-bathing but a metaphor for the ecstasy leading to an illuminated moment: "There is elevation in every hour," and "we have only to stand on the eminence of the hour, and look out thence into the empyrean" (J, I, 214). To be sure, all hours are not equally eminent; the coincidence of an ecstasy and a vision is rare, and one's whole life must be devoted to awaiting the occasion:

If by patience, if by watching, I can secure one new ray of light, can feel myself elevated for an instant upon Pisgah, the world which was dead prose to me becoming living and divine, shall I not watch ever? Shall I not be a watchman henceforth? If by watching a whole year on the city's walls I may obtain a communication from heaven, shall I not do well to shut up my shop and turn a watchman? (J, II, 471)

Thoreau's profession was that of watchman, and he had to be always on the alert for the feeling of elevation and a "new ray of light." The job was arduous and unending:

Not only narrow but rough is the way that leadeth to life everlasting. Our experience does not wear upon us. It is seen to be fabulous or symbolical, and the future is worth expecting. Encouraged, I set out once more to climb the mountain of the earth, for my steps are symbolical steps, and in all my walking I have not reached the top of the earth yet (J, III, 35).

The perfect Pisgah-sight, equivalent for Thoreau to the "abode of the present" (J, II, 74), was a moment of total ecstasy and illumination, and it was worth attending. One might say that his dedication to the job approximated, *mutatis mutandis,* that of the great mystic philosopher Plotinus. Indeed, in his *Journal* for 1840 Thoreau made the following notation:

Plotinus aimed at ἐπαφήν, and παρουσίαν ἐπιστήμης κρείττονα and τὸ ἑαυτὸν κέντρον τῷ οἷον πάντων κέντρῳ συνάπτειν (J, I, 139).

Plotinus aimed at "contact" (or "apprehension") and the "greater presence of knowledge," and at "uniting his own center with the center of all things." It would seem that Thoreau decided early to make this his own program. Being "on the mount" was a way of describing that "contact" with the One of Plotinus which led to the "greater presence of knowledge." Like Plotinus, what Thoreau brought back from his experience of union with the center of all things was teasingly ineffable.

The union that Plotinus advocated was one involving a man's total being: the coincidence of ecstatic feeling with perfect vision. This was Thoreau's goal as a naturalist—a difficult goal and not one that he could depend on attaining always. It remained his principal occupation, as he suggested in the following letter to Blake in 1857, five years before his death:

With regard to essentials, I have never had occasion to change my mind. The aspect of the world varies from year to year, as the land-scape is differently clothed, but I find that the *truth* is still *true,* and I never regret any emphasis which it may have inspired. Ktaadn [Mt. Katahdin] is there still, but much more surely my old conviction is there, resting with more than mountain breadth and weight on the world, the source still of fertilizing streams, and affording glorious views from its summit, if I can get up to it again.[9]

As always, the natural world is the source of Thoreau's intense delight, which finds its perfect end in the moment of illumination —the final stage in Thoreau's mystic quest, when the heat of ecstasy has been transformed totally into light. This is certainly what he means here by the somewhat curious use of "emphasis." The world is still to be depended upon, and he does not regret what it has always inspired, an "emphasis"—literally, an appearance—exactly equivalent in its root meaning to "epiphany." This vision it was that Thoreau always and finally aimed for, as he confessed to Blake in 1848: "My only integral experience is in my vision. I see, perchance, with more integrity than I feel." [10]

To judge by his writings, Thoreau had a fair amount of success in attaining this integral and integrative experience. In his *Journal* for 1841, for instance, he relates how noteworthy an event a moment of illumination could be for him:

Whole weeks or months of my summer life slide away in thin volumes like mist or smoke, till at length some warm morning, perchance, I see a sheet of mist blown down the brook to the swamp, its shadow flitting across the fields, which have caught a new significance from that accident; and as that vapor is raised above the earth, so shall the next weeks be elevated above the plane of the actual . . . (J, I, 300–301).

That "new significance"—accidental, and a part of the phenomenal world—transforms the actual in a major way, as Thoreau was to note the following year:

All sights and sounds are seen and heard both in time and eternity. And when the eternity of any sight or sound strikes the eye or ear, they are intoxicated with delight. Sometimes, as through a dim haze, we see objects in their eternal relations (J, I, 359).

9. Thoreau, *Correspondence*, pp. 491–492.
10. *Ibid.*, p. 222.

The delight, then, of seeing things under the aspect of eternity elevates the ordinary events of Thoreau's life. Moreover, "we are never so visionary as to be prepared for what the next hour may bring forth" (W, IV, 301). The shift in vision may occur at any hour and is sudden: "The change from foulness to serenity is instantaneous. Suddenly an influx of light, though it was late, filled my room" (J, I, 400). Here the illumination takes place in his chamber, but Thoreau's best descriptions of epiphanic moments are of outdoor occurrences. In them there is an almost eerie mingling of exact detail and visionary suggestion:

Some distant angle in the sun where a lofty and dense white pine wood, with mingled gray and green, meets a hill covered with shrub oaks, affects me singularly, reinspiring me with all the dreams of my youth. It is a place far away, yet actual and where we have been. I saw the sun falling on a distant white pine wood whose gray and moss-covered stems were visible amid the green, in an angle where this forest abutted on a hill covered with shrub oaks. It was like looking into dreamland. It is one of the avenues to my future. Certain coincidences like this are accompanied by a certain flash as of hazy lightning, flooding all the world suddenly with a tremulous serene light which it is difficult to see long at a time (J, II, 106–107).

Sometimes his descriptions are actually dramatic:

The pines standing in the ocean of mist, seen from the Cliffs, are trees in every stage of transition from the actual to the imaginary. . . . As you advance, the trees gradually come out of the mist and take form before your eyes. You are reminded of your dreams. Life looks like a dream. You are prepared to see visions. And now, just before sundown, the night wind blows up more mist through the valley, thickening the veil which already hung over the trees, and the gloom of night gathers early and rapidly around. Birds lose their way (J, II, 119).

One senses the presence of powers which are on the verge of exposing themselves; but at the crucial moment, the wind stirs, the world is engulfed in darkness, and we are left with a keen sense of loss—loss of the vision, that moment of illumination which was always so highly significant for Thoreau:

I do not know that knowledge amounts to anything more definite than a novel and grand surprise, or a sudden revelation of the insufficiency of all that we had called knowledge before; an indefinite sense of the grandeur and glory of the universe. It is the lighting up of the mist by the sun (J, II, 168).

The importance of the epiphanic moment, then, is simply that it constitutes the highest way of knowing—precisely that "greater presence of knowledge" aimed at by Plotinus. But unfortunately this knowledge is ineffable in philosophical or scientific terms: "Your greatest success will be simply to perceive that such things are, and you will have no communication to make to the Royal Society" (J, XII, 371). Still, Thoreau would find himself perpetually teased and perplexed by his experience:

If any part of nature excites our pity, it is for ourselves we grieve. . . . We get only transient and partial glimpses of the beauty of the world. . . . Beauty and music are not mere traits and exceptions. They are the rule and character. It is the exception that we see and hear. Then I try to discover what it was in the vision that charmed and translated me. What if we could daguerreotype our thoughts and feelings! for I am surprised and enchanted often by some quality which I cannot detect. I have seen an attribute of another world and condition of things. It is a wonderful fact that I should be affected, and thus deeply and powerfully, more than by aught else in all my experience . . . (J, VIII, 44–45).

Thoreau could grieve for himself that his "glimpses of the beauty of the world" were only partial and intermittent, and their nature ineffable. Nevertheless, the wonder was that the glimpses did come and that their arrival made such an enormous difference. The momentary experience might be no more than a vision of sunlight on pine needles, yet Thoreau could exclaim in ecstasy: "At sight of this my spirit is like a lit tree" (J, X, 305). The supreme value of the epiphanic moment for Thoreau was simply its power to effect a total transformation of his spirit from dejection to exaltation. It was the secret of his Transcendentalism, as he suggested in a letter to Blake in 1853:

I have had but one *spiritual* birth (excuse the word,) and now whether it rains or snows, whether I laugh or cry, fall farther below or approach nearer to my standard, whether Pierce or Scott is elected, —not a new scintillation of light flashes on me, but ever and anon, though with longer intervals, the same surprising & everlastingly new light dawns to me, with only such variations as in the coming of the natural day, with which indeed, it is often coincident.[11]

It was exactly the importance of this ever-new but perennial light, this *real* vision, that Thoreau had tried—somewhat mystifyingly, in the midst of a long series of quotations from the *Bhagavad-Gita*—to communicate to the readers of *A Week*:

The most glorious fact in my experience is not anything that I have done or may hope to do, but a transient thought, or vision, or dream, which I have had. I would give all the wealth of the world, and all the deeds of all the heroes, for one true vision (W, I, 145–146).

So much for his readers; the conclusion of the paragraph was clearly addressed by Thoreau to himself: "But how can I communicate with the gods, who am a pencil-maker on the earth, and not be insane?" Certainly his Concord neighbors thought him queer enough for racing around the woods to no apparent purpose; now Thoreau stopped to ask himself whether his being an equerry of epiphanies wasn't a rather precarious profession. Nevertheless, they were what he believed in, and his message remained unchanged in *Walden*:

If the day and the night are such that you greet them with joy, and life emits a fragrance like flowers and sweet-scented herbs, is more elastic, more starry, more immortal,—that is your success. All nature is your congratulation, and you have cause momentarily to bless yourself. The greatest gains and values are farthest from being appreciated. We easily come to doubt if they exist. We soon forget

11. *Ibid.*, pp. 296–297.

them. They are the highest reality. Perhaps the facts most astounding and most real are never communicated by man to man. The true harvest of my daily life is somewhat as intangible and indescribable as the tints of morning or evening. It is a little star-dust caught, a segment of the rainbow which I have clutched (W, II, 239).

Thoreau's statement of his theory is clearly somewhat more "poetic" and less direct here than in *A Week*; and it is perhaps in the earlier work, before his youthful exuberance was tempered by failure, that he truly succeeded in conveying the *"hypaethral* character" (J, I, 274) of his culminating Transcendental experience—total vision reached in nature through the five senses, a purely sensuous life. In *A Week* Thoreau could shout exultantly:

I see, smell, taste, hear, feel, that everlasting Something to which we are allied, at once our maker, our abode, our destiny, our very Selves; the one historic truth, the most remarkable fact which can become the distinct and uninvited subject of our thought, the actual glory of the universe . . . (W, I, 182).

Thoreau's uniqueness as a Transcendentalist resides in the fact that he attained the end of a Plotinian philosopher—the union of his own center with the center of all things—by purely Lockean means. And since the world was simply not prepared to "go to glory" with him (although he democratically offered everyone a ticket to his "Celestial Railroad" in *A Week* and *Walden*), he had decided early in life that it would be a sufficient career for him to go alone and send back news of what he found.

JAMES ARMSTRONG

✪

Thoreau as Philosopher of Love

Clifton Fadiman once remarked that Thoreau could get as much out of ten minutes with a chickadee as most men could out of a whole night with Cleopatra.

I think Mr. Fadiman intended to emphasize Thoreau's remarkable ability to squeeze the utmost in both meaning and pleasure out of the slightest experience, but his epigram has probably just as often been understood to imply that there was something unusual about Thoreau's sexual inclinations. I suppose it's only human to be curious about the love life of a man who in other respects led such a rich and satisfying existence. But neither he nor his biographers give us much satisfaction on this score. Although he speaks his mind freely on almost every significant and controversial topic, Thoreau has almost nothing to say about sex, and from the biographies we can only conclude that the closest he ever got to a woman in a romantic situation was the distance between the two seats of the rowboat in which he rowed Ellen Sewall around Walden Pond.

Psychologists have supposed—and a good many lay readers as

222

well—that Thoreau had a serious problem or even deficiency when it came to sex. Emerson and Channing seem to support this conjecture when they assure us that Thoreau never had any temptations to fight against. It has been suggested that he was a latent homosexual—"latent" meaning that whatever tendencies he might have had were never expressed. But I have always been suspicious of the whole concept of "latent" homosexuality. It's the easiest of accusations to make, and of course it cannot be disproved. (I have always believed, anyway, that there are far more latent heterosexuals among us.)

But whatever kind of sexuality Henry had, it was evidently more latent than potent. He was no stranger to sexual desire; he confessed that his acquaintance with women had not "always been free from the suspicion of lower sympathy" (Canby, *Thoreau,* p. 162). But lower sympathies, even if they were admitted, were to be repressed, not expressed. Unless some startling new information should come to light, we seem bound to conclude that he was a virgin. It remains for some imaginative novelist to do for Thoreau's sex life what Anthony Burgess did for Shakespeare's in *Nothing Like the Sun.* But then there's no denying that Burgess had a lot more to work with.

After the brief romance with Ellen Sewall when he was twenty-two, Thoreau seems never to have pursued another woman. We have so little information about his interest in Mary Russell that we can tentatively conclude that it didn't amount to much (a risky enough statement considering how quickly passionate love affairs can begin and end). There is no indication of any other romance in Thoreau's life—his "distinct no" to Miss Foord's suggestion of marriage indicates he had no interest in her—and we have the interesting deathbed reaction to his sister Sophia's mention of Ellen Sewall's name: "I have always loved her," he said. "I have always loved her."

Perhaps it would not be unfair to suggest that what he had always loved was his own Platonic idea of Ellen—for certainly in nearly everything complimentary he ever wrote about women he idealized them. The uncomplimentary things he wrote were mainly about the chatty young ladies people were always introducing him to:

The society of young women is the most unprofitable I have ever tried. They are so light and flighty that you can never be sure whether they are there or not there.

But when it came to Woman, his conception was courtly, or chivalric, at least in his habit of elevating the Woman he respected far above all taint of earthly things. To say he put this sort of Woman on a pedestal would be an understatement; he enshrined her among the stars.

I know a woman who is as true to me and as incessant with her mild rebuke as the blue sky—When I stand under her cope, and instantly all pretension drops off—& I am swept by her influence as by the wind and rain, to remove all taint. I am fortunate that I can pass and re-pass before her (as a mirror) each day—and prove my strength in her glances. She is far truer to me than to herself. Her eyes are like the windows of nature, through which I catch glimpses of the native land of the soul and from them comes a light which is not of the sun.

That Thoreau's tendency here is essentially Platonic is probably clear enough; just how Platonic it is I will explore later.

These are two poles of Thoreau's experience with women, then: on the one hand, a complete lack of experience in the physical expression of love; on the other hand, an incredibly idealized conception of Woman from which everything earthly has been purged. Brooks Atkinson has said that Thoreau's essays on "Love" and "Chastity and Sensuality" (which Henry sent as a wedding gift to his friend Harrison Blake) are "long on idealism and short on experience." We might be tempted to say the same of Thoreau's love life as a whole. But such a conclusion would need a good deal of qualification, and that qualification would turn on the word "love."

If by "love" we mean "physical love," then it's true he was short on experience; how "long" he was on idealism about sex is less clear, in view of his almost total reticence on the subject. His most explicit statement, from his essay on "Love," is this:

The subject of sex is a remarkable one, since, though its phenomena concern us so much, both directly and indirectly, and sooner or later, it occupies the thoughts of all, yet all mankind, as it were, agree to be silent about it, at least the sexes commonly one to another. One of the most interesting of all human facts is veiled more completely than any mystery. It is treated with such secrecy and awe as surely do not go to any religion. I believe it is unusual even for the most intimate friends to communicate the pleasures and anxieties connected with this fact,—much as the external affair of love, its comings and goings, are bruited. . . .

And it's clear that Thoreau is not about to lift the veil.

So he has virtually nothing to say about sex itself; on the more general subject of "sensuality," he is entirely negative. For example:

All sensuality is one, though it takes many forms. . . . It is the same whether a man eat, or drink, or cohabit, or sleep sensually. They are but one appetite, and we only need to see a person do any one of these things to know how great a sensualist he is ("Higher Laws," *Walden*).

Love and lust are far asunder. The one is good, the other bad. . . . Love and lust are as far asunder as a flower garden is from a brothel ("Chastity and Sensuality").

Sexual desire is clearly something to be denied; in Thoreau's mind, it has nothing to do with love.

The fact that Thoreau has so little to say about sex is no doubt attributable not only to his lack of first-hand experience, but also to his lack of second-hand or vicarious experience. He read voluminously, and he seems to have assimilated most of what he read. But in his Victorian age, an age when even Shakespeare was expurgated, he had little opportunity to read any literature that dealt openly with sexual matters. Even if he had had the opportunity, it is unlikely that he would have used it. Nothing but the most reverent treatment of the subject could have pleased him. When his friend Channing tried to tell him dirty stories, he told Channing to shut up. He said he could not "respect the mind that can jest on this subject."

But if by "love" we mean the *emotion* of love, apart from sexual desire, then although Thoreau is certainly long on idealism here, he is not, on the other hand, short on experience. On the contrary. Not only do we have evidence of his tender feelings for Ellen Sewall and Mary Russell (in his *Journal* and in the poem "To a Maiden in the East"), but we also have considerable documentation, in letters and journals, of his love for several older women. And it's not too much to call it love. Qualify it with "Platonic" if you will, but there is no better name for the feeling he expresses and describes in his writing. Even "friendship" is not enough. And where love is concerned, Thoreau is neither inexperienced nor reticent.

That he loved Lydian Emerson strongly and deeply is apparent from his letters to her. And if the language he uses makes some readers uncomfortable about the possible extent of his relationship with Emerson's wife, let them remember that not only Henry's sense of honor and loyalty, but his sexual inhibitions as well, should preclude any suspicion of the least impropriety. He is writing here in the language of what is sometimes called Courtly Love, sometimes Platonic Love:

My very dear Friend,
    I have only read a page of your letter and have come out to the top of the hill at sunset where I can see the ocean to prepare to read the rest. It is fitter that it should hear it than the walls of my chamber. The very crickets here seem to chirp around me as they did not before. I feel as if it were a great daring to go on and read the rest, and then to live accordingly. There are more than thirty vessels in sight going to sea. I am almost afraid to look at your letter. I see that it will make my life very steep, but it may lead to fairer prospects than this.
    You seem to me to speak out of a very clear and high heaven, where any one may be who stands so high. Your voice seems not a voice, but comes as much from the blue heavens, as from the paper.

My dear friend it was very noble in you to write me so trustful an answer. It will do as well for another world as for this. Such a voice is for no particular time nor person, and it makes him who may hear it stand for all that is lofty and true in humanity. The thought of you will constantly elevate my life; it will be something always above the horizon to behold, as when I look up at the evening star. I think I know your thoughts without seeing you, and as well here as in Concord. You are not at all strange to me. . . .

Both in this and in another letter to Lydian Emerson (both of which he wrote to her from Staten Island in 1843, after spending two years in the Emerson household), Thoreau speaks of the "elevating" influence she has had, and continues to have, on his life:

You have helped to keep my life "on loft," as Chaucer says of Griselda, and in a better sense. You always seemed to look down on me as from some elevation—some of your high humilities—and I was better for having to look up.

And in the Platonic scheme of things, this is the essential power of love—to lift us up, to raise us to higher and purer things.

But before looking at Thoreau's Platonism more closely, I would like to insist again that in the *emotion* of love, he was not at all short on experience. There were other women besides Lydian Emerson—like her, older than Thoreau; like her, intelligent, sensitive, well-read. And with these women, he was able to *talk*. They could listen to his observations and ideas with interest and sympathy, and they could provoke him with observations of their own. Thoreau was not eager to hear *most* women talk, but there were some to whose conversation he listened with pleasure.

Sometimes his enjoyment was impersonal, as when he arrived late to hear a lecture by the feminist Caroline Healey Dall, after having told Emerson that he thought most women had nothing to say. "Why Thoreau," said Emerson, "I thought you were not coming." Thoreau replied, "But *this* woman had something to say!"

But the personal, intimate conversations with close female friends were even better. Lydian Emerson's sister, Lucy Jackson Brown, seems to have been one of Thoreau's favorite women. In one letter to her he writes:

Pray let me know what you are thinking about any day,—what most nearly concerns you. Last winter, you know, you did more than your share of the talking, and I did not complain for want of an opportunity. Imagine your stove-door out of order, at least, and then while I am fixing it you will think of enough things to say.

What makes the value of your life at present? what dreams have you, and what realizations? You know there is a high tableland which not even the east wind reaches. Now can't we walk and chat upon its plane still, as if there were no lower latitudes?

Then there is Mary Moody Emerson, Emerson's brilliant and eccentric maiden aunt, whom Thoreau called "the wittiest and most vivacious woman that I know." Though she was very strait-laced in religion, and would rebuke Thoreau for not speaking of God with sufficient solemnity, she was tolerant of ideas generally. She was also a conversationalist who stimulated, rather than squelched, her companion. "It is perhaps her greatest praise and peculiarity," wrote Thoreau, "that she, more surely than any other woman, gives her companion occasion to utter his best thought."

But here perhaps the word "admiration" better describes the relationship than "love." At any rate, there was mutual enjoyment, and the instances of this kind of relationship are numerous enough to indicate that Thoreau was certainly not shy or backward with women, that he enjoyed their company immensely when they offered *intellectual* companionship, and that some women, at any rate, found him a delightful companion.

Since we are not speaking now of *sexual* love, we might also recall the numerous close friendships Thoreau had with men: Charles Stearns Wheeler, Jones Very, Bronson Alcott, Ellery Channing, Emerson, Edward Hoar, Harrison Blake—to mention a few. Did he *love* these men? Some of them, without a doubt— as long as they rose to the high expectations with which he met them. And that "love" and "friendship" are virtually interchangeable words for Thoreau will become evident, I think, in a few passages we will consider in a moment.

It is clear, then, that Thoreau had experience in love. And because he had this experience and reflected on it seriously (often with great anxiety) and because chaste and Platonic love and friendship, at least, were not bowdlerized from the literature he read, he was able to compare his own experiences and observations on love with those of poets and philosophers of all the ages. Out of this reading and thinking and talking and feeling, Thoreau managed, at a relatively early age, to distill some of the most beautiful and eloquent statements on friendship in our literature. And if he sometimes seems a little too high-flown, a little too ethereal, we should be hesitant about scoffing. To attempt to define the nature of love is to rush in where angels fear to tread; but to criticize another man's attempt to do so is the sheerest effrontery.

It is easy to find contradictions in Thoreau's statements about love and friendship. This should not be surprising, for like Emerson, he contradicts himself throughout his writings and is not the least bit troubled about doing so. (On this point he might well have borrowed Walt Whitman's words: "Do I contradict myself? Very well, then, I contradict myself. I am large. I contain multitudes.")

But then he is certainly guilty of some absurdities—though whether or not a given statement is absurd must be a very subjective judgment. There are some things to bear in mind, however, about these absurdities and contradictions. First, that anyone who risks writing on such a complex and emotion-charged subject is bound to arrive at some conclusions beyond the reach of logic or common sense. Second, that Thoreau was undergoing some profound emotional traumas when he wrote many of these statements: for example, the sudden death of his brother John, and his estrangement from Emerson. Third, that Thoreau's writings on love and friendship span many years and many moods. Some of his ideas change with further experience and further thought.

What is of value for us will remain; the rest will be dismissed and forgotten as it fails the test of our own experience. My claim is only that there is much worth considering, much worth remembering. I think Thoreau knew a great deal about love and friendship. If his standards, his expectations, are impossibly high, it is because he deliberately set them at that level. Who knows what we are capable of? Thoreau never claimed to know. And if friendship to him was always a tragedy, it is because the essence of tragedy is simply that: the difference between the best we can imagine and the best we can achieve.

II

I have said that Thoreau's notions of love and friendship resemble both the Platonic idea of love and the theories of Courtly Love in the Middle Ages. Let me explain.

In the dialogue of Plato called the *Symposium,* Socrates tells how he has been instructed in the matter of love by a very wise woman named Diotima. Diotima tells him that love is a natural attraction our souls have for the Good, the True, and the Beautiful, which are simply three facets of the same divine Perfection. But in the young and inexperienced person, this natural inclination is not yet developed; the development can be enhanced and encouraged by conscious awareness and understanding of what is happening and what *should* happen. The soul begins, perhaps, by loving a single beautiful object—a person, for instance, toward which it is irresistibly drawn. But the soul soon learns that the beauty, or goodness, or truth which it perceived in this one person is also in other persons, and so its love expands to include more than one person. Then the soul sees that truth and beauty and goodness may be found in the natural world and in human institutions, and so it learns to love these things too—insofar as they contain elements of the good, the true, and the beautiful. From the love of institutions the soul proceeds—as if climbing a ladder —toward a love of "higher" things: of laws, for example, or of mathematical principles or musical harmonies. Eventually, of course, the goal of this ascent of the Platonic ladder is for the soul to love *pure* goodness, truth, and beauty—in other words, to love the principle, or the idea, or the *form* of these things, no matter where or how they may be embodied or expressed.

Pure Platonism, then, does not condemn the love of beautiful things or beautiful persons, nor does it deny sexual love. In fact, Diotima speaks explicitly (in terms too plain for some modern readers) of a man's natural love and desire for some handsome youth. In ancient Greece, the word "love" was as commonly applied to a homosexual attraction as to a heterosexual one.

But St. Paul and the early Church fathers changed all that. They discovered much in Plato that they admired and found perfectly consistent with Christianity. The Good, the True, and the Beautiful, for example, toward which all human souls naturally aspired, was simply another way of saying God. But orthodox Christianity has never been very comfortable about sex, for a number of complex reasons, and by the time Christianity had assimilated Platonism, the sexual element had been entirely expunged, and we were left with the ethereal "Platonic love" into which no suspicion of sexual desire must ever enter. Even the language was changed. Plato's word for love had been *eros,* but Christian love was *agapé,* which means something like "brotherly love," or more commonly, *caritas,* or "charity."

Christian Platonism won many adherents among the young and high-minded through the centuries. John Milton was one of the most ardent devotees of this system, and was particularly infatuated with the idea of chastity, by which he meant virginity. Probably the best exposition of Christian Platonism in the Renaissance occurs in *The Book of the Courtier* by Baldassare Castiglione, translated into English in Shakespeare's day by Sir Thomas Hoby. In one section of the book a bright young nobleman named Peter Bembo explains that Beauty is only "the outward bound and circumference" of Goodness, so that a beautiful woman is almost certain to be good, and vice versa. And he explains the growth and progression of love with the ladder metaphor, just as in Plato's *Symposium.*

Castiglione is not quite so negative about the physical aspects of love as most Christian Platonists, but he handles the whole subject with lightness and restraint, and goes only so far as to allow Peter Bembo to admit that kissing may be permitted in a relationship of pure and chaste love, as a means of bringing the souls of lovers into closer contact. There's a good deal of pussyfooting going on here, as you can see, and though Castiglione has a "dirty old man" scoffing at Bembo's exclusion of sexuality from his discourse on true love, the other participants in the discussion support Bembo's view completely. With books of this sort as the standard reading matter of the educated classes, it's not difficult to see why so many generations of our ancestors have been so confused about sex.

Courtly Love is quite another thing, in its original form, as it developed in southern France in the eleventh century. Sex was its focus and its reason for being. But by the time it was assimilated into the mainstream of Western culture, it had been considerably watered down. It is from the tradition of Courtly Love that we get most of our modern ideas of "romantic" love. "Romantic" originally meant "as in the old romances," and these romances were verse tales of love and adventure, told by such poets as Chrétien de Troyes, author of *Perceval, Lancelot,* and several other notable stories.

Courtly Love developed as an antithetical system to Christian Platonism. It was centered upon the sexuality that Christian Platonism lacked. It seems to have been invented among certain ladies of the courts of various French noblemen—with the assistance of various poets and ardent young men—possibly as a rationalization of the extramarital affairs that often developed between the ladies of the court and young noblemen or even pages.

But what particularly distinguished Courtly Love was that it was a highly formalized system, with rituals and dogmas as strict as those of Christianity and often remarkably parallel to those of Christianity. The code of conduct for the lover and his lady was extremely rigid. In the first place, there were high qualifications for the lovers; not just any churl could play the game. And then the whole love affair had to be conducted by certain rules; the utmost secrecy and decorum had to be observed, for example, and each lover was expected to have a confidant to serve as a go-between and adviser. The young man had to court his lady according to a prescribed system, and the lady was expected to set certain tasks for her lover to perform in order to prove his love. If either lover failed to abide by the rules of the game, courts of love were convened to try the accused party and decide punishment if he or she were found guilty. The goal of the whole game, of course, was sexual intimacy, and the whole thing was made deliciously spicy by all the obstacles and intrigues. At the same time, it considerably elevated the status of the woman, and protected her from being treated merely as a piece of property. In lifting the relationship between the sexes above the merely utilitarian, it made a religion of love—a religion whose high code and beautiful objects of worship were strongly appealing to those whose idealism found no home in the Church. As the highest of human achievements, a true love demanded the purest dedication, the kind of dedication a young man like Thoreau would be capable of.

One other aspect of Courtly Love deserves attention: ideally it was expected to occur between a married woman and a younger, unmarried man. The primary reason for this was that it was not believed that true love could exist within marriage. True love must be freely given and freely received, and any element of duty, or constraint, or obligation—as in marriage—was fatal to true love.

So Courtly Love emphasized woman—and preferably a mature married woman—as the proper object of love for a young man. The complicated rules governing the conduct of such a relationship necessitated a good deal of conversation between the lovers—the young man being expected to sue for the gratification of his passion in the most eloquent language possible, and the lady being expected to test and temper the quality of his love until she was satisfied that he was worthy of her. Language and dialogue were important to Courtly Love, just as they are a natural part of the Platonic tradition. In both cases the suitor must understand what it is he seeks, and why, and if his understanding is originally deficient, he is enlightened in the course of the lovers' conversation. In both systems the concept of true love is an elevated one, a noble ideal, and in both systems desire must be complemented by understanding.

Just as Christianity had assimilated Platonism, so Christian Platonism eventually assimilated Courtly Love, and the result was that in much of the literature of Courtly Love, the Lady remains chaste and unattainable—too pure, too good to be dishonored by her gallant and self-sacrificing lover, or prevented from receiving him by some tragic circumstance. Thus, because the affair was never consummated, it became suitable, even elevating, reading for the young Christian lady or gentleman who was thereby simultaneously instructed in the tragic suffering of adulterous affairs and in the ennobling effect of a love that remained entirely on a verbal plane.

Thoreau inherited this peculiarly amalgamated tradition, as to some extent we all have. It was a scheme that helped to shape his life and thought, and then proved admirably suited to serve the mind and heart it created.

III

Thoreau's philosophy of love and friendship has three basic tenets:

(1) Physical attraction or desire has nothing to do with true love or friendship.

(2) The friends or lovers must be persons of exceptionally noble character and sensitivity.

(3) A truly complete and satisfying friendship or love relationship, if achieved, cannot be sustained long at its highest level.

Let me illustrate these beliefs of Thoreau's by quoting some relevant passages.

Although he expressed frank admiration for Whitman's poetry, he confessed to some serious reservations about Whitman's "sensuality," complaining that Whitman was not writing about *love* at all:

There are 2 or 3 pieces in the book [the second edition of *Leaves of Grass*] which are disagreeable to say the least, simply sensual. He does not celebrate love at all. It is as if the beasts spoke. I think that men have not been ashamed of themselves without reason . . . (Letter to Blake).

In a passage previously quoted from "Higher Laws," he condemns sensuality of any kind:

All sensuality is one, though it takes many forms. . . . It is the same whether a man eat, or drink, or cohabit, or sleep sensually.

And he suggests that the best thing to do with sexual energy is to sublimate it:

The generative energy, which, when we are loose, dissipates and makes us unclean, when we are continent invigorates and inspires us. Chastity is the flowering of man, and what are called Genius, Heroism, Holiness, and the like, are but various fruits which succeed it ("Chastity and Sensuality").

But what about marriage? Surely sex is permissible there? But no. . . .

If it is the result of a pure love, there can be nothing sensual in marriage. Chastity is something positive, not negative. It is the virtue of the married especially. All lusts or base pleasures must give place to loftier delights. They who meet as superior beings cannot perform the deeds of inferior ones ("Chastity and Sensuality").

Thoreau's antisensualism is extreme here, and though we may be used to his overstatement in other contexts, this is hard to take. But it clearly indicates that he will have nothing to do with physical contact in a love relationship. To put it more positively, he insists simply that true love must be chaste. Here he is very much in the tradition of Christian Platonism, and though most Platonists happily exempt the marriage bed from their antisensual strictures, there are some, even today, who go as far as Thoreau.

The most interesting things Thoreau has to say about love come out of his second basic belief—that true friends or lovers must be nobly elevated and rarely matched. He finds it hard to believe that people will marry under less exacting conditions than his own:

Considering how few poetical friendships there are, it is remarkable that so many are married. It would seem as if men yielded too easy an obedience to nature without consulting their genius ("Love").

It is "poetical friendships" that Thoreau wishes to establish, and the fullest exposition of his ideas occurs in the "Friendship" essay added to the Wednesday section of *A Week on the Concord and Merrimack Rivers* in 1848. He is not talking about the common man's notion of friendship—"To say that a man is your Friend, means commonly no more than this, that he is not your enemy." Such a friendship is based on mutual advantage—what each can get from the other; little is required of either but basic honesty and a lack of animosity.

But a true, "poetical" friendship requires, to begin with, that the partners be equal to each other:

Friendship is, at any rate, a relation of perfect equality. It cannot well spare any outward sign of equal obligation and advantage. The nobleman can never have a Friend among his retainers, nor the king among his subjects. Not that the parties to it are in all respects equal, but they are equal in all that respects or affects their Friendship. The one's love is exactly balanced and represented by the other's. Persons are only the vessels which contain the nectar, and the hydrostatic paradox is the symbol of love's law. It finds its level and rises to its fountain-head in all breasts, and its slenderest column balances the ocean.

It is not only the metaphysical image of the "hydrostatic paradox" [1] that recalls John Donne here; we might also be reminded

1. The principle (depending on the law of uniform pressure of liquids) that any quantity of a perfect liquid, however small, may be made to balance any quantity (or any weight), however great.

of "The Good-morrow," in which Donne insists that love will last only if the partners contribute to it equally:

> Whatever dies was not mixed equally;
> If our two loves be one, or thou and I
> Love so alike that none do slacken, none can die.

Then Thoreau's thought takes a surprising turn. Insisting repeatedly that it is nearly impossible to find one other soul with whom one can establish a true friendship, he goes boldly on to consider whether a true friendship can exist as well among three as between two.

We shall not surrender ourselves heartily to any while we are conscious that another is more deserving of our love. Yet Friendship does not stand for numbers; the Friend does not count his Friends on his fingers; they are not numerable. The more there are included by this bond, if they are indeed included, the rarer and diviner the quality of the love that binds them. I am ready to believe that as private and intimate a relation may exist by which three are embraced, as between two.

And here, of course, he is being perfectly Platonic—surely you can love two mistresses or wives as well as one, and the love can be mutual all the way around. Theoretically this sounds wonderful, and once or twice I have tried very hard to believe it myself. But it's like believing you are going to write the great American novel: you haven't actually done it yet, but you're sure you have it in you.

(Thoreau may have been thinking, when he wrote this, of his friends Waldo and Lydian Emerson; within a year or two, however, he apparently abandoned his dream.)

But no matter how noble the friends are, Thoreau continues, their friendship makes them nobler; it elevates them above their ordinary state—"It will make a man honest; it will make him a hero; it will make him a saint." And this is the effect of friendship that he claims most often for himself—that *he*, at least, has been inspired, uplifted, and made a better man by the examples and the expectations of his friends.

High expectations are crucial to Thoreau's idea of friendship. A true friend idealizes us; he sees us as better than we are. And the beneficial effect of this is that we tend to grow—whether consciously or not—to measure up to our friend's ideal image of us.

We are sometimes made aware of a kindness long passed, and realize that there have been times when our friends' thoughts of us were of so pure and lofty a character that they passed over us like the winds of heaven unnoticed; when they treated us not as what we were but as what we aspired to be.

And later he adds:

I value and trust those who love and praise my aspiration rather than my performance. If you would not stop to look at me, but look whither I am looking and further, then my education could not dispense with your company.

But this does not mean that friends see or value each other falsely; on the contrary. They see each other's true potential, and behave as if they expect that potential to be realized; but at the same time they see each other's faults with a terrible frankness.

Friends must *know* each other truly; a friendship cannot exist where the knowledge is only partial. To fail to know both your friend's virtues and his faults is to insult him unforgivably. "This want of perception is a defect which all the virtues of the heart cannot supply."

Friendship does not excuse or forgive faults, says Thoreau. This is hard doctrine. But it is wise. For one thing, it is consistent with his insistence on complete honesty between friends: "Between whom there is hearty truth there is love; and in proportion to our truthfulness and confidence in one another, our lives are divine and miraculous, and answer to our ideal."

Thoreau is impatient with gentlemanly "good manners," not only in friends, but even in acquaintances:

Men are very generally spoiled by being so civil and well-disposed. You can have no profitable conversation with them, they are so con-

ciliatory, determined to agree with you. They exhibit such long-suffer-
ing and kindness in a short interview. I would meet with some provoking strangeness, so that we may be guest and host and refresh
one another. It is possible for a man wholly to disappear and be
merged in his manners. The thousand and one gentlemen whom I
meet, I meet despairingly and but to part from them, for I am not
cheered by the hope of any rudeness from them. A cross man, a
coarse man, an eccentric man, a silent, a man who does not drill
well,—of him there is some hope.

And he cannot ignore or excuse his friends' faults:

Confucius said, "To contract ties of Friendship with anyone is to
contract Friendship with his virtue. There ought not to be any other
motive in Friendship." But men wish us to contract Friendship with
their vice also. I have a Friend who wishes me to see that to be right
which I know to be wrong. But if Friendship is to rob me of my eyes,
if it is to darken the day, I will have none of it. It should be expan-
sive and inconceivably liberalizing in its effects. True Friendship can
afford true knowledge. It does not depend on darkness and ignorance.
A want of discernment cannot be an ingredient in it. If I can see
my Friend's virtues more distinctly than another's, his faults too are
made more conspicuous by contrast. We have not so good right to
hate any as our Friend. Faults are not the less faults because they
are invariably balanced by corresponding virtues, and for a fault
there is no excuse, though it may appear greater than it is in many
ways.

But at the same time, he and his friends are under mutual obligation not to advertise their faults to each other, nor to expect
indulgence:

The sorest insult which I ever received from a Friend was, when
he behaved with the license which only long and cheap acquaintance
allows to one's faults, in my presence, without shame, and still
addressed me in friendly accents.

Perhaps it is becoming clear that Thoreau is as much a Puritan
and absolutist about friendship as D. H. Lawrence is about sex.
Certain things are strictly forbidden.

And so it's no wonder, we conclude, that Thoreau found that

friendships couldn't last. Who could meet such exacting standards? Yet friends who know each other truly and deal honestly with each other are not unreasonable in their expectations, he insists: "For a companion I require one who will make an equal demand on me with my own genius. Such a one will always be rightly tolerant." Friends respect each other's individuality and integrity: "They cherish each other's hopes. They are kind to each other's dreams."

But the requirements for a poetical friendship continue to multiply, and we find ourselves overwhelmed by all the rules and regulations. *Of course,* no one could be expected to live up to all those demands. But then it suddenly dawns on us: they are not demands at all. Thoreau is not prescribing rules for conducting an ideal friendship; he is simply describing what happens in such a relationship. These are not rules you can consciously obey; your behavior must be natural, intuitive; it must come out of your character. Otherwise, it is false and insincere.

Friendship cannot be planned, nor friends selected: Friendship takes place between those who have an affinity for one another, and is a perfectly natural and inevitable result. No professions nor advances will avail. . . . Impatient and uncertain lovers think that they must say or do something kind whenever they meet; they must never be cold. But they who are Friends do not what they *think* they must, but what they *must.*

Does friendship need proofs? Certainly, says Thoreau: "Friendship is a miracle which requires constant proofs." Yet the proofs cannot be consciously determined; they simply happen, and our friend recognizes them for what they are: "He never asks for a sign of love, but can distinguish it by the features which it naturally wears." In fact, there are after all, surprisingly, no "laws" of love, no rules for conduct: "A true Friendship is as wise as it is tender. The parties to it yield implicitly to the guidance of their love, and know no other law nor kindness."

Although the love relationship described by Thoreau has as much *form* as the relationship of Courtly Love, it is a natural, organic form, not a mechanical one, a form proceeding not from

Reason but from Understanding, a form created not by following several dozen explicit rules, but by yielding to the influence of one divine law.

IV

Perhaps we may have objections to some of this. Thoreau may not take us with him all the way. Even with the greatest sympathy for his purpose, we may sometimes find his philosophy unacceptable or incomprehensible. So far, except for his strictures on sensuality (a very considerable exception), I can find no very basic objections to his beliefs about the way in which true lovers behave with each other. But there is one article in his catalogue that seems to me a naïve error—entirely too mystical, too unrealistic. Lovers or friends should never have to discuss any aspect of their relationship, he says: the relationship is too sacred to talk about. Everything must be understood without the need of words. "Love is the profoundest of secrets. Divulged, even to the beloved, it is no longer love" ("Love").

This is one paradox I cannot accept. Never say "I love you"? Never "Let me count the ways"? Thoreau continues:

I require that thou knowest everything without being told anything. I parted from my beloved because there was one thing which I had to tell her. She *questioned* me. She should have known all by sympathy. That I had to tell her was the difference between us,—the misunderstanding ("Love").

The feeling is probably a familiar one to all of us. We long for that total sympathy and understanding—perhaps mostly so that we will not need to explain ourselves when we don't want to.

> 'Tis pity if the case require
> (Or so we say) that in the end
> We speak the literal to inspire
> The understanding of a friend.[2]

2. From "Revelation" from *The Poetry of Robert Frost*, edited by Edward Connery Lathem. Copyright 1934 by Holt, Rinehart and Winston, Inc. Copyright © 1962 by Robert Frost. Reprinted by permission of Holt, Rinehart and Winston.

But to expect to be known without revealing ourselves is to expect what no human being can give us. Those who like to play at hide-and-seek, says Frost, "must speak and tell us where they are."

Thoreau tells us pretty much where he is in his writings. But he was not ready to tell his friends where he was; he expected them to know. The cooling of his friendship with Emerson has this symptom; Thoreau didn't want to talk about it, didn't want to explain anything.

I had two friends. The one offered me friendship on such terms that I could not accept it, without a sense of degradation. He would not meet me on equal terms, but only be to some extent my patron. He would not come to see me, but was hurt if I did not visit him. He would not readily accept a favor, but would gladly confer one. He treated me with ceremony occasionally, though he could be simple and downright sometimes; and from time to time acted a part, treating me as if I were a distinguished stranger; was on stilts, using made words. Our relation was one long tragedy, yet I did not directly speak of it. I do not believe in complaint, nor in explanation. The whole is but too plain, alas, already. We grieve that we do not love each other, that we cannot confide in each other. I could not bring myself to speak, and so recognize an obstacle to our affection.

And all that Thoreau says about the "tragedy" of love or friendship relates to this feeling of estrangement for reasons that cannot be discussed. We are left wondering if the end of the friendship is as inevitable as he concludes it is. His friendships *are* tragedies, to be sure. But is there a tragic flaw, an error? Is this where he misses the mark?

Whatever Thoreau's disappointments and tragedies in love and friendship, he gives us much to think about. He speaks sincerely and feelingly, and much of what he says vibrates with the sure, clear tone of truth; we feel it in our pulses. The quotable and memorable statements abound in the "Friendship" section of *A Week*. This one stays with me: "They cherish each other's hopes. They are kind to each other's dreams." Thoreau's words remind us of other men's words about love and friendship, and of our own unspoken thoughts as well. And perhaps we too long for the friend we can address in some such words as Thoreau imagines:

I never asked thy leave to let me love thee,—I have a right. I love thee not as something private and personal, which is *your own,* but as something universal and worthy of love, *which I have found.* O how I think of you! You are purely good,—you are infinitely good. I can trust you forever. I did not think that humanity was so rich. Give me an opportunity to live.

You are the fact in a fiction,—you are the truth more strange and admirable than fiction. Consent only to be what you are. I alone will never stand in your way.

This is what I would like,—to be as intimate with you as our spirits are intimate,—respecting you as I respect my ideal. Never to profane one another by word or action, even by a thought. Between us, if necessary, let there be no acquaintance.

I have discovered you; how can you be concealed from me?

Afterword: Some Random Thoughts on Thoreau's Personality

To help round out the picture, I would like to discuss a few aspects of Thoreau's personality a little further before bringing this volume to a close. I shall not attempt a full-fledged analysis of his personality, but rather will make a few brief comments both on what has been said and what has been unsaid in the preceding essays.

Several of the writers have alluded in one way or another to Henry Thoreau's supposed love for Lydian Emerson, Ralph Waldo Emerson's second wife. The legend of his love was originated by Henry Seidel Canby in his *Thoreau* (Boston: Houghton Mifflin, 1939, pp. 155–163). Other than several letters which Thoreau wrote Mrs. Emerson (which Raymond Adams, the dean of American Thoreau scholars, said shows that "there was a slight mother-fixation about the Thoreau–Lydian Emerson relationship, but nothing more"), Canby's only "evidence" is a fragmentary Thoreau manuscript entitled "A Sister," which is now in the Huntington Library in San Marino, California. Unfortunately Mr. Canby was never able to prove that that "sister" was Mrs. Emerson. It could just as well have been his actual sister, Helen, who died just about the time of the composition of the manuscript, or it could even be a personification of Nature, so

inconclusive are Thoreau's references. At any rate, Canby's theory
has been discounted by virtually every major Thoreau scholar.

A large number of critics have blamed Thoreau's mother for
his maladjustments in life. There is little question that she was
the dominant member of the Thoreau household, but I think
there has been a tendency to overemphasize the extent of her
domination simply because these critics have based their judgments of Mrs. Thoreau on the statements of Frank Sanborn in
his biographies of Thoreau. They have not been sufficiently aware
of the fact that Sanborn was strongly prejudiced against Mrs.
Thoreau. As an antidote to his depiction of her one should read
Jean Munro LeBrun's "Henry Thoreau's Mother," which was
first published in the Boston *Advertiser* of February 14, 1883,
as a reply to Sanborn's biography, and which has not received the
circulation it deserves. Mrs. LeBrun was for many years a
familiar of the Thoreau household. Her essay is too long to reprint here in its entirety, but a few paragraphs will give its essence:

I think the characteristics which chiefly impressed those of us who
knew Mrs. Thoreau best, were the activity of her mind and the
wideness of her sympathy. . . . She was also an excellent mother
and housewife. In the midst of poverty she brought up her children
to all the amenities of life, and, if she had but a crust of bread for
dinner, would see that it was properly served. Mr. Sanborn says
patronizingly, "she had sentiments of generosity." She certainly had,
though I should scarcely have spoken of it in that way. Year after
year, on Christmas and Thanksgiving days, she invited to her table,
not the rich who would return her hospitality, but her poorer neighbors from whom she could expect no return. She was never so poor
or so busy that she did not find ways of helping those poorer than
herself. Such was her influence in this respect that it was felt by
all who came in contact with her, and one young girl was heard to
say, "When I grow up, I will do like Mrs. Thoreau. I will give my
gifts to those who need them, and I will invite to my table the poor
rather than the rich, who are sure to have plenty of invitations
without mine."

And yet she did not confine her hospitality to the poor; people of every kind and degree were welcomed under her roof.

Her efforts in the anti-slavery cause are well known. She was unsparing in her denunciation of the fugitive slave law, and was one of the first to give aid and comfort to fugitives. . . . When she became interested in a poor servant-girl, she placed money in the bank for her, and encouraged her to add little sums to it from time to time. And when she made her will, every dollar was disposed of conscientiously where she thought it would do the most good, and in no way merely for her own pleasure. It was no mere impulse which made her do these things, but a high and noble principle. There was no poor man or woman who came in contact with her to whom she did not do some good.

She had her faults, as which of us has not? but her aim was high. She expressed herself frankly at all times, and she sometimes told disagreeable truths; perhaps she felt it a duty to do so. She had the courage of her convictions, and she certainly never hesitated to condemn a fault. It was done in all honesty to bring about a reform. She was much more likely to say severe things to people than of them. This does not make a person popular. She was a great talker, and she occasionally said sharp things; but what was this in comparison with her virtues? She was quick-witted and observing, and naturally had more to say than some of her neighbors. She was never guilty of mean and petty gossip. She was not uncharitable, and could readily forgive a fault if she saw any signs of repentance. On the whole, I think few women have done more good and less harm in the world than Mrs. Thoreau.

Thus she was hardly the dragon that Sanborn would have us suppose.

The question has sometimes been raised as to whether Thoreau was a homosexual. Had he been at all homosexually active, it would have been impossible for him to hide that fact in a town as small as Concord. To the best of my knowledge, no one has ever found the slightest hint of any suspicion on the part of his fellow townsmen. The argument that mid-Victorians would have been too prudish to mention any such suspicions even if they had had them is not a valid one, for a few years after Thoreau's death

Concordians raised a brouhaha over the homosexual activities of one man, and ran him out of town.

I must admit that the poem "Sympathy" which Thoreau wrote in 1839 in tribute to the eleven-year-old Edmund Sewall seems pretty strong evidence of homoerotic inclinations. J. Z. Eglinton, for example, in *Greek Love* (New York, 1964, p. 367), calls it "unequivocal in both its descriptions of [homosexual] desires and its confession of Thoreau's inability to make them known." Apparently Ralph Waldo Emerson was disturbed enough by the implications of the poem (or was he just plain naïve?) that he created out of whole cloth the story that Thoreau had written the poem about Ellen rather than Edmund Sewall—though he was hard put to explain why its subject is male rather than female. But, on the other hand, Edmund's own parents were apparently not at all disturbed by the poem and later enrolled Edmund as a student in the Thoreau boarding school—something it is hard to imagine their doing if they had the slightest suspicion that Thoreau was sexually attracted to their son. They obviously considered his admiration of Edmund to be intellectual rather than physical.

Some have cited Thoreau's *Journal* passage recording his "pleasure" at seeing young boys swimming in the nude as an indication of a more than casual physical interest in members of his own sex. While it may indicate an interest, it does not document an activity. And Havelock Ellis, in his monumental *Studies in the Psychology of Sex*, cites this particular passage from Thoreau, not as an example of homoerotic interest, but rather as an example of an enlightened attitude toward nudity. On the basis of the known evidence, I think we can conclude that Thoreau was not an active homosexual, and if he had homoerotic inclinations, he was apparently successful in suppressing or sublimating them.

Was Thoreau a prude? Many have thought so and can cite good evidence in defense of their position: he acted the complete prig when his friend Ellery Channing tried to tell him off-color jokes. Although he went into almost endless detail in *Walden* about every other facet of his housekeeping facilities at the pond, he was too reticent to even mention his toilet facilities. When he found a phallic fungus, his dismay and disappointment with Mother Nature for permitting such an obscenity to grow is amusing to any modern reader. His essays on "Love" and "Chastity and Sensuality" are, as Brooks Atkinson has observed, "Long on idealism and short on experience—in general a silly blunder," and his opening statement in "Love": "What the essential difference between man and woman is, that they should be thus attracted to one another, no one has satisfactorily answered," is, as Joseph Wood Krutch has said, "a real howler."

Yet, on the other hand, Thoreau could be astonishingly un-Victorian and outspoken at times. He teased Bronson Alcott about the derivation of his family name from Allcock. He was one of the few in his day to defend Walt Whitman's erotic poetry. He may have been privy about his own privy, but he devoted pages and pages of his *Journal* to a scientific study of the scatology of Concord wildlife. In *Walden* he chastised his readers for not emulating the Hindus in circulating rule books on "how to eat, drink, cohabit, void excrement and urine, and the like." (Shades of the *Kama Sutra*!) And when he found the phallic fungus, despite his expressed dismay, he made so realistic a drawing of it in his journal that the editors suppressed it when they published the text. Most surprising is the fact that he was, to a certain extent, a practicing nudist, often wading the length of the rivers of Concord completely naked and exalting some of the virtues of Adamitism. (Modern nudists look upon him somewhat as their patron saint and have devoted a number of articles to him in their various publications.) If then Thoreau was a prude—or should we say a typical mid-Victorian—in some respects, he was surprisingly unprudish and in advance of his time in others.

There is an incident too in Thoreau's life that it seems to me has not been sufficiently explored. It is the curious case of sympathetic illness he experienced just after the death of his brother

John. John died one of the most painful of deaths—from tetanus —in his brother's arms on January 11, 1842. Eleven days later Henry too became ill, exhibiting all the symptoms, including lockjaw, of his brother's disease. So intense was the illness that doctors gave up all hope and told the family that they could but await the end. But then suddenly after a few days there was a turn for the better and he slowly recovered, though he was confined to his bed for a month and even by mid-April was too weak to work in the garden. He went through many months of depression. For several years thereafter he dreamed "tragic dreams" on the anniversary of John's death. For the rest of his life he still choked, and tears came into his eyes, at the mention of his brother's name. His first book, *A Week,* as is well known, was written as a memorial tribute to John, even though, in the tradition of the elegy, John is never specifically mentioned by name within its pages. The illness, it is hardly necessary to say, was psychosomatic and is not unprecedented in medical annals, but such an overwhelming reaction to his brother's death is certainly deserving of further analysis by those who would understand Thoreau's personality.

It is surprising how often modern psychologists refer to Thoreau. For example, Henry Clay Smith in his *Personality Development* (New York, 1968, pp. 163–167) uses Thoreau as an example to illustrate his definition of an introvert—"a person of high aesthetic values and low economic values, who has a strong inclination toward meditative and reflective thinking." If this is accepted as a definition of "introvert," it fits Thoreau to the proverbial "T."

When A. H. Maslow made his well-known study of what he called "self-actualizing" people, that is, people who succeeded in a "full realization of human potential," he too chose Thoreau as an example—although he added that he was not certain that Thoreau completely fulfilled the definition. But when he went on to describe the self-actualizers as individuals who "have the wonderful capacity to appreciate again and again, freshly and naïvely,

the basic goods of life with awe, pleasure, wonder, and even
ecstasy, however stale these experiences may have become to
others" (*Motivation and Personality* [New York, 1954], p. 214),
it would be indeed difficult to find a better description of at least
one aspect of Thoreau's personality.

Paul Carroll, in a brief digression in *The Poem in Its Skin*
(Chicago, 1968, pp. 182–184), advances an interesting theory
about Thoreau's personality:

> How was it that a man of such genius for moral realities and
> for creating great American prose was also such a mean failure in
> private life?
> At everything he tried or seemed to want, Thoreau failed: he failed
> . . . as schoolmaster; he failed as suitor of Miss Ellen Sewall; he
> failed as lecturer at the Concord Lyceum; and he failed at the one
> career he seemed to care the most about—that of man of letters. . . .
> What accounts for these failures? It would be romantic to claim
> that Thoreau's failures came solely as the result of his refusal to com-
> promise his principles; it would be more realistic to try and under-
> stand why his contemporaries failed to recognize and reward the
> extraordinary man he was. In other words: How much of Thoreau's
> failures were the fault of the traditional villain—the hostile and/or
> pigheaded square world—and how much were they the fault of
> Thoreau's own attitude?
> Everyone knows the shameful history of the square world in its
> encounters with men of genius such as Thoreau. . . . Clearly the
> square world of 19th century Concord was not about to shower recog-
> nition or prizes on Henry Thoreau, who kept reminding that world
> [that] there were deeper and more exciting scenes for a man to enjoy
> than the accumulation of cash, clothes and conventional geegaws.
> But how much of Thoreau's fate as a chronic loser also resulted
> from that sour, unhappy side of himself which encouraged him to
> act like a skulker? . . . The implication of [Robert Louis] Steven-
> son's criticism is that Thoreau skulked because the world refused to
> admit the genius which at the time only he knew he possessed. As
> a result, he wasted a lot of time and energy in looking down his
> nose at his fellow citizens. In particular, he looked down on two
> important qualities which make one's life a success (at least in the

common sense of the term). Everyone knows what those qualities are: the desire to earn what one wants, and the ability to force one's contemporaries to recognize achievement in having earned what one wants. Instead of putting his considerable gifts to work to earn what these qualities can achieve, Thoreau chose to skulk and remain a loser. . . .

The Thoreau Complex, then, is one which embodies the sour jealousy and quiet desperation of a man of great or strong gifts who refuses to put those gifts or strengths to the test by earning the success he deserves.[1]

Mr. Carroll tells us that he derives his picture of Thoreau from Stevenson's famous essay, but he was apparently unaware that Stevenson publicly retracted that essay, saying that it had been written without a full knowledge of the facts of Thoreau's life. Nonetheless there is an element of truth in Mr. Carroll's theory. Take, for example, Thoreau's attitude toward his lack of success on the lecture platform, which Mr. Carroll alludes to. In his *Journal* Thoreau says:

After lecturing twice this winter I feel that I am in danger of cheapening myself by trying to become a successful lecturer, *i.e.*, to interest my audiences. I am disappointed to find that most that I am and value myself for is lost, or worse than lost, on my audience. I fail to get even the attention of the mass. I should suit them better if I suited myself less. I feel that the public demand an average man, —average thoughts and manners,—not originality, nor even absolute excellence. You can not interest them except as you are like them and sympathize with them. I would rather that my audience come to me than I should go to them, and so they be sifted; *i.e.*, I would rather write books than lectures. That is fine, this coarse. To read to a promiscuous audience who are at your mercy the fine thoughts you solaced yourself with far away is as violent as to fatten geese by cramming, and in this case they do not get fatter.

Or, again:

1. "The Thoreau Complex Amid the Solid Scholars" from *The Poem in It's Skin* by Paul Carroll. Copyright © 1968 by Paul Carroll. Used by permission of Big Table Publishing Company.

I am from time to time congratulating myself on my general want of success as a lecturer; apparent want of success; but is it not real triumph? I do my work clean as I go along, and they will not be likely to want me anywhere again.

These seem almost textbook examples of the "skulker," and Thoreau's skulking, while by no means a major element in his personality, is not limited to his lack of success on the lecture platform.

Many have commented on Thoreau's amazing cheerfulness in the last months of his life when he knew well he had but a short time left to live. He wrote Myron Benton, "I *suppose* that I have not many months to live; but, of course, I know nothing about it. I may add that I am enjoying existence as much as ever, and regret nothing." His sister Sophia wrote of him, "Henry . . . is so happy that I feel as if he were being translated rather than dying in the ordinary way of most mortals." Sam Staples said he "never saw a man dying with so much pleasure and peace." When his Aunt Louisa asked if he had made his peace with God, he replied, "I did not know we had ever quarreled." And when Parker Pillsbury tried to turn his thoughts to an afterlife, he replied, "One world at a time."

It is thus enlightening to note that Dr. Arthur C. Jacobson, in an article on "Tuberculosis and the Creative Mind" (*Medical Library and Historical Journal,* V [1907], 225–230), states that it is a characteristic of victims of tuberculosis "to bear their burdens of disease most cheerfully," adding, "Every practitioner is familiar with the extraordinary trait which enables the advanced consumptive to declare that he feels 'bully' when his temperature is 104°. . . . In no other disease *with equally extensive lesions* is the psychical and consequently the physical status equally exalted."

After examining Thoreau's personality from so many angles in this book, I hope we have arrived at a greater understanding of both his life and his works. We have found—that is, if we were not already well aware of the fact—that he was very human. He had some of the flaws and weaknesses that all of us possess, yet he had strengths that are rarely to be found. For those who would idolize and idealize him, it is not pleasant to realize that he could be crusty and erinaceous at times, and that some of his most pungent criticism may have been instigated by some of his own weaknesses and failures. But to point out these flaws in his life in no way destroys his greatness. Henry Salt, Thoreau's most sympathetic and understanding biographer, has aptly said:

The blemishes and mannerisms of Thoreau's character are written on its surface, easy to be read by the indifferent passer-by who may miss the strong and sterling faculties that underlie them. His lack of geniality, his rusticity, his occasional littleness of tone and temper, his impatience of custom, degenerating sometimes into injustice, his too sensitive self-consciousness, his trick of over-statement in the expression of his views—these were incidental failings which did not mar the essential nobility of his nature. We shall do wisely in taking him just as he is, neither shutting our eyes to his defects nor greatly deploring their existence, but remembering that in so genuine and distinctive an individuality the faults have their due place and proportion no less than the virtues. Had he added the merits he lacked to those which he possessed, had he combined the social with the individual qualities, had he been more catholic in his philosophy and more guarded in his expression, then we might indeed have admired him more, but should scarcely have loved him so well, for his character, whatever it gained in fullness, would have missed the peculiar freshness and piquancy which are now its chief attraction—whatever else he might have been, he would not have been Thoreau.[2]

2. Henry S. Salt, *Life of Henry David Thoreau,* pp. 297–298 (London: Bentley, 1890). Reprinted by permission of Haskell House Publishers.

Selected Bibliography

The standard editions of Thoreau's works are the so-called Manuscript and Walden Editions of *The Writings of Henry David Thoreau* (both editions are printed from the same plates) published by the Houghton Mifflin Company of Boston in 1906 in twenty volumes (of which the last fourteen are the *Journal*). *The Collected Poems of Henry Thoreau,* edited by Carl Bode, has been published in a revised edition by the Johns Hopkins University Press (1964). *The Correspondence of Henry David Thoreau,* edited by Walter Harding and Carl Bode, was published by New York University Press in 1958. All these editions, however, will soon be superseded by the forthcoming *Collected Works of Henry D. Thoreau* to be published by Princeton University Press under the aegis of the National Endowment for the Humanities and the Center for Editions of American Authors of the Modern Language Association.

Thoreau scholars have been so productive in recent years that it is all but impossible for any but the specialist to keep up with their work. However, *A Thoreau Handbook* by Walter Harding, published by New York University Press in 1959, provides a guide through this vast ocean of material and it is supplemented by the quarterly *Thoreau Society Bulletin* (Geneseo, N. Y.: State

University College, 1941–) which includes a running bibliography of current Thoreau scholarship.

As for biographies of Thoreau, the most recent is Walter Harding's *Days of Henry Thoreau* (New York: Knopf, 1965). Most important among the earlier biographies are Henry Salt's *Life of Henry David Thoreau* (London, 1890; New York, 1969); Henry Seidel Canby's *Thoreau* (Boston, 1939); Frank B. Sanborn's *Life of Henry David Thoreau* (Boston, 1917); and Ellery Channing's *Thoreau, the Poet-Naturalist* (Boston, 1873).

Contributors

RALPH WALDO EMERSON (1803–1882) and Thoreau saw each other almost daily—from 1837 when Thoreau returned to Concord from college until his death in 1862—and for two years (1841–1843) Thoreau lived in Emerson's house. Although their friendship had its ups and downs, it was never completely ruptured, and in the last years of Thoreau's life it attained a quiet serenity. On Thoreau's death, his sister Sophia asked Emerson to give the funeral address. Later revised for publication, it became the best-known and most influential depiction of Thoreau's personality and character. And since Emerson liked to think of his friend as primarily a Stoic, it unfortunately created the stereotype of Thoreau as cold, unfeeling, and negative. Although this essay first appeared in the *Atlantic Monthly* in 1862, I have chosen as my text the revised version of the Centenary Edition of Emerson's works.

DANIEL RICKETSON (1813–1898), a well-to-do New Bedford, Massachusetts, Quaker, collected literary friends and counted Emerson, Whittier, and the British essayist Howitt among his acquaintances. But the major friendship of his life was that with Thoreau. Reading *Walden* a few days after its publication in 1854, Ricketson wrote Thoreau a rather fawning letter suggesting they become acquainted. Thoreau took his time in replying and they eventually met in December of that year. From then until Thoreau's death in 1862, they corresponded and visited sporadically, with Ricketson always the more intent of the two. His chronic hypochondria often turned off Thoreau's enthusiasm, but they did share a mutual interest in the study of natural history and in the furtherance of the cause of antislavery.

SAMUEL STORROW HIGGINSON (183?–1907) was a pupil in F. B. Sanborn's private school in Concord in the late 1850's and there became acquainted with Thoreau through their mutual interest in natural history. His sketch was published in the *Harvard Magazine* shortly after Thoreau's death and while Higginson was still an undergraduate at Harvard College.

JOHN WEISS (1818–1879), son of a Jewish barber in Worcester, Massachusetts, was Thoreau's classmate at Harvard and later became a prominent Unitarian clergyman. In July, 1865, he reviewed four of Thoreau's books for the *Christian Examiner,* opening his review with the reminiscences of Thoreau included in this volume. Weiss was a *bon vivant* and active "man about campus" in his college days, and there is little evidence that he was at all close to the then shy and somewhat retiring Thoreau—a fact which undoubtedly somewhat colors these reminiscences.

WILLIAM ROUNSEVILLE ALGER (1822–1905), a Unitarian clergyman in Boston, knew Thoreau slightly, but obviously sympathized not at all with his philosophy.

GEORGE W. COOKE (1848–1923) was a Unitarian clergyman in Lexington, Massachusetts, who wrote frequently of the Transcendentalists. Nowhere is the dichotomy in reactions to Thoreau's personality better epitomized than in these two interviews gathered by Cooke. I have never succeeded in identifying his two interviewees.

ANONYMOUS. "The author of this article, who prefers to leave it unsigned, was an intimate personal friend of the late Miss Sophia E. Thoreau, the sister of Henry D. Thoreau. The two friends often visited each other. Their acquaintance and friendship began when Miss Thoreau was thirty-two years of age, and continued unbroken until her death in 1876. The author of the article during this period made frequent visits to the Thoreau home in Concord, none of them very brief, and many of several weeks' duration, and participated with absolute freedom in the family life," noted the editors of *Outlook* when they first published "Reminiscences of Thoreau"—"In

Virtue of Noble Living" in this volume. To the best of my knowledge, the author of the article has never been further identified.

EDWARD WALDO EMERSON (1844–1930), son of Ralph Waldo Emerson, was for many years a general practitioner in his native town of Concord and won both the confidence and admiration of his fellow townspeople. Sometime in the later years of the nineteenth century, he realized that the people who could personally remember his friend Henry Thoreau were getting fewer and fewer, and that many sources of information about Thoreau's life were being lost. Thus he determined to be a Boswell and gather up all the information he could while it was still available. Whenever, in the rounds of his professional duties, he came upon a person who could remember Thoreau, whether as a teacher, a lecturer, a surveyor, or a neighbor, he interrogated that person at length, and then as soon as he got home made a record of his conversation. These notes provided the backbone of his delightful little volume, *Henry Thoreau as Remembered by a Young Friend* ([Boston: Houghton Mifflin, 1917], reprinted by the Thoreau Lyceum of Concord in 1968).

DANIEL GREGORY MASON (1873–1953) wrote the essay that appears in this volume shortly after his graduation from Harvard College. He went on to become a well-known music critic and composer. As a young man he was commissioned to write a short biography of Thoreau for the Beacon Biography series, but for some unknown reason the book was never published. If we are to judge by this essay, it might well have helped to overcome the resistance to Thoreau's ideas and personality that was so rife about the turn of the century. Mason continued his interest in Thoreau throughout his life and one of his better-known compositions is the "Chanticleer Overture," based on Thoreau's *Walden*.

CHARLES IVES (1874–1954) is one of the greatest names in American music. Although he anticipated Schoenberg and Stravinsky in their experiments in polytonality and atonality, he has achieved widespread recognition only since his death. His second pianoforte sonata, *Concord, Mass., 1845*, is generally considered his masterwork. He accompanied its publication with a volume entitled *Essays Before a Sonata*, for which the essay included in this book was written as a commentary on the "Thoreau" movement of the sonata. Ives shared with Thoreau a prickly individualism that makes this one of the most Thoreauvian essays on Thoreau.

LEO STOLLER (1921–1968) taught at Wayne State University. His essay, a portion of a chapter from his *After Walden: Thoreau's Changing Views on Economic Man,* discusses one facet of what Thoreau himself thought to be the major problem of his life. As Thoreau said, "The whole duty of life is contained in the question how to respire and aspire both at once." Here Stoller discusses the dilemma Thoreau faced when he found surveying to be a satisfying source of income but then realized that his surveying was bringing about the destruction of the Concord woods he loved so much.

Professor Stoller's tragic death in 1968 brought an all-too-early end to the career of one of the most thoughtful of contemporary Thoreau critics.

RAYMOND D. GOZZI completed a doctoral dissertation in 1957, *Tropes and Figures: A Psychological Study of David Henry Thoreau,* under the direction of Professor Gay Wilson Allen at New York University. Although the dissertation has never been published, it has become one of the most discussed studies of Thoreau's personality because many of the ideas in Professor Gozzi's dissertation have been made generally available through Carl Bode's essay "The Half-Hidden Thoreau" (*Massachusetts Review,* IV [Autumn 1962], 68–80, and reprinted several times elsewhere). But rather than reprint Professor Bode's summary, effective as it is, I have chosen to print two chapters from the dissertation. These chapters were selected by Professor Gozzi as being most representative of the dissertation as a whole.

J. LYNDON SHANLEY is concerned with one of the most discussed points of Thoreau's life: whether his later years were happy or unhappy, and whether by his late thirties he had lost his creative genius. The case for such a disintegration of Thoreau's personality is discussed most fully in Sherman Paul's provocative *The Shores of America: Thoreau's Inward Exploration* ([Urbana: University of Illinois, 1958], particularly pp. 255–279). But it seems to me that most of Professor Paul's arguments are effectively answered in Professor Shanley's essay. Professor Shanley, a former president of the Thoreau Society, is an associate dean of Northwestern University.

JOEL PORTE. Porte's essay, from his *Emerson and Thoreau,* is in

absolute antithesis to the opening essay in this volume by Ralph Waldo
Emerson. Porte's book, a study of the relationship and a contrast of
the personalities of Emerson and Thoreau, argues that Thoreau was
not the Stoic Emerson thought him to be, but rather the most sensuous
of all the Transcendentalists. Mr. Porte is an associate professor of
English at Harvard University.

JAMES ARMSTRONG teaches literature and composition at Fullerton
Junior College in Fullerton, California. He taught previously at
Macalester College in St. Paul, Minnesota. His publications include
an article on Robert Frost and two college readers, *Voyages of Discovery* and *The Curious Eye.*

WALTER HARDING was born in Bridgewater, Massachusetts, in 1917, graduated from the Bridgewater State Teachers' College in 1939, and received his M.A. and Ph.D. respectively at the University of North Carolina and Rutgers University. Among his many publications are *Thoreau: A Century of Criticism, Thoreau's Library, The Correspondence of Henry David Thoreau* (edited with Carl Bode), *A Thoreau Handbook, Thoreau: Man of Concord, A Thoreau Profile* (with Milton Meltzer), *The Thoreau Centennial, The Days of Henry Thoreau, Emerson's Library,* and *A Checklist of the Editions of Walden.* Professor Harding has also contributed to numerous periodicals. He is on the faculty of the State University College at Geneseo, New York.

✪

AÏDA DIPACE DONALD holds degrees from Barnard and Columbia and a Ph.D. from the University of Rochester. A former member of the History Department at Columbia, Mrs. Donald has been a Fulbright Fellow at Oxford and the recipient of an A.A.U.W. fellowship. She has published *John F. Kennedy and the New Frontier* and *Diary of Charles Francis Adams.*